LEARNING AS A WAY OF LEADING

LEARNING AS A WAY OF LEADING

Lessons from the Struggle for Social Justice

Stephen Preskill

Stephen D. Brookfield

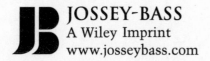

JOSSEY-BASS
A Wiley Imprint
www.josseybass.com

Published by Jossey-Bass
A Wiley Imprint
989 Market Street, San Francisco, CA 94103-1741—www.josseybass.com

Jossey-Bass books and products are available through most bookstores. To contact Jossey-Bass directly call our Customer Care Department within the U.S. at 800-956-7739, outside the U.S. at 317-572-3986, or fax 317-572-4002.

Jossey-Bass also publishes its books in a variety of electronic formats. Some content that appears in print may not be available in electronic books.

ISBN 978-0-7879-7807-5

Library of Congress Cataloging-in-Publication data available from publisher upon request.

Printed in the United States of America

FIRST EDITION
HB Printing 10 9 8 7 6 5 4 3 2

The Jossey-Bass

Higher and Adult Education Series

CONTENTS

Preface

In this book—our first together on leadership—we explore the form of leadership that most interests us: social activist leadership, or leadership for social justice. This is a form too rarely explored in the leadership literature. We both have had our fill of reading about the success stories of leaders who are appointed by organizational gatekeepers (boards of trustees, majority shareholders, boards of directors, and so on) to be the visionary exemplar who takes the organization to new heights. The leadership we are interested in is what springs naturally from a social movement, what, following Gramsci (1971), can be called organic leadership. This is leadership from below, where the leader is part of a collective that through dialogue crafts a vision to challenge dominant ideologies, structures, and practices. In organic leadership, the leader is concerned less with being the progenitor of a branded vision that is announced and imposed from above, and more with helping members of the organization, movement, or community realize what talents, knowledge, and skills they can contribute to a vision they themselves have generated.

For several years, we have experimented with using brief biographies to document the lives of social activists. We have tried to capture concrete actions and accomplishments of these activists that encapsulate the essence of a certain kind of leadership, one that focuses on learning. We are particularly interested in how leaders learn, how they support other people's learning, and how all of this deepens their social impact. Over the last three to four years, we have written at least a dozen biographical portraits of learning leaders, some of which were published individually in academic journals or presented at conferences, others that simply languished in our files. As we considered a book that might incorporate these articles, we began to analyze the specifics of how these activists learned and found that there were a number of learning tasks that recurred across these portraits. The learning tasks that we identified as a result of this analysis, together with most of the biographical portraits that we had previously written, became the basis for this book.

So the book that finally emerged from all of this work, the book that you now have in your hands, features leaders who are constantly learning from the world around them. They do this in part because they get great satisfaction from learning, but they do it primarily to bring about transforming changes that advance justice and promote the common good. This is a book about leaders who use what they have learned to secure people their basic rights, combat racism, overturn economic inequality, prevent corporate and governmental pollution of the environment, create forms of democratic socialism, and help people more fully realize themselves as human beings. It is a book about the kind of people we most admire and whom, despite our best efforts, we could never hope to emulate. Yet even as we accept our own limits in the face of their greatness, we are inspired by their selfless actions and animated by their passion and commitment. We have learned from the leaders profiled in this book and in some negligible way have become better people as a result of studying their lives.

In this book, we focus on nine leaders whom we believe were among the greatest activists in the twentieth century and who, by virtue of their thirst for knowledge, empowered millions of others to continue their own learning for the cause of social justice. As great as they were and as daunting as they seem, these leaders led most of all by encouraging thousands of others to lead alongside them. They were radically inclusive figures, open to a multitude of voices and perspectives, and eager to find ways for everyone to lead at least some of the time. How they learned to lead in this way and how they learned to partner with so many others to bring about massive social change is the focus of this book.

ORGANIZATION OF THE BOOK

Apart from our introductory and concluding material, each chapter in the book is divided into halves. In Chapters Two through Ten, the first half of each chapter comprises an analysis of a particular learning task. The second half profiles a learning leader who exemplifies this task. As a means of ensuring that there is some consistency across the learning tasks we examine, in Chapters Two through Ten the first half is structured around our responses to the same eight questions:

1. How do we define the particular learning task?
2. What are the benefits of the learning task?
3. How does a leader develop the ability to practice the learning task?
4. Where have we seen the learning task practiced?
5. How have we and others lived the learning task?
6. What blocks or prevents the practice of the learning task?
7. What are the perils and pitfalls of practicing the learning task?
8. How do we address the tensions, problems, perils, and pitfalls associated with the learning task?

These questions allow us to examine the learning tasks of leadership from many angles, explore their multiple meanings, and perhaps most of all share how challenging, even gut-wrenching, it can be to learn and practice these tasks. None of these tasks is ever fully achieved. Thus, the questions are also designed to temper our idealism and blunt our creeping triumphalism. Leading in this way is always flawed and invariably fraught with ambiguity. In other words, we hoped these questions would keep our discussion of these learning tasks as "real" and as grounded in the everyday world of practice as possible.

In the second half of each chapter, we profile in more detail one particular leader who for us exemplifies the learning task examined. These leaders, in order of appearance, are Jane Addams, Nelson Mandela, Septima Clark, Ella Baker, Myles Horton, Aldo Leopold, Mary Parker Follett, Paul Robeson, and Cesar Chavez. Although all of the leaders practiced all of the learning tasks to one degree or another, each one of them is strongly identified with pursuing consistently one of the particular learning tasks we identify. As a result, each portrait is framed to underscore how skillfully and distinctively the profiled leader practiced the learning task that is the focus of their respective chapter.

OVERVIEW OF CHAPTERS

Chapter One is our opening statement on the topic of leaders who are learners. It is here that we situate our focus on learning leadership within other leading theories of leadership; argue for a democratic, power-with approach to the study of leadership; introduce the nine learning tasks that are addressed individually in Chapters Two through Ten; and identify the nine leaders who are to be profiled.

Chapter Two centers on learning to be open to the contributions of others. Here we contend that maintaining a stance of radical openness to new ideas, perspectives, experiences, and values is an essential part of being a learning leader. As with many of the learning tasks, we also spend some time problematizing the task of openness and exploring how openness can sometimes hinder our activism as well as help it. On the whole, though, we try to make the case that no leader can be a learner and no learner a leader without developing the capacity for openness. Our exemplar of learning openness is Jane Addams, the founder of Hull House and one of America's most admired women at the beginning of the twentieth century. Few leaders were as willing to open themselves to learning from such a dizzying array of sources. Addams was particularly noteworthy for attracting a brilliant community of female activists to Hull House who were just as likely to guide her toward new understandings as they were to learn from her mentoring.

Chapter Three takes up the task of critical reflection and advances the view that virtually all significant leading that seeks to make a positive difference in organizations and communities includes a strong component of critical reflection. Without maintaining a standard to which a community of learners holds itself—such as redistributing power to promote the common good, or countering the political, economic, and racial hegemony that diminishes human flourishing—leadership for learning and for social justice cannot make meaningful progress. Critical reflection asks us to scrutinize the assumptions we make about power dynamics, our own use of power, and how we accept (without being aware of it) assumptions and practices that harm us and benefit the most powerful.

The exemplar for Chapter Three is Nelson Mandela. In an analysis of Mandela's autobiography, *Long Walk to Freedom*, we explore the assumptions Mandela held—and modified—concerning the best way to end the minority rule of the White Nationalist Party and usher in a free South Africa. Mandela's willingness to reappraise assumptions about excluding Whites from the ANC, about whether to use nonviolent or violent means to bring about change, about when to open negotiations with the repressive regime, and about renouncing the armed struggle, had enormously significant repercussions for millions of people. It is hard to imagine a more profound example of the exercise of critical reflection.

Chapter Four examines the task of learning to support the growth of others. Exploring the theories of servant leadership and developmental leadership, we highlight leaders who believe their main job is to help people realize their fullest possible potential as human beings. In particular, this entails attentive listening, thoughtful questioning, creating opportunities for sharing life stories, championing the purposes of co-workers, and staying curious about each other's experiences. Septima Clark, lifelong teacher, civil rights activist, and cofounder of the Citizenship Schools, which helped to breathe new life into the Civil Rights Movement, is the person we focus on as the exemplar of these tasks. Having committed her entire life to helping people develop the skills and knowledge they would need to flourish as human beings, and to challenging the vicious manifestations of White supremacy, Clark was particularly noted for practicing the learning task of supporting the growth of others.

Chapter Five tackles the challenging task of learning collective leadership. Collective leadership is impossible without a shared vision of what people together hope to accomplish. Once that vision is identified, all group members must accept some leadership role, even as they also agree sometimes to put their own individual interests aside for the sake of the group's agreed goals. Under true collective leadership, there is no one person that everyone looks to as leader. Interdependence prevails to such an extent that every group member is seen as critical to the group's success. As we indicate, this is almost impossible to do, but approximations of it can be incredibly exhilarating and inspiring.

The great Ella Baker, a fierce proponent of civil rights and a tireless advocate of shared leadership, is the person particularly identified in this book with the learning task of collective leadership. Long before it was written about or much practiced, Baker lived the idea that every group needed many leaders. Rather than one single person being the leader, leadership worked best, she asserted, when the group as a whole found a way to lead. Baker devoted her life to achieving the end of eliminating racism. Her means was always collective leadership.

Learning to analyze experience is the topic of Chapter Six. Here the focus is on people coming to appreciate the value of their own experiences. Leaders and followers together delve deeply into that experience and mine it for new insights into how social forces and structures have impeded their progress. They also learn to work with others in pooling and sharing that experience in order to see how people might organize differently for the common good. The curriculum for analyzing experience is the curriculum of people's lives. Exploring this curriculum critically and collaboratively helps us understand better how to organize and lead to secure the changes we seek.

Myles Horton and the school he founded, the Highlander Folk School, are explored in this chapter. Horton encouraged the people who gathered at Highlander to tell stories about themselves and reflect on the meaning of those stories. He urged them to listen to each other's stories, analyze them, and take lessons from them. He particularly wanted people to see how similar their experiences were and how these commonalities could be explored critically, but communally, to offer insights that would direct efforts for future change. Horton is best known for practicing the learning task of analyzing experience.

Chapter Seven shifts the focus to learning to question. Learning to question ourselves and others is the springboard for learning to question the status quo. Questions are a valuable way to explore alternative values, goals, and actions, and they help make possible the sharing of important new information. They are, as we say, "the engine of knowledge creation." We contend that the more we question each other constructively and discerningly, the more likely we are to stay alert to new ideas and new possibilities. Few leaders brought as much passion and inquisitiveness to their work as Aldo Leopold, the great environmentalist and author of *A Sand County Almanac*. Long before it was fashionable, Leopold was tenacious about conservation and ecological balance. Because he was both humble about his own knowledge and intensely curious about the world, he developed the lifelong habit of asking hard, insightful questions. He is thus most closely associated with the task of learning to question.

The task of learning democracy is explored in Chapter Eight. We accept from the start that democracy is more honored as an abstract concept than it is lived out in reality. In a society dominated by top-down organizations, and one in which the decisions of boards of multinational corporations may have great long-term impact on our lives, democracy is not often part of our national experience. Certainly, the money-dominated constant campaigning for funds that passes as the political process today is a laughable and distorted facsimile of anything that resembles true democracy. We suggest in this chapter that we are most likely to learn about democracy in small-scale settings: families, neighborhoods, schools, and community associations. Here we can learn about the power of all voices being heard and sometimes observe leaders who think little about their own individual contributions and more about inviting others to add value. Learning to make the most of everyone's strengths, democratic leaders help communities become more imaginative and proactive.

Mary Parker Follett, still widely read for her lively ideas about democracy, is the learning leader introduced at the end of this chapter. Like so many of the other leaders profiled in this book, Follett had great faith in the knowledge, experience, and wisdom that ordinary people could add to a group's capacity to deliberate and reach fair decisions. Her work focused on finding ways to make the most of what such people had to offer in a variety of organizational and community settings. In this book, she is particularly identified with the task of learning democracy.

In Chapter Nine, we consider what it takes to sustain hope in the face of struggle. Rejecting naïve hope or knee-jerk optimism, we insist that learning leaders practice hope as a critical discipline in which the injustices of the past and the inequities of the present not only are acknowledged but become the foundation on which a more positive future is to be constructed. We further affirm that

leaders must learn to find hope in the heroic struggles of the
so-called ordinary people they interact with everyday.

Paul Robeson, an admired and feted leader who saw how his
success was being ideologically manipulated to convince Black
Americans that substantive racial advancement had occurred, is
our exemplar of practicing hope. The more his fame propelled
him into international tours and travel, the more he learned of the
growing anticolonial movements around the world and their link
to fighting White supremacy in the United States (and vice versa).
His growing public and private commitment to socialism, and his
refusal to disavow the Soviet Union, meant that when the U.S.
State Department confiscated his passport (as he faced the House
Un-American Activities Committee) he was, in effect, an exile in
his own country. We examine how Robeson's loss of income and
public pillorying did not destroy his hope that sooner or later
Black and White workers would see their common interests and
unite within labor unions to force democratic change.

Learning community, the focus of Chapter Ten, is the leadership learning task that encompasses all the others. It cannot
be learned or practiced without openness, a willingness to reflect
critically, a desire to support others' growth, an attempt to lead
collectively, a focus on analyzing experience, a readiness to ask
provocative questions, a determination to work democratically, or
a practice of critically tempered hope. In this chapter, we feature
the moral, strategic, and tactical leadership of Cesar Chavez during the California farm workers movement of the 1950s and 1960s.
His commitment to developing community, his concern for the
poor people who drove the farm workers movement, and his growing skill as a community organizer allowed him to emerge as one
of the most important union leaders of recent times. Additionally,
his commitment to nonviolence as the most effective route to
social justice gave his leadership an integrity and staying power
that has few equals.

The final Chapter Eleven includes a brief reaffirmation of
some of the book's key themes; a few sobering thoughts on how
hard it is to write about leadership as a shared, collective process
while keeping the focus on individual leaders; and two personal
codas about our ongoing struggle to practice what we preach—to
model (however feebly) learning leadership.

Our Audience

As educators, we wrote this book for our students. Virtually all of them are leaders in some manner who have devoted themselves to creating environments to help people learn. So the first audience that comes to mind for this book are people like our students who find themselves in leadership positions in a variety of educational and community organizations and who are constantly searching for better ways to connect learners to new ideas and experiences and more invigorating pedagogical practices.

Because so much of this book is also about social activism and social change, it is also for people who are intent on making change for the common good, who are committed to involving many people from diverse origins in a quest for more humane and just living arrangements for all. It is also true that this book is for people who are frustrated by standard, conventional, top-down leadership practices and who are looking for more democratic, inclusive, and appreciative ways for people to lead together. Undoubtedly, this book is as well for those who love to learn as an intrinsic good and are looking for leaders, and for communities where learning is prized and treated as a true collaborative endeavor. Such communities create numerous opportunities for people to reflect deeply on experience and do some powerful and incisive thinking together.

In the end, it probably isn't an exaggeration to say this book is for just about anyone who wants to make a difference for the public good by joining with others to bring about positive change. The people profiled in this book saw wrongs they wanted to right and knew they could not accomplish this alone. They knew they had to ally with others of like minds, to energize and inspire them, help them find their authentic voices and their best selves, and bring them together to identify with each other's struggle until the pressure for transforming action could not be denied. Who makes change, how this change happens, and how continuous learning supports efforts for that change are all explored in this book. Those who care about social change but are baffled by it and want to understand it a little better, or those who have always wondered what it would be like to be a part of a movement for change, would do well to read the stories and the analyses that make up this book.

Acknowledgments

Stephen Preskill (Stephen P) is immensely pleased that this book is being published; it represents his best thinking on the links between learning and leadership and captures well what he hoped to say about the leadership of social justice. But none of this would have been possible without the coauthorship, chapter contributions, support, collegiality, critical acumen, editing skill, and friendship of Stephen D. Brookfield. Stephen P has racked up a lifetime of debts to Stephen B that he can never repay, but he must at least say that he is deeply grateful to him for doing so much to make this final product better. He dedicates this book to him with profound admiration and appreciation.

The following people read significant portions of this book, were extremely supportive, or did something to help keep this project moving in a positive direction. Stephen P is very grateful to Stan Agustin, Robert Baade, Allison Borden, Varda Brahms, Karen DeMoss, Lee Francis, Kathy Glyer, Sam Howarth, Robyn Humara, Gael Keyes, Yann Lussiez, Michael Morris, Mary Sellers, and in particular Hallie Preskill. He also wants to thank numerous students at the University of New Mexico for reading early portions of the manuscript or for participating in some way in supporting this project. Finally, Stephen P spent the summer of 2006 in New York City writing a key portion of this book. It was a wonderful summer in many ways, not least because he felt so productive and New York is such an exciting, stimulating, and energizing city. The best thing about that summer, however, was sharing it with Karen, who proved to be such an inexhaustible source of inspiration, encouragement, and love. So she remains to this day. To her he is eternally grateful.

Stephen D. Brookfield (Stephen B) offers his greatest acknowledgment to Stephen Preskill for conceiving this book and inviting Stephen B along on his journey of learning from the leaders we profile. Stephen B also thanks his bandmates in The 99ers, Molly Holley and Colin Selhurst, for understanding when rehearsals needed to be cut short and gigs refused because of deadlines imposed by manuscript completion. Finally, Stephen B thanks Kim Miller for always being ready to remind him that the adulation of the crowd (or at least the scattered groups he is sometimes invited to address) means nothing next to the microreality of his daily actions and choices.

We both know that thanks to editors often appear to be ritual-istic, but we hope that our gratitude for David Brightman's always supportive, and helpfully critical, perspective is read as genuine. David was unfailingly helpful, full of useful ideas for the book's organization, and ready to ask provocative questions that helped us make the book what it is. In contrast to most acknowledgments that add a disclaimer to the effect that the people named had no responsibility for how the book finally appeared in print, we want to affirm that this is David's book as well as our own.

New York City   STEPHEN PRESKILL

St. Paul, Minnesota   STEPHEN D. BROOKFIELD

THE AUTHORS

STEPHEN PRESKILL

Stephen Preskill is currently the chair of the Department of Education at Wagner College. For nine years, he was an elementary and middle school teacher before earning his doctorate from the University of Illinois at Urbana-Champaign in 1984 in educational policy studies, with an emphasis in the history of American education. From 1984 to 1989, he taught at Carleton College in Northfield, Minnesota, and from 1989 to 1994 he was a member of the educational leadership faculty at the University of St. Thomas in St. Paul, Minnesota. For thirteen years, he taught at the University of New Mexico in Albuquerque and served as Regents' Professor in the Department of Educational Leadership and Organizational Learning from 2004 to 2007. During the past year, he held the Jane Simmons McKimmon Professorship of Leadership Studies at Peace College in Raleigh, North Carolina.

This is his second book for Jossey-Bass and his third book overall. With Stephen D. Brookfield, he co-wrote the first and second editions of *Discussion as a Way of Teaching: Tools and Techniques for Democratic Classrooms* (1999, 2005). With Robin Smith Jacobvitz, he coauthored *Stories of Teaching: A Foundation for Educational Renewal* (2001). Preskill's main research activities have focused on the history of American educational reform, teacher and leader narratives, the connections between learning leadership and democracy, and how discussion-based teaching supports democratic processes. He has published more than forty articles in a variety of social science journals.

STEPHEN D. BROOKFIELD

The father of Molly and Colin and the husband of Kim, *Stephen D. Brookfield* is currently Distinguished University Professor at the University of St. Thomas in Minneapolis-St. Paul, Minnesota. He received his B.A. degree (1970) from Coventry University in modern studies, his M.A. degree (1974) from the University of Reading in sociology, and his Ph.D. degree (1980) from the University of Leicester in adult education. He also holds a postgraduate diploma (1971) from the University of London, Chelsea College, in modern social and cultural studies and a postgraduate diploma (1977) from the University of Nottingham in adult education. In 1991, he was awarded an honorary doctor of letters degree from the University System of New Hampshire for his contributions to understanding adult learning. In 2003 he was awarded an honorary doctorate of letters from Concordia University for his contributions to adult education.

Brookfield began his teaching career in 1970 and has held appointments at colleges of further, technical, adult, and higher education in the United Kingdom, and at universities in Canada (University of British Columbia) and the United States (Columbia University, Teachers College, and the University of St. Thomas). In 1989, he was Visiting Fellow at the Institute for Technical and Adult Teacher Education in what is now the University of Technology, Sydney, Australia. In 2002, he was Visiting Professor at Harvard University Graduate School of Education. In 2003–04, he was the Helen Le Baron Hilton Chair at Iowa State University. He has run numerous workshops on teaching, adult learning, and critical thinking around the world and delivered many keynote addresses at regional, national, and international conferences. In 2001, he received the Leadership Award from the Association for Continuing Higher Education for "extraordinary contributions to the general field of continuing education on a national and international level."

He is a four-time winner of the Cyril O. Houle World Award for Literature in Adult Education: in 1986 for his book *Understanding and Facilitating Adult Learning: A Comprehensive Analysis of Principles and Effective Practices* (1986); in 1989 for *Developing Critical Thinkers: Challenging Adults to Explore Alternative*

Ways of Thinking and Acting (1987); in 1996 for *Becoming a Critically Reflective Teacher* (1995); and in 2005 for *The Power of Critical Theory: Liberating Adult Learning and Teaching* (2004). *Understanding and Facilitating Adult Learning* also won the 1986 Imogene E. Okes Award for Outstanding Research in Adult Education. These awards were all presented by the American Association for Adult and Continuing Education. The first edition of *Discussion as a Way of Teaching: Tools and Techniques for Democratic Classrooms* (2nd ed. 2005), which he coauthored with Stephen Preskill, was a 1999 Critics Choice of the Educational Studies Association. His other books are *Adult Learners, Adult Education and the Community* (1984), *Self-Directed Learning: From Theory to Practice* (1985), *Learning Democracy: Eduard Lindeman on Adult Education and Social Change* (1987), *Training Educators of Adults: The Theory and Practice of Graduate Adult Education* (1988), *The Skillful Teacher: On Technique, Trust and Responsiveness in the Classroom* (2nd ed. 2006), and *Teaching Reflectively in Theological Contexts: Promises and Contradictions* (co-edited with Mary Hess, 2008).

CHAPTER ONE

THE ESSENCE OF LEARNING LEADERSHIP

Think of the word *leader*. (Don't spend more than five seconds letting images flit through your consciousness.) What pictures does this word conjure up? Do you see a man? Or do you see a woman? Is that man or woman adopting a posture that seems strong, confident, bold, assertive? What do those attributes look like in your mind? Is the person you're thinking of White? Is she or he wearing a suit or uniform? Stephen Preskill (Stephen P) grew up in the United States, and the leader who most quickly jumps to mind for him is Franklin Delano Roosevelt, declaring to the American public that the only thing we have to fear is fear itself. Stephen Brookfield (Stephen B) grew up in England, and a picture of a cigar-chomping Winston Churchill bedecked in military regalia jumps into his head. If you are a White person (as the two of us are), the chances are you have been so successfully socialized by patriarchy and White supremacy that these are the sorts of people you will think of. If you are a union member or socialist, you may also think of other people—Eugene Debs, or Aneurin Bevin, for example. If you are African American, Malcolm X, Harriet Tubman, Paul Robeson, Ella Baker, Marcus Garvey, Septima Clark, W.E.B. DuBois, Angela Davis, or Martin Luther King may be the names that pop up. Or perhaps women such as Eleanor Roosevelt, Indira Gandhi, Golda Meir, or Margaret Thatcher suggest themselves. Interestingly, on the basis of a wholly unscientific polling one of us did of his women friends and colleagues (all of whom had graduate degrees, knew of the insidious nature of patriarchy, and considered themselves feminists), not a single woman was mentioned in the first three names of leaders each of these women gave. Churchill, John Kennedy, and Joseph Stalin were the most frequent.

Our contention in this book is that the images of leadership—indeed, the very words *leader* and *leadership*—have been culturally framed to equate effective leadership with authoritarian control imposed by those at the apex of a hierarchy. A smooth and seamless ideological manipulation has ensured that those we automatically think of as leaders are precisely the people who represent the interests of the status quo: males from upper-class families who function as protectors of wealth and privilege. One need only think of the Bush dynasty in the United States; in the last twenty years it has produced two presidents and the governor of a swing state that ensured the election of his brother to the presidency in the face of allegations of serious electoral fraud. The Kennedy dynasty had the project of combating Jim Crow practices forced on them by events, but they too were drawn from the same narrow spectrum.

Churchill, Roosevelt, Kennedy, Bush, Stalin: these figures represent a distressingly narrow view of how people in organizations and communities get things done. According to this view, leaders are highly directive people who relay commands to their subordinates, expecting them to be carried out with dispatch and efficiency. Typically, leaders are also the people who have titles—CEO, president, chairman of the board, and principal being some of the familiar designations. In this perspective, leaders are thought to be ahead of their followers and in some important way distant from them. It is no accident that the Kennedys were portrayed as living within a magical bubble (Camelot) in much the same way as monarchies have been portrayed throughout history. Leaders are presented as being somehow higher, smarter, and more advanced than their followers, with a breadth of experience and depth of wisdom they use to help followers see the light of the leader's more progressive vision. Yet, ironically, leaders are also very often associated with maintaining the status quo, with creating an environment where stability and harmony are the highest values.

The conventional concept of leadership comprises the four elements critiqued by Raelin (2003) in his analysis of a culture that prizes and practices directive, top-down leadership. In Raelin's view, people automatically assume effective leadership to be serial (exercised by one person at a time, passing the baton on to the next generational leader), individual (only ever exercised by a single individual), controlling (fiercely pursuing the leader's vision of how others should live and how a community or organization should function), and dispassionate (viewing as necessary "collateral damage," the wrecked lives of those individuals, cultures, or communities that are uprooted, excluded, or disenfranchised in the pursuit of a set of desired goals). Conventionally defined leadership is practiced by a single, distinct figure positioned at the top of a hierarchy, what Foucault (1980) called sovereign power. This person directs the organization or movement's operations, relying minimally on subordinates, and imposing his or her vision on others. He or she is determined to be perceived as unemotional, confident, unwaveringly commanding, and bordering on arrogant. Separate and mysterious, conventional leaders avoid getting too close to their constituents so as to keep them subordinate.

Our contention is not only that leadership doesn't have to be this way but that it can't be sustained this way if meaningful and lasting changes for the common good are going to occur. In an era in which people routinely expect to be lied to by those in power, we need leaders who strive to place learning at the center of their work. Such leaders know in their bones that they have much to learn and that the people likely to be their best teachers are the co-workers they see and collaborate with everyday. They also see encouraging the learning of others as the central responsibility of leadership.

Our assumptions about leadership are (as you will no doubt have gathered by now) radically different from the conventional model. Our chief claim is that leadership can be practiced by anyone in any kind of movement, community, organization, or institution. It is part anarchist, part collective, part democratic, and constantly rotating. Leadership is not necessarily a function of a hierarchy or bureaucracy; nor does a single person in a position of authority have to exercise it. It is, rather, a relational and collective process in which collaboration and shared understanding are deemed axiomatic to getting things done. Leadership has little to do with formal authority or where one is in the chain of command, and a great deal to do with forming and sustaining relationships that lead to results in the common interest. Furthermore, leaders are not necessarily the most prominent or vocal members of a group; they are often quite deferential, leaving space for others to voice their concerns and contribute their ideas.

Leadership as it is explored here encourages change, even pushes for it, especially when the status quo demeans people or fails to give them opportunities to employ fully their experience and talents. The leaders the two of us prize most (once we've done some ideological detoxification on the automatic images that come to our minds) are critically aware of our failures as a society to serve all people well. For Stephen P, a prime example would be Ella Baker because in her quest to make American society more just and equal she never drew attention to herself, acknowledged the thousands of others who contributed to this ongoing struggle, and demanded that power be centered in the group, not the individual. For Stephen B it would be Paul Robeson or Nelson Mandela because of the strength they displayed in their unwavering commitment to combating White supremacy and global capitalism (in Robeson's case) and White supremacy and the complete economic and political disenfranchisement of his country's majority population (in Mandela's case). Both men paid a heavy price for their commitment. For Robeson it was the loss of livelihood, public vilification for much of his adult life, and increasingly debilitating depression (which his son argues was the result of the CIA and FBI's administration of drugs and covert encouragement of "treatment" by electro-shock therapy). For Mandela the price was spending most of his adult life in prison, unable to see his children and then grandchildren growing up, and unable to grow old with his wife.

The leaders we are interested in know that a vision for more humane and just communities is desperately needed and that leadership entails people coming forward who are able and eager to work with others to create such communities. They also know that leadership is often facilitative rather than directive, and that good leaders learn to create an environment conducive to people's growth and inviting of everyone's participation in the fashioning of change to promote the public interest. But more than anything else, the leaders we are interested in are learners. They revere learning, they learn from their experience and from their co-workers, and they are constantly sharing with others the fruits of what they have learned. They also regard as paramount the responsibility to encourage the learning of others.

Because leaders who learn know how beneficial and broadening learning is for everyone, they work to create mechanisms, structures, strategies, and opportunities to support individual and communal learning. Although they express a variety of motives for wanting to lead, these learning leaders communicate clearly and often that learning isn't only a means to some end; sometimes it is an important end in itself. Co-workers who are leaders can be threatening to entrenched administrators because they often use cogent, well-prepared arguments to challenge things as they are. They have an excellent grasp of the relevant facts and they know how to use them to make the best possible case for how things might be different. Under the best of circumstances, such leaders are invaluable to organizations and institutions. Yet because they seek to question and even overthrow the status quo, those who resist change view them with suspicion, particularly the unrepresentative minority whose interests are threatened. On the other hand, those who lead by virtue of learning encourage and support such co-workers and find multiple ways for them to have an impact on the direction of their shared enterprise.

What are some of the ways learning leaders demonstrate their commitment? Well, they listen with close attention, observe with a discerning eye, and read texts of all kinds—including the texts of people's experiences—with critical acumen. They are constantly on the alert for new information, novel insights, deepened understanding. For these learning leaders, everything learned is potentially grist for the leadership mill. They try constantly to make connections between what they have learned, the issues that matter to them most, and the goals they are trying to achieve as leaders. Nothing is too trivial or insignificant, at least at first, to be taken into account and used in some way to lead more effectively or to bring about change more proactively. Such leaders do not hide their enthusiasm for what they are learning, either. They eagerly and overtly share their reflections on experience, what they are reading, what new ideas they are coming up with, what interesting connections they are making, and how they are revising earlier ideas and practice because of new learning. They do this in part because they are unabashed lovers of learning. But they also do so for strategic effect, to stir up their co-workers' excitement about their own learning and its potential for stimulating creativity and furthering change.

The raison d'être for modeling a public commitment to learning is to induce co-workers to launch their own learning projects. Everything that learning leaders do should be linked in some way to supporting other people's learning. This includes supplying resources, bringing compatible collaborators together, connecting learning to purposeful and meaningful work (paid and unpaid), and offering ongoing incentives for this learning to continue. These actions are intended to induce some change deemed important by the community, movement, or organization. This kind of intrinsic reinforcement should never be underestimated by learning leaders, particularly when it is linked to proof that an act of learning is contributing to something that matters to the community as a whole. Most significant of all outcomes, perhaps, are the long-term relationships that occur as a result of working together on learning projects. Such relationships not only increase one's willingness to learn and lessen one's vulnerability about admitting ignorance but also fuel future projects and public work. As relationships deepen, the distinction between leader and follower blurs, with so-called positional leaders and followers freely exchanging roles as leader-follower, teacher-student, and speaker-listener. In this way shared, openly displayed learning is beneficial to the whole community.

FOUNDATIONS OF LEARNING LEADERSHIP

The idea that leaders should place learning at the center of their practice is not new or original. Learning as a defining component of leadership has been practiced and conceptualized in all kinds of social movements, revolutions, and organizations. In this section, we review five of the most frequently cited models of leadership that we feel contribute to this idea: transformational, symbiotic, developmental, servant, and organic leadership.

TRANSFORMATIONAL LEADERSHIP

The relational emphasis we have outlined is central to James Mac-Gregor Burns's original formulation of transforming leadership (1978). In contrast to transactional leadership (which he characterized as an exchange that is temporary, instrumental, and nonbinding), transforming leadership signifies a long-term relationship between leaders and followers that produces significant change, raises leaders and followers to higher levels of motivation and morality, and encourages followers to assume leadership roles themselves. Transactional leadership leaves the power relations between leaders and followers unchanged. Transforming leadership produces a climate in which followers are constantly becoming leaders by virtue of the ideas they put forward, the actions they take, and the learning they engage in. Burns indicates that one of the markers of transformational leaders is their capacity to learn from their followers, to be willing students to their followers' teachings. Such leaders have developed the seemingly paradoxical ability "to lead by being led" (p. 117) as they unite with followers to pursue goals that transcend self-interest and that seek to further some notion of the common good.

SYMBIOTIC LEADERSHIP

Building on this reciprocal conception of leadership, Matusak (1997) contends that "the relationship of leader and follower is symbiotic; that each role benefits greatly the interdependent nature of the relationship; that the leader today may be the follower tomorrow" (p. 27). For her, leadership is at its best when leader and led feel inspired and energized to do great things together, to scale new heights of collective accomplishment, and to share roles of responsibility that reflect much more positively on the group as a whole than on any one individual. Leaders who learn carefully cultivate a dynamic in which everyone enjoys the opportunity to be a leader at least some of the time. This dynamic is collective and requires a partial submerging of the self inside the group, a losing of oneself for the sake of the whole. It means that anyone can contribute at any time as leader, follower, innovator, protégé, mentor, guide, witness, or scribe. All of these roles are necessary and valued, and who does what is irrelevant as the group becomes a collective unit. In a collective dynamic, individual interests are fused with a sense of the common good, and identity is derived from participation in a shared, mutually satisfying endeavor.

DEVELOPMENTAL LEADERSHIP

Belenky, Bond, and Weinstock (1997) augment these notions of reciprocity and collectivity in their book *A Tradition That Has No Name*. Here they explore the implications of what they label developmental leadership, a tradition that focuses on quietly and self-effacingly developing the leadership potential in others. Developmental leadership targets the silenced and overlooked members of communities, to help them find their voice and take a more active role in shaping their individual and collective destinies. Enthusiastically open to the contributions of others, especially those who have repeatedly been displaced and ignored by the majority, developmental leaders are disciplined learners, eager to reexamine old assumptions and reconsider ingrained practices. They take the lead in questioning, reevaluating as they try to see things from new vantage points, and working tirelessly "to get others to do the same. They are such good listeners, because they see themselves learning from everyone, no matter how young, inexperienced or silenced a person might be" (p. 272). Developmental leaders value constructed knowing, the process by which groups of people come to new understandings about themselves and the larger world through the give and take of spirited dialogue. Such leaders are drawn from both genders, with Myles Horton (founder and creator of the Highlander Folk School) an exemplar of the process.

SERVANT LEADERSHIP

Still another leadership practice that underscores learning leadership is servant leadership. The servant leader stands in sharp contrast to the conventional leader. The conventional leader aspires to lead because of a need for power or material wealth or for some other extrinsic desire. Such a leader is a leader first. The test of leadership of this kind may be found in such things as productivity figures, movement up school league tables, or the volume of legislation signed into law. The servant leader is a servant first and reluctantly accepts a leadership role in order to support and assist those who remain unserved. The test of the servant leader's effectiveness is the extent to which followers' actual needs (which may differ markedly from official definitions of what these needs are) are realized. Robert Greenleaf (1977), one of the leading articulators of this theory, says that the key questions for the servant leader are: "Do those served grow as persons? Do they, while being served, become healthier, wiser, freer, more autonomous, more likely themselves to become servants? And what is the effect on the least privileged in society; will they benefit, or, at least, not be further deprived?" (pp. 13–14).

With regard to servant leadership, we caution against overemphasis on autonomy; it can undercut the collective dynamic referred to earlier. But we affirm the importance placed on furthering the interests of those most disregarded by the majority. We are also aware that there are situations in which meeting people's felt and expressed needs is the last thing we should be doing. In a consumer society in which people judge their own, and others', worth by the amount of goods they possess, we must challenge the need to engage in the pursuit of ever more expensive designer possessions. In a racist society, the last thing we need to do is affirm White supremacy by supporting the needs of those who wish to overturn affirmative action, which they view as discriminating against White males.

One of the defining qualities of servant leaders is their inclination to listen first. Listening, according to Greenleaf, is a discipline that must be steadfastly practiced and, despite lack of immediate results, consistently employed. It is the central practice of servant leaders because "true listening builds strength in other people" (p. 17). On a related note, servant leaders use words sparingly. They have learned how inadequate speech can be, how feebly it captures the richness of lived experience. Their art is learning how to say just enough, without excess or embellishment, to help the listener connect the words that are spoken to her or his own experience. O'Toole (1996) argues that even some leaders typically viewed as distant and charismatic were noted for their listening ability and for their willingness to take dissent seriously.

He makes this case for such Rushmorean figures as Washington, Jefferson, Lincoln, and, to a lesser extent, Theodore Roosevelt. O'Toole observes that these presidents listened "to their followers and encouraged dissenting opinion among their advisors." Accordingly, they all chose their cabinets carefully to reflect a broad range of opinion and used them "to test ideas, explore all sides of issues, and to air the full range of opinion" (p. 29).

Matusak (1997) adds that leaders who listen must do so fully and genuinely. When leaders are authentic listeners, they remain open to new and different ideas. They convey that they believe what another person has to say is important, that they are interested in it even if they disagree with what is said. They strive to understand this person's rationale and realize that it is valid within the speaker's frame of reference. This is a leadership implementation of the critical theorist Jürgen Habermas's ideas (1973) regarding the four validity claims that must be met for communication to be authentic. Habermas believes that to communicate authentically speakers strive to use language that stands the best chance of being understood by hearers; this is the claim of *comprehensibility*. Authentic speakers also do their best to give the fullest possible information about the matter under consideration; this is the claim of *truth*. The extent to which speakers follow the rules of talk that prevail in a discussion community is a third feature of authentic speech; this is the claim of *rightness*. Rightness is crucial because communication is impossible without people observing the intuitively understood norms and rules governing speech, a sort of broadly accepted road map of talk. Finally, we need to know that the people speaking to us are sincerely interested in making themselves understandable and in understanding us in return; this is the claim of *authenticity*. To Habermas and Matusak, meeting these claims is crucial to establishing and sustaining trust.

Embedded in the practice of servant leadership is a criterion by which societies are judged. For Greenleaf, "caring for persons, the more able and the less able serving each other, is the rock upon which a good society is built" (p. 49). The test of the servant leader is the extent to which this person is generous and giving, so that her effect is an enlargement of kindness and joy. At the center of such leadership are the intertwined notions of collectivity and compassion. Compassion is, after all, a collective phenomenon, rooted in the sense that others' flourishing and one's own happiness are inseparable. But caring and compassion are not to be sprayed indiscriminately; rather, they are to be directed specifically at the most marginalized, underserved, and despised sectors of the populace.

Servant leaders view diversity as a strength to be savored and appreciated, not a problem to be overcome. For De Pree (1989), "an understanding of the diversity of people's gifts, talents, and skills" underlies every interaction and decision. Understanding diversity includes knowing how diminished we all are when voices go unheard, and how important it is "to begin to think about being abandoned to the strengths of others" (p. 9). A thoughtful approach to diversity calls on us to celebrate the talents and gifts each person brings to the community, and challenges leaders, in particular, to learn that "the art of leadership lies in polishing and liberating and enabling" (p. 10) those talents and gifts for the benefit of all. Again, in servant leadership the importance to genuine diversity of the least heard voices is paramount.

Organic Leadership

The idea that all have something to contribute to leadership is at the heart of the thought of the Italian political activist Antonio Gramsci. Gramsci was a founder member of the Italian Communist Party, a journalist for socialist newspapers, and a strategist for the factory council movement in 1920s Turin, which advocated direct worker control of industries such as the Fiat motor company. In 1926, while a Communist deputy in the Italian parliament, he was arrested by the fascist government (Mussolini had come to power in 1922) and placed under police supervision. In May 1928, he was tried as a political prisoner, with the prosecutor reportedly declaring "for twenty years we must stop this brain from working." He spent the rest of his life in prison, interspersed with brief spells in hospital, until dying in 1937 in a sanitarium days after his full release finally became legal. There could hardly be a more dramatic illustration of Zinn's (1990) observation that "how we think is . . . a matter of life and death" (p. 2).

Gramsci developed the concept of the organic intellectual to describe the kind of people we profile in this book. Where he talks about organic intellectuals, we talk of organic leaders, drawn from a movement or community, remaining tied to it even though their work may take them out of it, and spending their life fighting a war of position (as Gramsci called it) on their group's behalf. Organic intellectuals were "elites of a new type, which arise directly out of the masses, but remain in contact with them" (p. 340). These leaders are able to formulate and communicate a strategy for political revolution in terms that the working class or racial minorities can understand, because they are themselves formed by working-class culture or their racial membership. The end result of this effort is establishment of a new hegemony reflective of working class interests.

Building on Marx, Gramsci contends that unless a cadre of organic leaders emerges to act as a catalyst for revolutionary change, a group, class, or race will remain one *in* itself (one tied together by virtue of habit and culture) rather than one *for* itself (with a self-conscious awareness of its interests that is held by the majority of the group). Organic intellectuals bring the necessary leadership to help people realize their true situation of oppression and to prompt them to decide to change this through organized, mass political action; in other words, to become groups for themselves. The existence of organic leaders is crucial to the awakening of revolutionary fervor. In Gramsci's view, the dynamics of a large-scale political movement are such that "innovation cannot come from the mass, or at least at the beginning, except through the mediation of an elite" (p. 335). Organic intellectuals have the responsibility to help people understand the existence of ruling-class hegemony and the need to replace this with a hegemony that reflects the wishes of the majority. This is precisely how Nelson Mandela framed his life's work: to ensure that the majority of South Africans constituted a government reflecting their interests.

To lead effectively, organic intellectuals need the capacity to empathize with the condition of the oppressed. They must be capable of "feeling the elementary passions of the people, understanding them and therefore explaining and justifying them" (Gramsci, 1971, p. 418). This is why it is so difficult for well-meaning middle-class radicals to become organic leaders. Despite Paulo Freire's oft-quoted injunction (1973) for middle-class activists to commit class suicide so they can work in an authentic way with the peasantry and other oppressed groups, this transition is highly problematic. What of attempts to commit racial, rather than class, suicide? How can White adult activists ever experience the systemic racism visited daily on people of color? As Holst (2002) points out, discussions of organic leaders in the civil rights struggle that focus on Martin Luther King (the emblematic organic intellectual, in Cornel West's view) tend to ignore how the Civil Rights Movement "produced organic intellectuals from the Black share-croppers and working class throughout the South" (p. 85). Also, from an Africentric adult education perspective (Colin, 1988, 2002; Colin and Guy, 1998) racial suicide by Whites is a meaningless idea. The central definitional component of Africentrism (Asante, 1998a, 1998b) is that its proponents exhibit racial membership of the African Diaspora, a membership that ties them together by culture, tradition, and the experience of racism. Of course, Whites can be supporters and allies of struggles of people of color, and they may sometimes be invited to participate in them, but they cannot be movement organic leaders in Gramsci's terms.

As we think of leaders embedded within social movements, Gramsci's adumbration of the leader as organic intellectual has been helpful to us. To him the job of a leader who is an organic intellectual is to "organize human masses and create the terrain on which men [sic] move, acquire consciousness of their position, struggle etc." (p. 377). There is no pretense of neutrality or objectivity here, no compulsion to see the oppressor's point of view. The intellectual as organic leader works to galvanize working-class opposition and translate this into the formation of an effective revolutionary party. In this analysis, education is a site for political practice in which organic intellectuals can assist the working class in its revolutionary struggle.

Our emphasis in this book is on leadership that places learning at its center, and this certainly encompasses many of the ideals and practices encompassed in the preceding five models. For example, learning leadership involves placing one's own agenda and persona in the background and the goals of the movement, community, or organization in the foreground. The first priority of learning leaders when allocating resources is the development of their staff, and they themselves will willingly forgo personal opportunities to make sure others get what they need to meet new challenges. Studying the lives of such leaders as Ella Baker and Jessie De La Cruz, Ellen Cantarow (1980) summarized well what sets these leaders apart: "They have been behind-the-scenes leaders who have worked to build strength, self-confidence, skills, and commitment in others. [They] believe that while organizers and leaders may inspire people, help them think through problems and shape goals, it is finally the people themselves, at the grassroots, who must bring a future that is still only in our imaginings" (p. xli). This gives a clue to how middle-class White radicals can work as leaders. They can use their privilege explicitly and purposefully for the good of groups other than those they are drawn from, and they can work to place ego gratification aside as they pursue these purposes.

What is distinctive about learning leadership is that it highlights in bold relief commitment to, and practice of, learning. A capacity to learn from experience; desire to explore new areas of knowledge and practice; readiness to critique, revise, and sometimes even abandon past assumptions in light of new events or insights; and concern for the learning of members as the most important purpose of an organization, community, or movement—these things are what make learning a way of leading. In our view, an important practice of learning leaders is to consistently and publicly model their own commitment to and practice of learning. Some elements of this are difficult; you can't really invite colleagues over to your house to watch you read, or to see you come to fresh insights as you take a shower. However, you can speak in meetings or informal conversations about this reading or these insights and how they have affected your thinking and therefore your practice. In organization newsletters or movement rallies, you can reveal how your learning has challenged or confirmed assumptions you have about the way your community, organization, or movement can achieve its goals.

Perhaps the most important element of learning leadership, however, is being open to learning from the people around you and letting them see how crucial this is for your own practice and development. This last point cannot be overemphasized. Leaders love to learn from the people to whom they are responsible. They would rather learn than teach, rather listen than speak, rather absorb new ideas than unfurl the latest innovation. Such leaders are committed to collective group leadership, to leading by virtue of bringing to the forefront the multiple talents found throughout the community, not through the brilliance of the authority figure at the top. It is not easy to lead in this way, accustomed as so many are to a culture that says the leader is the one who takes charge and tells everyone else what to do. But it does not take long, if the leader is consistent, to lead by drawing on the group's strengths and by taking seriously their pent-up ideas for making change.

THE NINE LEARNING TASKS OF LEADERSHIP

In this book, we tell the stories of many actual community and organizational leaders who share a commitment to leading through learning. We have found that their success as learning leaders is dependent on a number of dispositions, capacities, and public practices. We have described these, using the language of learning, as the nine learning tasks of leadership as we conceive it. The first of these tasks, the one that is foundational for all others, is *learning how to be open to the contributions of others*. Once one is able to practice this habit, then the second learning leadership task—*learning how to reflect critically on one's practice*—becomes possible. Our contention is that critical reflection is intrinsically a social learning process in which the perceptions and interpretations of others are crucial. Only if one is open to the contributions of others can one gather the perspectives needed to practice critical reflection. A third leadership task is *learning how to support the growth of others*. In terms of what we wish for those whom we serve, the enhanced capacity for them to learn is paramount. From this perspective, the focus of traditional performance appraisals becomes not "How well did you do your job this year?" but "What and how did you learn this year?"

Connected to supporting the learning of others is the fourth task, that of *learning how to develop collective leadership*. Collective leadership flows from a culture in which engagement in, and sharing of, learning is an expectation and a priority. As people learn new skills, dispositions, and epistemologies, they inevitably become aware of how individual learning is both premised on and contributes to the learning of others. We cannot learn to be critically reflective, analyze experience, question ourselves, practice democracy, sustain hope, or create community without the necessary involvement of others. Once we start to see that the collective is the source of so much of our learning, our strength, and our identity, it is but a short step to realizing that leadership also resides in the collective. When our perception of learning as an individual phenomenon changes to one of learning as a group process, then the idea that leadership is like learning—something that moves around the community and is dependent on the involvement of others—becomes commonplace.

Task five, *learning how to analyze experience*, is a leadership practice that all the leaders profiled in this book exemplified to a high degree. One of the most difficult dimensions of this task is when its practice leads us to challenge old assumptions and then to reconfigure accepted practices. In the conventional notion of leadership, a leader is not supposed to change her mind too much. She should create a vision, commit to it, and then relentlessly pursue it through hell or high water. Changing your mind is not an option in this model because to do so is perceived as a sign of weakness, an indication that you don't have the guts to push your agenda, or that you must have misdiagnosed the situation to begin with. We are particularly intrigued with those activist leaders who manage to engage publicly in reflection on experience—especially when their analysis led to radical shifts in direction—without weakening people's confidence in them.

Learning how to question oneself and others is the sixth task, and once again we contend that it is impossible to practice this alone. First, one learns questioning by seeing how others do it. This is where an organization like the Highlander Folk School was so influential on generations of activists. In Highlander workshops, practically the only action that facilitators took was to ask an occasional question. Ella Baker, Septima Clark, and other women activists (Lewis, 1998) lived this task throughout their lives, though McDermott (2007) cautions that Highlander itself was not immune to internal sexism. Baker was never satisfied with her efforts to promote a bottom-up approach to learning and social change and continuously questioned how she could involve ordinary people in making important organizational decisions for the NAACP and SCLC. The environmentalist Aldo Leopold was also driven to constantly question his own ideas and get his students to reconsider how their assumptions about the natural environment often had multiple unforeseen consequences. The questions learning leaders pose challenge their followers to see complexities and interrelationships in major social issues and launch inquiries that stretch the bounds of their worldview. Moreover, this work is never done. What is learned one day is used the next as a bridge to considering a new set of understandings and challenges.

Learning democracy is the seventh task of learning leadership, and one that, like learning to question, never ends. Learning democracy requires, in the opinion of the adult educator Eduard Lindeman (Lindeman and Smith, 1951), studying a number of democratic disciplines. To live democratically one must learn to honor diversity, live with the partial functioning of the democratic ideal, avoid the trap of false antithesis (where we are always forced to choose between either-or, mutually exclusive options), accept the compatibility of ends and means (where we avoid the temptation to bypass the democratic process in the interests of speedily reaching a decision regarded as obviously right and necessary), correlate the functioning of social institutions (health, education, and social services) with democratic purposes, develop collective forms of social and economic planning, live with contrary decisions, and appreciate the comedy inherent in democracy's contradictions. For Lindeman, learning democracy was not just a leadership imperative; it was the central task of adult life.

When efforts to live democratically fail to reach full fruition (as is inevitable), then the eighth task—*learning to sustain hope in the face of struggle*—comes in to play. One of the dangers of learning leadership is that the longer one learns about leadership practice the more one becomes aware of just how deep and strong are the structural forces that oppose attempts to change the status quo. The development of radical pessimism (where realizing the forces ranged against us causes us to lose hope) is a danger facing all those who think and act critically. Prime examples for us of leaders who sustained hope in the face of unbearable animosity and political isolation are Paul Robeson and Nelson Mandela. As a result of being pilloried in the public press for his support of the

Soviet Union and his commitment to anticolonial struggles across the globe (as well as fighting White supremacy in the United States), Robeson was deprived of his passport and livelihood, forced to defend himself in front of the House Un-American Activities Committee, and labeled a traitor. Yet despite all these pressures, he remained steadfast in the certainty of his belief, his radical hope that the dawn of a nonracist, democratic socialist society was just around the corner. Mandela's imprisonment was not sought as an act of martyrdom; in fact, he went to great lengths to hide his identity so as to avoid capture. But when the government repeatedly promised him freedom so long as he refrained from political organizing, he consistently refused. Throughout his autobiography *Long Walk to Freedom* (Mandela, 1994), he writes again and again of how his hope—his faith even—that the dawn of a properly democratic South Africa was inevitable never wavered. Che Guevara is another who, though mired in the Cuban jungle, hopelessly outnumbered, plagued by illness, and working with a few comrades and hopelessly outdated weapons, never lost his conviction that his guerrilla army would win the support of the mass populace and lead to the inevitable overthrow of the Batista regime.

Our ninth and final learning task is *learning to create community.* The leaders we profile in this book all seek to build community and teach the value of community-based decision making and leadership. Each of them has an intense interest in building communities where people's experience and knowledge are honored and where opportunities for members to develop their talents and capacities are limitless. When Aldo Leopold spoke of the biotic community, he meant an environment in which each organism contributes an irreplaceable element and in which the loss of any part somehow diminishes the whole. This is how Myles Horton, Ella Baker, Mary Parker Follett, and Eleanor Roosevelt regarded communities of human beings. They set out to create conditions for every person to add something invaluable to the community of learners. In so doing, the group's success became dependent on each individual's contribution. Building communities in which the members of those communities are authentically empowered to make important decisions for themselves and their neighbors remains a chief objective of the work of leaders who learn.

In the first half of each of the following nine chapters, we share at some length our understanding of what each of these learning tasks involves and how leaders practice them. Our objective is to show as clearly and straightforwardly as we can how leaders, particularly those pursuing social justice, place learning at the center of practice. We explore in specific, concrete terms how learning leaders continue to engage, challenge, and appreciate their collaborators, as well as stimulate them to meaningful action. Our belief is that when leaders make learning the most salient habit in any community, movement, or organization, the members are much more likely to claim their own empowerment and change the world. A small part of this first section entails introducing remarkable learning leaders, nearby and distant, well known and anonymous, who have been highly successful in keeping their own learning going while also doing everything possible to sustain the learning of their comrades.

In the second half of each of these chapters, we explore at much greater length the story of a particular learning leader who exemplifies the learning task that is the focus of the chapter. Our objective is not to offer full-scale biographies of these leaders and activists but to include highly focused vignettes or portraits of those who saw learning as a central part of their quest to create a more just and equitable society. For these leaders, learning was not a byproduct of the social justice struggle, nor primarily a personal characteristic worth cultivating. Learning was central to that struggle both in moving it forward and as evidence that it was making a difference for those committed to it. These learning leaders constantly brought attention to their own learning when recounting their efforts to foment change. Furthermore, they saw their leadership as including a strong teaching component. Yet the most important parts of their teaching were learning how to ask stimulating questions and being open to the teachings of their students, members, and followers. Such an attitude, incidentally, aligns perfectly with Burns's contention that transformational leaders always remain open to being led by their followers.

The leaders we profile all stand out as thinkers and activists in pursuit of some kind of social transformation. For Ella Baker, the goal was to end racism and ensure that African Americans and oppressed peoples everywhere enjoyed all the rights and privileges to which they were entitled. For Septima Clark, it was to allow Black people the freedom to educate themselves and be full, active members of a democratic society. Jane Addams wanted everyone to have the basic necessities, which would allow them to take full advantage of all available educational opportunities and learn to work together in communities of learning. Paul Robeson, like Ella Baker, sought to end racism and ensure that people of all colors and classes identified their common interest in creating a democratic socialist society. Aldo Leopold's objective was to help people learn to conserve and appreciate the natural environment and develop the critical skills needed to oppose those bent on its destruction. Mary Parker Follett saw participatory democracy as the only sensible response to society's problems and wanted everyone to understand fully its many advantages. Cesar Chavez sought economic and social justice for farm workers and never wavered in his belief that with work and persistence that day of justice would eventually arrive. Nelson Mandela wanted nothing less than to overthrow White supremacy in South Africa and make it possible for Blacks to participate without restriction in the life of his country. Myles Horton sought to use progressive adult learning methods to help poor people from all over the south gain greater control over the economic, social, and political forces shaping their communities.

As we have said, all of these leaders put learning at the center of their efforts. They gauged their progress by the degree to which their constituents, collaborators, and colleagues continued to learn how to analyze and act on the problems facing them. These leaders, without exception, also maintained a broad outlook on their work, seeing it always as a struggle for their comrades' shared humanity and creating the political conditions most likely to bring about each person's flourishing. Even if they did not say so explicitly, they agreed with Myles Horton that anything they wanted for themselves, anything that might help them grow and thrive, they must also want for everyone else without exception. That is the kind of community they all believed in. That is the kind of society they all attempted to build. The learning tasks these remarkable leaders executed as they pursued this goal are the focus of this book.

Chapter Two

Learning to Be Open to the Contributions of Others

At the root of learning leadership is the practice of openness, which is why learning to be open is the first of the learning tasks we address in detail. Openness is the willingness to entertain a variety of alternative perspectives, be receptive to contributions from everyone regardless of previous attainment or current status, and create dialogic open spaces—multiple opportunities for diverse voices and opinions to be heard. When we practice openness, we try to hold in temporary abeyance our own assumptions and preconceptions so that we can consider fully what others want to contribute. This is not easy for leaders who are accustomed to having their say first or who are used to dominating the conversation. Leaders who are open have learned to stop talking and start listening to what others have to say. They strive to let words, ideas, and actions flow freely, actively, and publicly, inviting the contributions of others with a hospitable and lively enthusiasm.

Our interest in openness as a learning task of leadership makes us think first of public, community forums where openness is such a critical element of effective group deliberation. When people come together to talk, think, and make important decisions, leaders who practice openness do all they can to make room for many voices and opinions. They believe that every person in the organization or community has something valuable to teach and that everyone can contribute something for the good of the group. These beliefs are premised on the assumption that people develop a sense of belonging to a group as their contributions are invited and affirmed and that group members will consequently respond creatively to the challenge to think more deeply and act more boldly. Openness is premised on the idea that every voice is precious and that every person has knowledge to impart that can benefit the entire group. Unless leaders create opportunities for these contributions to be felt, the community as a whole is diminished.

Of course, there are potential dangers in this perspective, particularly in the naïve idea that the knowledge and experience people wish to contribute are always enriching. Experience is most emphatically not an unalloyed good, or inherently broadening. Depending on our conditioning, we can interpret our experience in a certain way to develop knowledge that confirms racist views, underscores an unquestioning adherence to authority, or builds the case that a selfish orientation is both realistic and morally defensible. Many times the practice of openness requires leaders to intervene to stop certain people from monopolizing the floor and drowning out the contributions of others. At other times it calls leaders to stand against an emerging and convenient consensus, to force people to confront their unacknowledged biases, or to challenge their naked self-interest.

Leaders who are guiding groups in learning to be open work in the same way as architects charged with fostering community among people working in a large, disorienting building with many closed doors. One of the first things such architects would demand is that the doors be removed from their hinges and that people be encouraged to move freely around the building. Although the terrain remains confusing, the ability to explore without constraint feels liberating and the chances for individual and small-group learning are greatly enhanced. No room now is off-limits; no route from one part of the building to another is now blocked. As people roam about and gain familiarity with a structure that had once seemed austere and unapproachable, they also begin to get to know one another better. In helping each other come to know a formerly forbidden place, they gain access to one another's lives as they are drawn into building community.

As we shall see in Chapter Eight, openness and democracy are inextricably intertwined; you can't have one without the other.

However, we do realize that merely removing doors is not enough. There must also be spaces in the building where people can huddle with allies, free of surveillance, to challenge prevailing agendas and interpretations. If doors are removed and the most privileged are allowed to eavesdrop, or to broadcast their views loudly, nothing is achieved other than confirming the status quo and heightening surveillance so that subversive and revolutionary perspectives are prevented from forming. This is a point advocates of Foucault make in their critique of open plan offices, and it is the reason Stephen B prefers teaching with the door closed.

As important as it is to maintain openness in public forums, leaders must also learn to be open in more personal contexts. Being open in an encounter with another individual requires the leader to let the other person take the lead in the conversation, to be willing to have that individual set the agenda. When leaders create opportunities for such one-on-one exchanges, they must quiet their natural impulse to talk about themselves and their accomplishments and to create a climate for honest, heartfelt expression on the part of others. Similarly, leaders must set aside time for observing and being with others, surrendering personal agendas and highlighting nonjudgmental receptiveness.

Listening carefully is sometimes particularly necessary—but also difficult—when trying to understand the experiences and reasoning behind views we find distasteful or vicious. If we are in a relatively isolated position with little freedom to maneuver, or if we are vastly outnumbered by the conservative majority that wishes to prevent change, our only hope for survival and advancement is to know our enemies so well we can outthink, outplan, and outwit them. Listening carefully is therefore necessary if we are to understand the attitudes and instincts of those powerful members of a community who are working strenuously to deny democracy. It is a necessary disciplined study for us to take the most effective action possible to oppose their interests. Attentive listening helps us identify weak spots and contradictions that can then be worked on to undermine the automatic assumption of power and authority that the most privileged quickly claim.

For leaders who work in a competitive, hierarchical, privatized environment, listening in this way is therefore a political as well as a communicative project.

As we have said, one of the most difficult challenges facing leaders striving to be open is the issue of remaining open to ideas that are anathema to them. To find ways to hear out others—however boring, hateful, long-winded, or pernicious they appear—can tax even the most committed leader. But if it is the case that people can learn from anyone, no matter how unlikely the teacher may appear to be at first glance, then the willingness to hear out others who seem to be diametrically opposed to our own views is critical. As we all know, this is much easier to espouse than to do. Most of us are more than willing to entertain ideas that are familiar and that will probably endorse our own. But a radical commitment to learning demands that we maintain a commitment to openness, regardless of the source or our initial reaction to what another person puts forward.

Of course, one of the hardest aspects of openness is deciding when too much transparency can work against the democratic interests and agenda one is trying to advance. Warning those in power who wish to retain their entrenched privilege exactly how one is going to go about extending democracy and abolishing this privilege is naïve and foolish. So we acknowledge there are limits to openness depending on the political situation within which we work. Openness is fine when there is a commitment to openness on the part of others. But when our commitment to openness is used against us as an excuse to allow voices of bigotry, authoritarianism, and self-satisfaction to broadcast uninterruptedly, then openness is counterproductive.

THE BENEFITS OF OPENNESS

In his book *Leading Without Power*, Max De Pree captures the value of openness with poignant concision. "A closed organization is a tragedy," he says. "An open one holds enormous promise" (1997, p. 12). Why is the absence of openness such a tragedy? A closed environment forestalls opportunities for people to learn from each other. If people can't share their mutual discoveries, the community cannot grow and the incentive to learn withers.

Communities and organizations that are closed sap enthusiasm and joy.

If leaders are able to encourage climates or structures that allow expression of new ideas and unfamiliar perspectives, opportunities for learning abound. Openness can create opportunities for unimagined initiatives to be tried. It can shake people up, getting them to think outside the box, and value what they have rejected or avoided in the past. More important, it can create an environment where dissenting voices are genuinely welcomed and where the clash of opposing viewpoints can be witnessed. This sort of disequilibrium provokes creative thought and action and gives people the chance to try out new ways of seeing and doing. It is a chance to experiment, to play the "believing game," as Peter Elbow (1986) has called it, in which, for a limited time, we think, speak, and act as if we adopted a controversial or unfamiliar perspective. To be open is to create possibility, fuel hope, behave as if the options for the future are virtually unlimited.

How a Leader Develops the Ability to Practice Openness

Leaders are best positioned to develop openness when they value and understand its potential benefits. In short, to practice openness, leaders must rank it highly as an intrinsic part of professional behavior or effective change agency. Stories, anecdotes, parables, and legends—narratives of all kinds—can be shared to show what happens in organizations and communities when small experiments are attempted throughout the membership. Meetings can be redesigned to invite a variety of views without bringing premature closure. As movements and organizations are strategizing, a plan of wide reading can be suggested, including studying materials that directly challenge current policies and practices. Two powerful leaders of guerrilla armies, Nelson Mandela and Che Guevara, both attest to the power of reading for the practical life-and-death decisions guerrilla leaders routinely need to make. One-on-one conversations can also be arranged that allow ideas and personal experiences to be shared more freely and extemporaneously. At present, this is what the discipline of executive coaching does, but it is available only for those privileged few at the top levels of an organizational hierarchy. Openness requires movements and organizations to find ways to encourage such coaching (often called mentoring) that are available to all, not just an advantaged elite.

WHERE WE HAVE SEEN OPENNESS PRACTICED

When he thinks of openness, Steve P recalls his experiences back in the early 1990s with a dean of education at a medium-sized Catholic university in the upper Midwest. This dean made a point of not imposing his political or ideological agenda on his faculty, but on giving them the widest possible scope to make their own decisions and set their own agendas. In fact, this dean did have an agenda: to put deliberative and decision-making authority, to the greatest extent possible, in the hands of faculty. Almost without exception, the decisions that emerged from such deliberations received the full, unwavering support of this dean. His unalterable commitment to openness was undoubtedly connected to other values that he held dear: trust in the ability of this faculty to make sound and sustainable decisions; respect for how much this faculty could accomplish when given free rein; love for the faculty's passions and convictions about the purpose and meaning of education at its best. The openness this leader so clearly espoused unleashed in many of us the sense that we could accomplish anything, and that in the process of striving to do so we could joyfully perform our work at a greatly heightened pitch of shared satisfaction. In other words, the openness practiced by this dean, and its attending values of trust, respect, and love, produced a higher degree of professional contentment in many of Stephen P's School of Education colleagues than most of them had ever known.

Clearly, this dean put a great deal of faith in openness. He believed that unheard perspectives would be shared, that greater collaboration would be fostered, and that opportunities for colleagues to learn from each other would be increased. For many whom this dean led, these benefits were readily apparent. For others, however, the sometimes disorienting discussions that accompanied such openness were distracting and even disturbing. They preferred a more predictable and orderly environment in which positional leaders set the direction to be followed, with little input from subordinates. We understand the basis for this point of view, but we question its long-term value. Like lecturers who never solicit ideas from their students, leaders who do not create spaces for followers to be heard fail to take advantage of the multiple viewpoints that can be found in their communities and lose out on the creative ideas that inevitably reside there.

These approaches to leadership are rooted in differing assumptions about people. One view seems to assume that people aren't all that creative or imaginative, that they don't add much value to the organization or movement, and so inviting their opinion isn't going to make much difference. The other view is premised on the idea that the brains of movement or organizational members are teeming with ideas and creative plans for addressing organizational or movement problems. Finding ways to tap into those ideas and plans helps the movement and excites and motivates co-workers by acknowledging their contributions to the group.

How We and Others Have Lived This Openness

One of the ways we try to live openness is in our one-on-one advisement of graduate students as they approach a topic for a master's paper or doctoral dissertation. As we work with such students, our goal is to put our own interests and passions aside and do everything we can to draw out theirs. This is challenging, for a number of reasons. One is that we want them to choose a topic that parallels our own interests. Another is that they are used to being manipulated by their instructors and playing the game of pleasing authority figures. They are highly attuned to all the signals, visual and verbal, that indicate when to concur with their teacher's suggestions and let their own goals and desires go unrealized. Often a kind of dance results in which they make every effort not to step on the instructor's toes and thus take part in the exchange in a wary, half-hearted manner. Under such conditions figuring out what students are passionate about can border on the impossible. But if we work at it, old habits of students deferring to authority figures and withholding their true desires can be supplanted by a different, much more open model of instructor-learner relations. Listening actively to students and striving to hear what truly engages them is part of the process. But so is echoing, paraphrasing, and restating what students are trying to tell us, not to serve our own purposes but to help them find a voice and a purposeful project that is ultimately of meaning to them.

The Talking Practice group both of us were involved with at one time (we called it "Talking Teaching") is another example of how we've tried to live openness. This group was wholly voluntary and met once or twice a month during lunch. It had no purpose other than for its members to talk about whatever teaching practice was on their mind on that day. Without a formal agenda or need to produce an institutionally approved bottom line, both of us felt that this group enabled some of the most open conversation we had ever enjoyed in our lives.

The Critical Incident Questionnaire (CIQ) we have used in classrooms and meetings as a formative evaluation tool is another attempt at openness. The CIQ is a single-page form that is handed out to students once a week at the end of the last class you have with them that week. It asks five questions:

1. At what moment in class this week did you feel most engaged with what was happening?
2. At what moment in class this week were you most distanced from what was happening?
3. What action that anyone (teacher or student) took this week did you find most affirming or helpful?
4. What action that anyone took this week did you find most puzzling or confusing?
5. What is it about the class this week that surprised you the most? (This could be about your own reactions to what went on, something that someone did, or anything else that occurred.)

The CIQ takes about five minutes to complete, and students are told *not* to put their name on the form. They are also told that at the next class we will share the group's responses with them. After we have collected the CIQ responses, we read through them, looking for common themes, comments that indicate problems or confusion, and anything contentious or needing further clarification. Major differences in students' perceptions of the same activity are recorded as well as single comments that strike us as particularly profound or intriguing.

At the start of the first class of the next week, we spend three to five minutes reporting back to students a summary of the chief themes that emerged in their responses. If students have made comments that cause us to change how we teach, we acknowledge this and explain why the change seems worth making. We try also to clarify any actions, ideas, requirements, or exercises that seem to be causing confusion. Criticisms of our actions are reported and discussed. If contentious issues have emerged, we talk about how they can be negotiated so that everyone feels heard and respected. Quite often students write down comments expressing their dislike of something we insist they do. When this happens, we know we must take some time to reemphasize why we believe the activity is so important and to make the best case we can about how it contributes to students' long-term interests.

We have also used the CIQ as a meeting evaluation tool when we chaired departments. The process is the same as in a classroom: the last order of business is completion of the CIQ and the first item on the next meeting's agenda is the CIQ report. One difference is that we insist that we as head of the department not collect the forms. Instead, department members take it in turn to collect them and then present the summary of responses at the next meeting. For us this has worked well to bring the subterranean rumblings of dissent that usually follow meetings out into the open where they can be addressed directly.

In a perfect world, the problem of discovering the true passions of others probably wouldn't be very difficult. But in our organizations and communities the dominant ideologies of individualism, competition, and privatism, and the structures these ideologies inform, have erected many barriers to self- and group realization. Leaders who are open must understand that there is much history, culture, and habit to be challenged before people can begin an authentic process of making the most of their abilities. Talking about developing self-knowledge and self-awareness is valuable, but we rarely take the time that is necessary to allow these things to emerge.

WHAT BLOCKS OR PREVENTS THE PRACTICE OF OPENNESS

In our experience, openness is rarely practiced, so it seems that almost everything potentially blocks it or threatens it. Administrators who want to control the organization they are responsible for rarely see much virtue in openness. It is easier and safer for them to keep a lid on the perspectives that are expressed, to squelch the impulse for creativity or originality. We hear it again and again. When someone has an idea or wants to try a new initiative, the supervisor or the person to whom this person reports sabotages it. It is fairly clear that the greatest obstacle to openness is a leader who doesn't want it, who fears how easily it might undermine his or her authority.

Size gets in the way of openness. It intimidates people, making them less likely to speak up, less inclined to express an alternative point of view. Size contributes to a perception that conditions are not open, even when they are. The larger the organization, the less likely it is that new ideas and dissenting views will be disseminated. Even if there is a degree of openness within some pockets of the organization, this will not be experienced widely. Sustaining openness requires a persistent and resourceful leader who knows where these pockets are, who pushes stubbornly for them to be opened further, and who does not become discouraged in the face of resistance. In an important way, the learning task of being open is also enabled by the learning task of sustaining hope in the face of struggle.

Openness is also threatened by the fact the opportunities to practice it are so rare. In an age of automaton conformity (Fromm, 1941), one-dimensional thought (Marcuse, 1964), and omnipresent surveillance (Foucault, 1980), most people have learned an ideology of compliance and self-censorship. Their energies are devoted to *not* being thought of as different, to *not* stepping out of line, and to being regarded as a team player—in other words, to being conformist. Even the much favored analogy of a team player, as Fromm (1956) argued, is highly controlling, implying as it does that a team player always sublimates her own passions and convictions to the overall team project, even if she is afflicted with severe misgivings about its rightness. Our view is that being an effective team member requires us to challenge a prematurely emerging consensus. It also calls us to create moments of deliberate dissonance in which members are forced to confront perspectives they would prefer to avoid.

WHAT ARE THE PERILS AND PITFALLS OF PRACTICING OPENNESS?

Part of the problem with any serious focus on openness is encouraging pernicious ideas. At least one view of openness would say that we must treat all opinions as the same, as all deserving of equal consideration no matter how harmful, hateful, stereotypical, or unsubstantiated they might be. Openness, according to this perspective, does not really permit leaders to endorse some ideas and censor others. In this line of analysis, there must be a blanket acceptance of all perspectives in the guise of an all-enveloping, unconditional positive regard for each person's dignity and worth. As Marcuse (1965) pointed out in his essay on repressive tolerance, this can lead to the unchallenged airing of hate-filled, racist, highly disrespectful viewpoints.

One could make a case that expressing such views is useful in that it helps us know exactly who the enemy is and how they think. Indeed, for the Australian Michael Newman (1994), defining the enemy is the whole point of adult education. One could also argue that before resolution of tension can begin, and before stereotypes can be countered, an airing of the basis for such tensions and stereotypes is healthy. This may indeed be necessary, but in the short run allowing such views to be expressed is enormously hurtful to the individuals and groups that are targeted and increases hatred and resentment to the extent that the possibility of dialogue across differences breaks down completely. It can also serve to legitimize deliberate suppression and marginalization of those viewed as different. Of course, openness implies and actively supports strong responses to repellent opinions, but this is not always enough. Nor is it guaranteed that such responses will come forward. The short-term damage to a small community can be devastating and irreversible.

Another drawback to openness is that it can have the effect of affirming the most conventional and commonly expressed viewpoints. If ideological manipulation has worked well, open expression of views leads to reassertion of the prevailing ideology or to privileging of a previously established consensus. Openness can also stall progress and movement. It is, at least in one sense, a license to express *any* viewpoint, however irrelevant or inconvenient. Any leader genuinely committed to openness must expect delays in deliberative processes and in reaching final decisions. Keeping the conversation open to hear every participant and ensure that every position is represented can be frustrating and incredibly draining. It can affect morale and curtail the momentum to move forward. Ironically, it can even undermine the push for openness by discouraging contributions from people who believe that by expressing one more point of view an important decision will be delayed or an already lengthy discussion will be prolonged.

It is not surprising that one of the leaders we profile (and who has been hugely influential on both of us) made a clear distinction between organizing (where openness can be self-defeating) and education (where openness is crucial and irreducible). Myles Horton felt that the exigencies of organizing meant one had to respond quickly and tactically to new developments, foreshortening the time otherwise available for consultation and conversation. At times such openness was a luxury organizers could ill afford (Horton and Freire, 1990). This point is developed even further in Ian Baptiste's articulation (2000) of a pedagogy of disempowerment (rather than empowerment) in which he argues that when one is working against powerful and entrenched interests the last thing one should do is be open about one's plans. To support his contention, he describes a situation in which he worked with a number of community groups on the south side of Chicago to assist them in reviving an area ravaged by pollution and migration. He admits to being committed to transparency, to having all his actions be above-board and subject to full public scrutiny. These liberal humanist sensibilities meant, "I succeeded only in playing into the hands of the government officials (and their lackeys in the community). They played me like a fiddle, pretending in public to be conciliatory, but wheeling and dealing in private" (p. 47).

We admit quite frankly that we have no final answers to the tensions and contradictions we describe. Perhaps the best we can hope for is that we can adopt strategies that limit the negative effects of practicing openness. Some way must be found to impose limits and time frames to prevent openness from becoming more of a problem than a solution, more of a constraint than an unleashing of possibilities. One way to do this is by creating periodic open spaces, places, and times where any idea can be put forward, any question raised, any practice tried. Punctuating organizational and community life with open space can bring new life and energy, while avoiding long, drawn-out, seemingly endless exchanges where no closure is ever reached. Brainstorming, the believing game, methodological belief (where for five minutes we agree to see another's view of life as true and consider what it would mean for our actions if this view were indeed the case), and various lateral thinking activities are common approaches. There is also a whole branch of work called future studies, where imaginative projections into the future are used to generate benchmarks by which we can judge current actions.

In the end, the value of openness for any group is so overwhelmingly strong that ways must be found to recognize and address problems without giving up on the basic idea. Leaders particularly must strive to model an openness that is humane and respectful. This kind of openness keeps the conversation moving in a variety of productive directions without allowing the exchange of ideas and information to undermine individual relationships or obstruct the goal of maintaining a cohesive community. Leaders have a special responsibility to practice an openness that allows the group to entertain a range of perspectives while also affirming the humanity and irreplaceable presence of every community member.

Jane Addams and the Practice of Openness

Jane Addams, the cofounder and director of Hull House (Chicago's most noteworthy settlement house), was renowned for her openness, the first of our learning tasks of leadership. In the years before World War I, Addams became arguably the most famous woman in America. The most important element in her life was her inclination to learn, her eagerness to profit from whatever others were willing to teach her. As a public figure, she modeled consistently a process of admitting her mistakes, slowly and patiently adopting a new point of view, and then explaining why her new perspective was more defensible than the old.

On September 19, 1889, with only the haziest sense of how they would proceed, Addams and Ellen Starr (a former classmate of hers at Rockford Female Seminary) opened Hull House at 335 South Halsted Street on the west side of Chicago. In these early years, Addams and Starr strove to furnish a space where the poor could gather to learn, commune, and envision a better life for themselves. But just as important (and Addams took a particularly strong stand in this regard), Hull House was a place for the educated residents to share what they knew, not primarily by telling or even by example but by living among plain people and learning from them, by "getting to know them and by trying to create with them a sense of community" (Diliberto, 1999, p. 163). At the center of this work, then, was the disposition of openness. Educated residents had to put aside their polished expertise and sense of superiority to acknowledge the power of ordinary, less well-educated people to enlighten them.

Throughout her life, Addams (1961) insisted that Hull House was created more to unleash the unexploited powers of young adults like her than to assist the poor. At Hull House, members of the working and middle classes came together to use what they had learned to improve society. In Addams's view, this was not primarily a patriarchal gesture in which the more privileged middle classes would lend a helping hand to the less-well-off working classes. It was a mutual, collaborative effort intended to enrich and broaden the lives of both groups, and to offer a vision of a beloved community in which each participant was actively contributing something valuable to the whole. You could almost say that in this way Hull House was an early exemplar of open space technology, in which participants generate and sustain their own communicative communities.

OPENNESS TO A COMMUNITY OF LEARNERS

As a proponent of collaborative learning and a practitioner of radical openness to new ideas and perspectives, Addams herself was unusually mindful of what others had to teach her. In a recent biography of her early years, Louise Knight (2005, p. 368) characterizes Addams as a careful listener who was known for her "questioning eyes" and "gentle inquisitiveness." Knight quotes one awestruck resident who said of Addams that she tried "to understand and interpret [everyone] correctly and graciously." Knight invokes Weber Linn, her nephew and an early biographer, who affirmed that "her real eagerness was always for understanding" (p. 368).

An earlier biographer, Allen Davis (1973/2000), also acknowledged that one of Addams's greatest gifts was her ability to change her mind as she sought to reappraise her assumptions regarding "the poverty she observed, the utter despair she witnessed during the depression of 1893" (p. 74). Much of this reappraisal was due to Addams's conversations with the women who were attracted to Hull House and came to reside there. The ones who stood out the most, who significantly reshaped Addams's social outlook and her professional priorities over time, were Florence Kelley, Julia Lathrop, and Mary Kenney. Each woman in her own way guided Addams toward new insights about herself and supported her in making contributions that directly addressed the country's most daunting problems.

In Allen Davis's (1973/2000) estimation, "More than anyone else Florence Kelley turned Jane Addams from philanthropist to reformer" (p. 78). Kelley assumed responsibility for the Hull House Labor Bureau, which trained immigrant women as domestics and quickly developed a rich and complementary relationship with Addams. These two women were very different. Addams maintained a calm, hopeful demeanor; Kelley was politically shrewd and full of visionary zeal. Addams was steady, balanced, and organized; Kelley was somewhat mercurial but also more imaginative about the future possibilities and how to bring them to fruition. However, thanks to Addams's own willingness to consider a range of views, their differences drew them together, rather than driving them apart. As Sklar (1995) observes: "Addams taught Kelley how to live and have faith in an imperfect world, and Kelley taught Addams how to make demands on the future" (p. 183). Because each was receptive to the contributions of the other, they created a dynamic energy and modeled a commitment to openness that caught the attention of staff and residents alike.

Their commitments to social justice were very real, though intriguingly different from one another. Addams saw social problems from many angles and tended to regard the interests of all participants sympathetically. Also, Addams abhorred conflict. Kelley, as Sklar (1995) notes, usually sided with the group she saw as most exploited, cast social conflict in stark contrasts of good and evil, and unhesitatingly "expressed anger against the causes of social injustice" (p. 185). This difference was not lost on Addams. Kelley's "ardent and provocative personality kindled a fire within Addams' aloof self-possession" (p. 185) that would over time provoke Addams to favor a more assertive progressivism that toiled against the causes of poverty, not just its outward manifestations. Both these developments would have been impossible without Addams's characteristic openness, which led her to frequently revisit and revise her commitments and practices.

Another Hull House resident who had a striking impact on Jane Addams' developing political activism was Julia Lathrop. On arriving at Hull House in 1890, she worked closely with community members and, under the influence of Florence Kelley, pursued a variety of institutional reforms to improve the lives of the immigrant families she knew so well. In 1912, she became the first head of the Children's Bureau and, in one commentator's words, "displayed a remarkable empathy for individuals combined with a pragmatic zest for the bureaucratic infighting necessary to achieve administrative and legislative reform" (Opdycke, 2000).

Allen Davis (1973/2000) believes Lathrop set an important example for Addams by maintaining a good sense of humor. Addams always had a rather solemn side to her personality and at times took herself too seriously. Lathrop "taught Jane how to appreciate the comic side of her experience and to laugh at her own predicament" (p. 76). In effect, she encouraged Addams to be open to the political and social absurdities that inevitably arose in settlement house work. But Lathrop, like Kelley, also assisted Addams in becoming more politically aware and active, and, when necessary, in taking a strong stand about policies and settlement house practices designed to serve the most vulnerable populations.

Addams's tendency to empathize with everyone's perspective could sometimes blind her to the people or groups enduring the most blatant exploitation. Lathrop was often the person likely to push Addams toward a political stance that held risks but that also could result in important gains for those with the fewest privileges. Taking such a stand was, of course, premised on Addams remaining open to its potential benefits and accepting its possible perils. Above all, Lathrop helped Addams see that the leaders at Hull House could not patronizingly extend to the community an array of services they thought would be beneficial. Rather, "Hull House had to be ready to meet whatever needs its neighbors presented" (Lagemann, 1985, p. 25). Under the influence of Lathrop and Addams, Hull House strove to embody a programmatic openness that meant being responsive to the expressed needs and wishes of community members.

Still another Hull House colleague who enlightened Addams in significant ways was Mary Kenney. Unlike Kelley and Lathrop, Kenney was solidly working-class and came from Irish immigrants. Around 1890, Kenney organized the Women's Bindery Union No. 1, holding early meetings in the backroom of a saloon. At her mother's urging, Kenney attended a function at Hull House, and although suspicious of the settlement house's wealth and privilege, she responded to Addams's invitation to help by mentioning the need for a meeting place for her union. Addams, sensing Kenney's resistance, unhesitatingly offered Hull House, launching a close and professionally rewarding relationship for both women. This act of unrestrained openness and the mutually satisfying relationship it engendered can hardly be overestimated. Addams went to great lengths to support Kenney's local. She made flyers and distributed them herself throughout the neighborhood. She worked closely with Kenney to improve working conditions for her union members, as well as many others.

Perhaps most significantly, she collaborated with Kenney in establishing the Jane Club, which eventually furnished inexpensive housing for as many as fifty working women at a time. One of the objectives of this cooperative boarding house was to offer protection for women who were out on strike and enduring weeks of little or no income. The Jane Club also had an educational function, not unlike Hull House itself. It gave young working women the experience of being in a collegelike residence where they could gather for meals and engaging conversation. Many years later, Kenney observed that it was Addams who "took the bitterness out of my life. For if she wanted to work with me and I could work with her it gave my life new meaning and hope" (quoted in Davis, 1973/2000, p. 79).

Of course, Mary Kenney's impact on Jane Addams was no less noteworthy. As much as Florence Kelley, Kenney "radicalized" Addams. Kenney broadened Addams's already open perspective even further and, in Davis's view, "made her sympathetic to organized labor, and helped her move from a position of wanting to comfort the poor—to one of a determination to eliminate poverty" (1973/2000, p. 79). Kenney also encouraged Addams to radicalize her openness, prompting her to reach out and help other laboring groups that were in need, solidifying the reputation of Hull House for championing women workers. When three dozen women walked off their jobs in the spring of 1892 to protest the levying of a thirty-five-cent fine for lateness, they did not hesitate to seek out Addams for help. According to Ellen Gates Starr, Addams didn't just offer moral support; she argued vigorously that the rights of these women had been peremptorily denied. She visited the firm where the protest had occurred and informed its managers that they had broken the law. She further "arbitrated before [the judge] and had the girls back in two days with the grievance removed and the world wiser and nobody the hungrier" (quoted in Diliberto, 1999, pp. 198–199).

Thanks in significant part to Kenney's powerful influence, Addams remained a loyal friend of organized labor and a strong advocate of social justice for working persons for the rest of her life. She believed wholeheartedly that isolated laborers were rendered helpless before the organized might of corporate monopolies and that such disparities of power and organization posed "a menace to the entire community" (Addams, 1960, p. 202). She came round to viewing that part of the public responsibility of any settlement house is to defend and support the most vulnerable, which invariably included, at that time, wage laborers. She played a key role, with the support of Kenney, Kelley, Lathrop, and others, in promoting worker efforts to organize themselves, and through such organizing to increase the likelihood that workers would receive a fair share of the yield that resulted from their labor.

Practicing openness required that Addams plunge herself into the social and political affairs of the city in order to learn as much as possible. She had to grasp the problems facing labor and understand how industry too often victimizes even the most innocent child. Openness gave her the strength to witness unblinkingly the corruption into which even the most refined social class has often sunk, and it prepared her to challenge society's powerful representatives for the sake of a social justice ideal that could benefit all. This radical openness was a product of the lessons she learned from Kelley, Lathrop, and Kenney, and so many others who were drawn to her listening, curious, responsive presence. Perhaps most of all, she discovered that her own openness to learning was the vital basis for her continued usefulness as a reformer and advocate.

OPENNESS TO TRANSFORMING EVENTS: THE PULLMAN STRIKE OF 1894

Jane Addams didn't just learn from people; she also learned from events. One of the most transforming events for her during these early years was the Pullman Strike of 1894. The conflict began when the workers who built the luxurious sleeping cars named after George M. Pullman went out on strike, owing to a series of wage cuts that Pullman himself demanded in the wake of the depression of 1893. As head of the American Railway Union (ARU), Eugene Debs led the ARU in a boycott of all Pullman cars, after a number of fruitless attempts to conciliate the matter with Pullman. The strike and the boycott wreaked havoc on an economy in which railroads dominated transportation. Riots broke out; chaos ensued. Against the advice of Governor Altgeld of Illinois, President Grover Cleveland sent in federal troops, ending the uproar but dangerously alienating working people everywhere. Addams herself commented in an article about the strike that the specter of class warfare disturbed many people and caused them to lose faith in the benevolent paternalism of Pullman. Indeed, Addams observed that the discussions following the strike were divided into two camps: those pleading for individual benevolence, presumably supporting Pullman; and those insisting on social righteousness, apparently championing the cause of the workers.

It is probably not too much of an interpretive leap to note that Addams was pointing to two contrasting positions or attitudes contained within her own social outlook. She struggled in her own life and work with the merits of these two positions but came to appreciate more clearly than ever as a result of the Pullman crisis the wisdom of the social justice perspective. Knight (1997) comments further that the Pullman Strike helped Addams grow out of her ruling-class sensibilities and see more clearly how "benevolence was a form of tyranny" (p. 130). But it took the fact of the workers' rejection of benevolence for her to see that a view embracing social justice and worker empowerment must prevail. Of course, without steadfast commitment to an open reappraisal of the values she had lived by, this realization and this shift in her social outlook would have been impossible.

At Hull House, Addams was both leader and learner, both social worker and sociologist, both intellectual and activist. Her open commitment to serving in whatever way would be useful meant she could throw herself into the fray of city politics or stand back and comment thoughtfully on the need for social and political reform. Despite the fact that she helped to usher in the profession of social work, her openness earned for her the reputation of a roving generalist who through the years was consulted on the widest possible range of issues. What allowed her to assume this role of public oracle was, above all, this openness: her curious and inquiring mind, her continuing quest for self-knowledge, her insatiable desire to learn more and apply what she learned to the problems of modern life. She was always ready to acknowledge her own mistakes and just as apt to learn from them. This willingness to learn allowed her, more so than other activists of her time, to grasp the underlying causes of social problems and then apply what she had so assiduously absorbed to the challenges facing her every day on Chicago's South Halsted Street.

CHAPTER THREE

LEARNING CRITICAL REFLECTION

Like motivation, learning, and the ability to think outside the box, critical reflection is now codified as one of several performance indicators of professionalism. Few leaders these days would declare themselves *not* to be critically reflective. It has become what philosophers call a premature ultimate; in other words, it is a term that, once invoked, inspires such reverence that it puts an end to any further debate.

But what exactly is critical reflection? Most people use it in a broad sense to refer to the process by which they think intensively about their practice. This includes making judgments about the strengths and weaknesses of actions taken to extend democracy, encourage collaboration, and so on. In this broad sense, critical reflection involves us learning to reflect *in* our practice (monitoring what we are doing and what adjustments we can make to support our colleagues' effectiveness) and learning to reflect *on* our practice (in which we look back retroactively on our actions to consider how they helped or hindered our aims). In this broad sense of the phrase, critical reflection is largely technical, concerned with scrutinizing the accuracy of the assumptions underlying our decisions, actions, and judgments.

However, as these comments suggest, it is not quite that simple. Critical reflection has a normative basis; that is, it is grounded in a set of values considered desirable by its advocates. After all, in a purely technical sense one could talk about becoming more critically reflective regarding how one persuaded others that a particular race was inherently inferior to another, or how best to convince skeptics that the efficiency of authoritarian control is always to be preferred over the messiness of democracy. Totalitarian leaders in various kinds of organizations, communities, and societies are quite capable of using critical reflection in its broadest, most technical sense to tighten their ideological manipulation of the masses; indeed, the most "successful" of them become highly adept at this.

For the two of us, then, critical reflection is inherently normative and must be directed toward the realization of certain purposes. One of the chief purposes for which Steve P employs critical reflection is to help him understand how best to acknowledge and enhance the humanity of his co-workers. For Steve, leaders engage in critical reflection to gauge how well they have helped colleagues act freely and creatively, communicate clearly, respond compassionately to others, continue their own lifelong quest as learners, and make the most of their abilities. People in organizations frequently refer to the constraints put on their ability to express themselves. Steve uses critical reflection to address this constraint and to help people think expansively about the challenges facing them. This means ensuring that space is allowed for people to take risks, converse with others regularly, and gain a sense of how their own learning projects relate to and complement what others are trying to do. Ultimately, Steve believes leaders reflect critically to help build a learning community in which all members feel they are growing as persons and co-creating new knowledge.

Stephen B interprets critical reflection from a critical theory tradition; for him its inherently normative character springs from its focus on understanding power and hegemony. When critical reflection investigates power and power relations, the emphasis is on how power is distributed, how it moves around a community, organization, or movement, and the degree to which it is used responsibly or abused. The concern here is to understand how power dynamics affect the ability of people—both leaders and followers—to do satisfying work for the common good and lead meaningful and productive lives. Where the investigation of hegemony is concerned, critical reflection's emphasis is on leaders understanding how they, and those they serve, internalize ideas, beliefs, and values they regard as commonsense, good for their interests, and broadly supported—and then realize how these ideas, beliefs, and values are subtly destroying them.

So the two of us link the practice of critical reflection to normative assumptions or standards regarding what constitutes good leadership. Even though our political inclinations differ, we both agree that critical reflection centers on the degree to which leadership enables people to act with agency. Our central reflective question is, What are leaders doing to support colleagues or community members in gaining meaningful control over their own work, their own learning, and their own lives? This question is, of course, problematic in that agency can be employed for a number of dubious or harmful purposes. To refer back to the examples quoted earlier, we are not interested in helping people exercise agency to ensure maintenance of White supremacy or patriarchy. The agency we want leaders to develop is agency to challenge these ideologies.

One of the most important lenses of critical reflection is the perception of colleagues and community members regarding how leadership is exercised. Leaders need to find some way of getting inside members' minds to understand what it is like to be a subordinate in this setting and to appreciate what followers most want from their leaders and from the organization. A simple and anonymous survey can be distributed periodically to community members to ask about their relationship with the leader and probe into the leader's ability to engage followers, the extent to which leaders display credibility and authenticity, or the degree to which leaders are seen to be contributing to achievement of movement objectives. Such a survey, of course, would have to be developed and measured against the vision that has been established for the organization. The focus would be on how well the leader is supporting a member's efforts to achieve individual and organizational goals. The key to the success of any such survey is a commitment to reporting—warts and all—the full range of positive and negative perceptions of leadership.

A leader committed to critical reflection takes seriously any evidence that co-workers are dissatisfied or that either the leader or the organization as a whole is not contributing to individual or collective growth. In the light of evidence that improvement is warranted, leaders publicly bring this evidence to the attention of organizational or community members and work with them to develop a plan for addressing concerns that are expressed. A responsive leader then reports periodically on the progress being made. This is a systemic application of the dynamic of the Critical Incident Questionnaire, which has already been discussed (Chapter Two). Critically reflective leaders research co-workers' concerns and show how they respond to them, thereby giving colleagues the respect they deserve.

A hallmark of critically reflective leaders is their ability to alter their practice in light of new information regarding the dynamics of power and presence of hegemony. This sometimes means abandoning previous operating assumptions. With relatively little concern for ego or saving face, they lead the effort to adopt new assumptions or move in a different direction. This is not easy, particularly once a structure is established or a set of practices has been found to be successful over time. Change is hardest when what needs to change seems to have worked for a long time.

A particularly hard dynamic is to commit to responsiveness and then have to stick to one's guns in the face of majority opposition. There are times when the will of the majority goes against one's surest instincts and commitments. In such a situation, it is important to realize that responsiveness is just that: *responding* to what one learns. One can respond to a concern in good faith by doing one's best to explain why the concern expressed does not warrant changing one's mind. Most emphatically, responding is *not* the same as capitulation to majority opinion. There will be times when being responsive means explaining and justifying why one cannot in good conscience do what the majority demands. Such times are never easy.

THE BENEFITS OF CRITICAL REFLECTION

Critical reflection is a survival tool of adult life, not a process that only leaders engage in. Without the ability to see how power and hegemony inscribe themselves in our daily actions and decisions—and to challenge how they suppress true democracy—we are at the mercy of seemingly random forces. Connecting the private life to the public event or the personal trouble to the political factor helps us keep self-laceration under control. Ideological control works most smoothly when (1) people can be manipulated into thinking that their own subjection is good for them, a desirable state of affairs, and (2) people come to believe that their marginalization is due to natural forces as much beyond their control as a hurricane or tornado. This is why mental health—let alone economic survival—depends on the ability to analyze things critically.

Becoming critically reflective also raises our chances of taking informed leadership actions. By informed actions, we mean actions that are based on assumptions that have been carefully and critically investigated. These actions can then be explained and justified to ourselves and to our colleagues or subordinates more convincingly. If a colleague asks us why we're doing something, we can lay out the evidence (experiential as well as theoretical) that undergirds it and make a convincing case for its accuracy. An informed action is also one that has a better chance of achieving the consequences intended for it because it is taken against a backdrop of inquiry into how people perceive what we say and do.

But the critically reflective habit confers a deeper benefit than that of procedural utility. It grounds not only our actions but also our sense of who we are as leaders in an examined reality. We know why we believe what we believe. A critically reflective leader is much better placed to communicate to colleagues and followers (as well as to herself) the rationale behind her practice. She works from a position of informed commitment. She knows why she does and thinks what she does and thinks. Knowing this, she communicates to others a confidence-inducing sense of being grounded. This sense of being grounded stabilizes her when she feels swept along by forces she cannot control. It can also help her stay true to her convictions in the face of massive obstacles: external cultural inhibitions, internal self-doubt, political opposition, and the sense of being alone. Many of the leaders we profile faced penalties, punishment, and opposition yet retained an inner core of a rationale—a set of unshakeable, critically examined commitments—that helped them endure hardships, keep hope alive, and exercise true independence of thought.

As valuable and beneficial as it is for leaders themselves to reflect critically, it is equally important that they support the development of critical reflection in their co-workers and colleagues. When critical reflection becomes a practice that is widely shared and honored, then the possibility is greatly increased that the whole organizational culture will learn to see how certain types of rhetoric and behaviors actually keep people down and what can be done to change them. Again, the assumption is that leaders want to include people in decisions more fully, build on their strengths, call on their creative capacities, and excite them about their role in creating a more powerful community, movement, or professional culture. But whatever our assumptions are as leaders, they must be examined and measured against what we are accomplishing. To the extent that leaders and others engage in this kind of critical reflection, the greater is the likelihood that something significant will happen.

How a Leader Develops the Ability to Practice Critical Reflection

Part of the problem with reflection as it is so often practiced is that it has no function other than to encourage thinking, generally in some material form such as a written journal or a tape recording. Without a method or a purpose, reflection is unsustainable. This is where *critical* reflection comes in. Critical reflection, growing out of other critical traditions, focuses the process of thinking on power, justice, empowerment, agency, self-realization, and community renewal. Those who engage in critical reflection must be prepared to confront the ways in which communities and organizations undermine justice, limit agency, concentrate power in the few, and discourage individual and community renewal. Leaders and others need to know how to collect data of all kinds—quantitative and qualitative—that point to the signs of justice or injustice, agency or disempowerment found in any group. Understanding how the community or organization is failing to serve its members well is the first step toward a proactive, democratic quest for locating and affirming the sources of the common good.

We hear a great deal about data-driven decision making in leadership, but usually the data collected and the decision-making mechanisms employed are punitive, driven by the suspicion that people are not working as hard as they should to achieve common goals. Such data collection is so removed from promoting the shared good for everyone that it can do more harm than good. Unless the data are tied to a set of goals constructed by the community as a whole, and unless those goals emphasize such humane concerns as mutual growth, shared appreciation, and serving those least well off, then data-driven decision-making becomes a counterproductive and even pernicious sham. Leaders, then, must constantly link their practices to the vision and accompanying goals that were created in concert with all organizational members. This vision must, in turn, be doggedly employed as a vital touchstone for tracking and gauging organizational and community progress.

WHERE WE HAVE SEEN CRITICAL REFLECTION PRACTICED

Martin Luther King, Jr., was remarkable for his ability to reflect critically on the Civil Rights Movement and his leadership. His vision focused on justice, nonviolence, and human dignity, and despite his occasional missteps his life and leadership consistently mirrored this vision. When he believed that civil rights were not enough and that economic rights must also be embraced, he spoke out boldly. Similarly, when the contradiction between his advocacy of nonviolence and his silence on the war in Vietnam grew too intense, he again spoke out against this war. What we know about the behind-the-scenes deliberations that preceded these decisions shows King carefully scrutinizing his own leadership and that of his advisors for evidence of inconsistency and failure to live out the vision that together they had so scrupulously charted. Taylor Branch meticulously charts this critical reflection in his trilogy of America in the King Years, *Parting the Waters* (1988), *Pillar of Fire* (1998), and *At Canaan's Edge* (2006).

Another example is the leadership of Myles Horton at the Highlander Folk School. Myles tried hard to live the idea that whatever he wanted or sought for himself should be similarly attainable for everyone else. He affirmed many times that no right or privilege should be accorded the few but that such things must always be enjoyed by the many. As he put it, "You can't have an individual right. It has to be a universal right. I have no rights that everybody else doesn't have. There's no right I could claim that anybody else in the world can't claim, and I have to fight for their exercising that right just like I have to fight for my own" (Horton and Freire, 1990, p. 105). He lived this belief by insisting on full integration of Blacks and Whites at Highlander workshops and by giving everyone at Highlander gatherings the same opportunity to participate and articulate strategies for promoting equal rights in their home settings. This striving for self-consistency, for keeping thought and action in line, was the result of intense and probing reflection on what it meant to practice democracy authentically. Horton learned that his voice was one among many, that his perspective must not enjoy privileged status. He learned to keep the focus on learners, not the facilitator; on followers, not the one provisionally designated as leader.

HOW WE HAVE LIVED CRITICAL REFLECTION

We have lived critical reflection primarily as teachers. For one thing, we use the Critical Incident Questionnaire to invite regular anonymous feedback from students, asking them to comment on those times when during the class they felt engaged, distanced, affirmed, puzzled, or surprised. We use the data we receive from students to comment publicly on how the class is helping or hurting students and what we can do as a community of learners to steer the class in a more helpful direction. In this way, we model the idea that together the class as a whole can have a degree of control over the quality of the learning environment created and that we as instructors are not only open to criticism but also want to use that criticism proactively to enhance everyone's learning. This is an opportunity as well to measure the class's progress against the vision for the class established originally in the syllabus. To what extent are we living up to that vision? How are we falling short?

We also make a point of offering public critiques of our teaching by comparing what has actually happened in class to our ideals of what a supportive learning community is like. Many times we have surprised students, four or five class sessions into a course, by announcing our own critique of our conduct, noting perhaps how we have too often dominated conversations or failed repeatedly to follow up on valuable questions that were raised.

During these times, we also note how we may have lost the opportunity to get more students involved in a sensitive discussion about race or social class, or how the racism inscribed in us has manifested itself in our actions. We do this not only because we believe such critical reflections are warranted but also to model this process and encourage others to follow suit.

One of Stephen P's memories of a leader practicing critical reflection was when the lead organizer for a group of community activists facilitated a discussion about the effectiveness of a recently taken community action. This particular action focused on a school reform conference in a medium-sized southwestern city and was designed primarily to bring attention to greater community and parental involvement in public education. But as the discussion about the action proceeded, it was clear how important it was to this organizer to maintain a critical perspective. Issues of how well the attendees actually represented the community's diversity came up, along with concerns that people were talked at too much and weren't able to set the agenda for many of the conversations. Similarly, worries arose that accommodations for Spanish speakers were not uniform and that the rhetorical tone of many discussions was jargon-laden and distancing. Most of all perhaps, this postaction discussion centered on the concern that participants were not encouraged to explore strategies for how to use the ideas introduced at the conference. Lamentably, the group concluded, there was only a half-hearted attempt to get people to commit to how they would think and act differently once they returned home to their neighborhoods. In this case of group critical reflection, all of the critical points that were broached focused on how the conference fell short of empowering participants and allowing them to take control over their own learning. In fact, this postaction conversation was structured in such a way that most of those in attendance did join in and did end up arriving at conclusions that were constructed and owned by the group itself.

WHAT BLOCKS OR PREVENTS THE PRACTICE OF CRITICAL REFLECTION

Maintaining a healthy commitment to criticism and critical reflection is quite difficult. It requires us to look hard at our practice, measure it against meaningful standards, and note shortcomings. It also obliges us to consider how we might do things differently. This can be exhausting, painstaking work, particularly where uncovering power and challenging hegemony are concerned. It hurts to uncover deficiencies and inadequacies and to realize that what you thought were empowering practices used for the good of all were experienced by the most marginalized as oppressive and constraining. It is challenging to pursue critical reflection when it involves the practices of a whole group in an organization or community; it is just as daunting to subject ourselves and our own individual practices to this kind of incisive scrutiny.

But aside from personal aversion to critical reflection, there are ideological, organizational, and bureaucratic reasons it gets blocked. For one thing, to be forthrightly critical about oneself or one's colleagues can be costly, leading to firings, poor evaluations or a lower pay increase. Frank criticism of our practice rarely leads to celebration of our analytical acumen. Rather it more often leads to more stringent accountability measures that tend to further entrench the status quo. To bring attention to problems and shortcomings in the place where we work is to invite the opprobrium of our supervisors and the wrath of our CEO. No matter how well grounded these critiques may be, such bad news is rarely welcomed, despite the fact that responding positively to such critiques could be a good long-term development. There is simply too much at stake, with respect to financing, resources, and power, for most leaders to look benignly on such critical reflections.

Finally, there are tremendous ideological barriers to critical reflection. Ideologically, we have learned that disagreeing with powerful authority calls our judgment into question, as when our opposition to an immoral invasion is labeled appeasement. As the two of us indicated at the beginning of Chapter One, we believe we live in a time when leadership is equated with the cult of the individual, or the cult of personality, where one person embodies strength, determination, boldness, and so on. This person is usually a White man. Focus groups, campaign strategists, and executive or "life" coaches all underscore the importance of appearing to be decisive. Even when the decision made is disagreed with by the majority (as was British Prime Minister Tony Blair's decision to invade Iraq), the appearance of decisive action earns a grudging respect.

WHAT ARE THE PERILS AND PITFALLS OF PRACTICING CRITICAL REFLECTION?

The first peril is undoubtedly the one of suffering the wrath and punishment of those who don't wish any sort of critique in their movement or organization. Practicing critical reflection, and encouraging it in others, can lead to the whole weight of authority falling down on our heads. It can get us fired, socially ostracized, professionally marginalized, and unable to develop allies. In some countries challenging authority gets people tortured or murdered. It is not too serious to say that critical reflection is sometimes a matter of life and death.

Another pitfall is the temptation to omit the critical part, to offer a series of reflections that either ignore power and hegemony or lack any connection to a compelling collective vision. Recording one's thoughts about an experience or an issue has merit. It is useful to have such a record to look back on, if for no other reason than to satisfy the impulse for nostalgia. But for leaders in organizations and communities, learning to reflect critically is not primarily a diverting way to pass the time. It is recommended to support ongoing learning and encourage meaningful change. Only when we reflect critically with respect to some broad organizational or community purpose—growth, agency, justice, empowerment, and so on—can the true value of critical reflection emerge. Only when we think in terms of how the policies and practices that organize our lives fail to live up to our ideals can we realize the benefits of reflecting critically.

Finally, critical reflection can sometimes induce a radical pessimism. This is the danger of wallowing in an excess of critique and thereby falling precipitously into the abyss of despair. Too much negative critique can yield too little hope. One of the challenges of this process is to moderate critique so that it is substantive and honest while leaving room for individual and collective agency. Once the critiques have been issued, people need to know what to do about them, how to act on them for the better. Perhaps there should be a rule that for every criticism put forward, for every critical reflection recorded, there must be an accompanying recommendation for how people can proactively respond to it.

For us, Cornel West's notion of critically tempered hope (West and Sealey, 1997) is crucial. This is a hope that is profound yet realistic, a hope in which we keep a broad compelling vision in our mind even as we work through the contradictions and contexts of everyday life. We develop our understanding of this hope further in Chapter Nine. For the moment, we would endorse West's argument that human energy is not an infinite resource and that activists need to make sure their energy is directed toward the most meaningful and realizable projects. Myles Horton (Horton and Freire, 1990) believed these were projects aimed at changing structures, rather than projects focusing on individual hearts and minds, important and satisfying though they may be. Structures and systems in large part determine behavior. Change the structures in which people live and you change their behaviors, even their instinctual responses. Anyone who has lived in an organization knows just how much the behavior of participants is in response to the reward structure in place.

Of course, to change structures you need collective energy. Only rarely can one person change a structure; it is something that usually needs collective will and effort. This is another reason that in Chapter Five we emphasize development of collective leadership as such a strong learning task. People acting in solidarity and unity can achieve far more than the same number of people individually expressing their anger and frustration. This is not just the basis of the labor movement; it is a fundamental principle of all kinds of leadership.

HOW TO ADDRESS THE TENSIONS, PROBLEMS, PERILS, AND PITFALLS ASSOCIATED WITH CRITICAL REFLECTION

Leaders committed to the practice of critical reflection are willing to examine their past and present experience in the light of an individual and collective vision. We must bring a critical lens to analyzing experience that focuses on how we have pursued our commitments to equity, justice, sharing of power, and mutual growth. This means scrutinizing our actions from as many angles as possible. These perspectives include not only our own reflections on our individual experience but also reflections by co-workers and leaders who are in situations similar to our own. We must be willing to read relevant literature as we ask ourselves hard questions and face up to the answers we reach, no matter how difficult or painful these answers might be.

We must do all this and more, it is true, but we must also somehow be gentle and patient with ourselves and others. It is not oxymoronic to talk of radical patience, of realizing that major structural change is a long haul (Horton, 1998), a long revolution (Williams, 1961). To allow the inevitable defeats and roadblocks to kill the energy for change is disastrous. One way older leaders like the two of us (and we hate to read that descriptor!) can help is by demonstrating that age does not necessarily bring about a "sobering up" to reality and loss of Utopian desire. The sense of urgency, the need to bring about positive change is there for both of us, but the need to laugh, to make light of our foibles is also crucial. Sometimes we need to tread softly when we encounter strong resistance or unreasoning fear and our space for movement or negotiation is limited. At other times we need to call on our deepest reserves of commitment when facing up to such resistance and fear.

Leading in a critically reflective key quickly moves past the misunderstanding that inconsistency is the hobgoblin of practice. In fact, we would argue that an accurate understanding of what we face as leaders—that is, of the fundamentally contradictory nature of human behavior and change agency within organizations, communities, and movements—*requires* inconsistency. For us, mindless and prideful consistency is the enemy of purposeful change. The only hope we have of knowing when flexibility or a 180-degree turn is a justified response to contextual complications, and not a convenient cop-out or excuse for cowardice, is through critical reflection. Of course, even then critical reflection teaches us never to be 100 percent sure that we have got that particular contradiction analyzed properly.

NELSON MANDELA AND THE PRACTICE OF CRITICAL REFLECTION

Nelson Mandela, the first president of a fully democratic South Africa, is now an iconic, fully paternal, figure. Yet at one time in his life he was officially labeled a dangerous and violent terrorist, a treasonable tool of the Communist Party. How can the same person receive the Nobel Peace Prize (in 1993) and have spent twenty-seven years in prison for inciting violence? Part of the reason for these contrasting perceptions of Mandela is his willingness to change course as he judged circumstances had changed. To opponents, this seems like cynical expediency; to supporters, a principled alertness. To those who know little of Mandela beyond a few glimpses of him in newsreel footage, it may seem as if Mandela is confused, lacking a firm grounding in core principles. The two of us, because we have chosen Mandela as an exemplar of learning leadership, clearly number ourselves among the millions of his supporters around the globe. But we have a slightly different take on Mandela's actions. Our contention is that he practiced the critical reflection we analyze as a regular feature of his leadership.

As a lawyer and movement leader who was eventually forced underground in his struggle for justice, Mandela faced a bewildering set of learning tasks in his exercise of leadership. He had to learn how to adapt the exercise of leadership to prison conditions, how to live with the awareness of the effects of his commitments on those closest to him (his family), how to put a guerrilla army together from scratch, how to wage a campaign of sabotage without producing loss of life, how to gauge when to hold firm and when to bend in negotiations, and how to decide when concealing his intentions from his closest allies was justified. Many of his decisions centered on appropriate use of force and forms of coercion and manipulation. He had to come to a plausible ethical justification for taking up arms, he had to discern how best to use the external pressure of world opinion to force concessions from the apartheid regime, and he had to decide when to keep his cards close to his chest in negotiations. On this last point, even his own ANC colleagues were unaware of his initial talks with the regime that led to establishment of universal franchise.

One of the earliest assumptions Mandela reappraised concerned his belief that the movement for a free South Africa must be one in which only Black South Africans should be involved—specifically, his belief that the African National Congress (ANC) should not admit Whites as members, nor cooperate with White groups (such as the South African Communist Party) that were also dedicated to the dismantling of apartheid. This assumption was based on Mandela's belief that the stain of racism had spread so deep into African consciousness that Whites would inevitably come to be seen as leaders within the ANC and thus come to occupy leadership positions. He felt that if Whites were initially involved as equals in the movement, they would move rapidly into leadership positions. One reason for this, he argued, was Black South Africans' unconscious perception of White superiority subliminally predisposing them to defer to White ideas. Mandela was also suspicious of Whites' intent, particularly White Communists, who he believed "were intent on taking over our movement in the guise of joint action" (Mandela, 1994, p. 108). Third, he had an Africentric skepticism of the relevance of a Marxist analysis to the African liberation struggle. His belief at this time in his life was that "it was an undiluted African nationalism, not Marxism or multiracialism, that would liberate us" (p. 108).

In the decade after the forming of the Youth League, however, Mandela experienced a number of events that caused him to revise his earlier assumption that the liberation struggle should be the preserve only of Black South Africans. The first was his numerous conversations with South African Communist Party members such as Moses Kotane, Ismail Meer, and Ruth First. As a result of these conversations, Mandela found that "my long-standing opposition to communism was breaking down" (p. 119) and that "I was finding it more and more difficult to justify my prejudice against the party" (p. 119).

Having had his skepticism of communists weakened through conversation and observation, Mandela was prompted to initiate a self-directed study of dialectical materialism. Here, the role of literature as a lens to aid in challenging assumptions is front and center. He describes reading Marx, Engels, Lenin, Stalin, and Mao and being stimulated by the *Communist Manifesto* (and exhausted by *Das Kapital*). He records how he found himself drawn to the idea of a classless society, which, to his mind, "was similar to traditional African culture where life was shared and communal. I subscribed to Marx's basic dictum, which has the simplicity and generosity of the Golden Rule: 'From each according to his ability; to each according to his needs' (Mandela, 1994, p. 120). He documents how the quasi-scientific underpinnings of dialectical materialism attracted him because, in his words, "I am always inclined to trust what I can verify. Its materialistic analysis of economics rang true to me" (p. 120). He also found in his reading of these texts a number of practical suggestions that seemed to him helpful to the struggles he was conducting. Finally, the Soviet Union's support for anticolonial struggles in Asia and Africa helped explain "why I amended my views of communists and accepted the ANC view of welcoming Marxists into its ranks" (p. 121).

As well as holding numerous conversations with communists and his own studies in dialectical materialism, Mandela was prompted to reexamine his assumptions about working with communists after reflecting on his own autobiographical experiences. The success of the mass action of March 1950, where more than two thirds of African workers stayed at home, was clear to Mandela, and he was forced to acknowledge that communists had played a significant part in planning and conducting this mass action.

By the 1950s Mandela had overturned his earlier assumption that the ANC struggle was best conducted by Black South Africans alone, and that Whites, particularly White communists, would inevitably take the movement over. He had come to see no contradiction between African nationalism and dialectical materialism and "found that African nationalists and African Communists generally had far more uniting them than dividing them" (Mandela, 1994, p. 121).

A second major assumption concerns Mandela's strategizing about how best to bring down the apartheid system. His early activist years were spent pursuing various paths of nonviolent resistance. They included strikes, boycotts, contraventions of the pass laws (which determined where Black South Africans could travel), and stay-at-homes. However, events caused him to conclude that mass civil disobedience was no longer effective, and that now a campaign of armed struggle was necessary. The choice of sabotage was deliberated and considered, on the assumption that a strategy involving the smallest loss of life would have the widest favorable reception. Mandela wrote, "Because it did not involve loss of life it offered the best hope for reconciliation among the races afterward" (Mandela, 1994, p. 282). The intention "was to begin with what was least violent to individuals but most damaging to the state" (p. 274), and the key to this campaign was the issuing of "strict instructions ... that we would countenance no loss of life" (p. 283).

Mandela's approach to the struggle was always dictated by a pragmatic concern to experiment with whatever means might speed the end of apartheid. Writing about the various discussions he had held on how best to put pressure on the South African regime, he summarizes his position thusly: "We should approach this issue not from the point of view of principles but of tactics, and ... we should employ the method demanded by the conditions. If a particular method or tactic enabled us to defeat the enemy, then it should be used" (p. 127). To Mandela, nonviolence was a tactic to be used as long as the situation demanded it. If it worked it would be used, if not it would be abandoned. As nonviolent tactics were met consistently with harsh violence, Mandela eventually concluded that a tactical change was warranted. In his view, "Nonviolent passive resistance is effective as long as your opposition adheres to the same rules as you do. But if peaceful protest is met with violence, its efficacy is at an end. For me, nonviolence was not a moral principle but a strategy; there is no moral goodness in using an ineffective weapon" (Mandela, 1994, p. 158).

How Mandela examined and changed his assumption regarding the effectiveness of nonviolence illustrated his capacity to alter the exercise of leadership in response to changing circumstances. On the one hand, he frequently articulates the need for a form of collective leadership similar to Ella Baker's notion of developmental leadership from the grass roots, which we profile in Chapter Five. Hence, one reason he gave for the move to armed struggle was the fact that this was happening anyway as Black South Africans were forming their own military units. Consequently, the ANC needed to be the organization directing their actions. In his view, "We have always maintained that the people were ahead of us, and now they were" (p. 272).

Contrarily, however, he also argued that leadership sometimes involved individual leaders moving against an already agreed and articulated collective policy. An example of this was the deliberate break he made with ANC policy when he gave a statement to the local and national South African press in May 1961 stating that the ANC was now closing the chapter on nonviolent policy and moving into a different phase of the struggle: armed resistance.

This readiness to forge an individual path against the wishes of ANC colleagues was also evident, as we shall see, in his later willingness to open secret negotiations with the apartheid government when there was no ANC mandate to do so.

A third assumption Mandela examined concerned his conviction that because the ANC was a collective no one person should step away from ANC policy to pursue a maverick course of action. Mandela began to question this assumption as the ANC and the apartheid government seemed locked in a stalemate. To break this impasse, Mandela embarked on a series of secret meetings with politicians from the South African government, which he chose not to reveal to his fellow prisoners or the ANC executive. This practice, which *Long Walk to Freedom* maintains was essential to opening the dialogue the armed struggle was fought to achieve, directly contradicted Mandela's own paradigmatic assumption concerning the collective nature of the anti-apartheid movement. In this instance, the end was seen as justifying the means.

This is an episode of critical reflection—a questioning of accepted assumptions regarding the operations of power and hegemony—that could not be more significant, involving as it did the future lives of thousands, even millions. Yet it did not involve any conversations with others. Instead it was a wholly internal process, guided only by Mandela's personal analysis of a drastically worsening situation and the appalling future it presaged. This situation was characterized by serious impediments to any negotiations. Both sides viewed opening discussion as a sign of weakness, even betrayal of their cause, and neither would come to the table until the other made significant concessions.

Mandela secretly met with Kobee Coetsee (the government's minister of justice) to discuss possible common ground that could be established to open negotiations. He told no one of what he was doing and wanted the process of negotiation to be under way before any ANC members learned of it. In his reading of the situation, it was necessary to take a giant leap ahead of the organization in order to move it in the direction that he felt it must go. This was an astonishing volte-face of leadership. Mandela's decades of leadership practice had been premised on the rock of his commitment to collective leadership. He had always argued that the ANC was a collective and that no individual was bigger than the organization. Yet here he was, if not deliberately lying to his closest, most trusted colleagues, then at least not being entirely open or truthful with them. His justification: "I knew that my colleagues upstairs would condemn my proposal, and that would kill my initiative even before it was born. There are times when a leader must move out ahead of the flock, go off in a new direction, confident that he is leading people the right way" (Mandela, 1994, p. 526).

Long Walk to Freedom also explores how Mandela examined and then changed assumptions he had about the role of Whites in the maintenance of apartheid. Initially, in his capacity as co-founder and later president of the Youth League of the ANC, he acknowledged, "I was angry at the white man, not at racism" (p. 112).

Through the two lenses of reading literature and conversations with allies and colleagues (particularly individuals involved in the South African Communist Party such as Moses Kotane and Joe Slovo), he came to rechannel his anger in a new direction. He came round to the view that Whites' behaviors and actions were caused by a system of White supremacy. If such supremacy was a systemic phenomenon, reasoned Mandela, then the people within it—oppressors as well as oppressed—were products of the system. This did not absolve individuals of their collusion in, or direct committing of, racist acts, but it did imply that such people were potentially able to change. If the system produced these behaviors, then logically a change in the system would produce a change in behavior. If the logic of this assumption is extended even further, it leads to establishment of the Truth and Reconciliation Commission, in which the possibility of amnesty was offered to perpetrators of crimes on both sides of the struggle.

This analysis of behavior as systemically produced, and therefore potentially open to being systematically changed, underscored Mandela's pronouncements in the lead-up to the first fully democratic South African election of 1994 (which resulted in the ANC forming the government). Mandela constantly reminded people again and again that "the liberation struggle was not a battle against one group or color, but a fight against a system of repression" (p. 620). This reminder was a major element in his strategy to convince Whites that they had as much of a role to play in a free South Africa as did their Black fellow citizens. On release from prison, he faced reporters' questions that made it plain they expected him to voice anger and hate toward Whites. Instead, Mandela claimed, "In prison my anger toward whites decreased, but my hatred for the system grew. I wanted South Africa to see that I loved even my enemies while I hated the system that turned us against one another" (p. 563). In many ways, the future of the country rested on Mandela's ability to educate people to accept this systemic analysis. If he could persuade them of its accuracy, there was a chance that the transition to democracy could be accomplished with a minimal loss of life and relative absence of atrocities.

Mandela's readiness to reflect critically on his own assumptions regarding the practice of leadership can be seen to have had enormously positive outcomes for South Africa. Whatever the future might offer regarding subsequent assessments of his presidency, and notwithstanding the obvious problems of assuming that an autobiography stands as an objective account of history, there can be little doubt that Mandela's practice of critical reflection affected the lives of millions. It is hard to imagine a more striking example of this aspect of learning as a way of leading.

CHAPTER FOUR

LEARNING TO SUPPORT THE GROWTH OF OTHERS

A central task of leadership is learning to support the growth of others. But growth in and of itself is not always desirable. In a finite world of limited space and resources, supporting everyone's right to grow—if this is defined by having bigger houses, bigger SUVs, more territory, and more possessions—is untenable. Sooner or later something has to give, and when it does it is usually the least powerful members of a community who end up doing the giving. So for us growth, like critical reflection, is always normative, grounded in an ideal of what development entails.

From our point of view, leadership itself is a normative practice focused on the project of increasing people's capacity to be active participants in the life of their communities, movements, and organizations. The purpose of leadership is to sustain the desire of people to go on contributing, as both leaders and followers, to everyone's overall benefit. This may include openly expressing dissent from action taken by some in the organization. Leadership that discourages active involvement in the organization, that leads to withdrawal or silence, would, according to this view, have to be counted as misleadership or antileadership. There may also be times when supporting the growth of the most marginalized means restricting, even opposing, the growth of the most powerful. In the White Supremacist world of post-war South African society, the growth of the most powerful needed to be restricted by the African National Congress (ANC) for true growth (as we define it) to occur. Marcuse (1965), among many others, argued that had the growth of the German Nazi Party been curtailed in the 1930s the world would have avoided the slaughter of millions.

The implications of our argument for the desirability of supporting growth are that people need to feel an integral part of the groups to which they belong, and groups need their members to participate as actively as possible. An organization that invites and supports people to bring all their talents, experiences, and creativity to bear on the challenges faced by the organization is going to be a better-run, healthier place, more likely to be able to serve people well. When people are actively contributing to the welfare of the organization and know their involvement is making a difference, they feel better about themselves and readier to take risks in expanding their horizons. In a word, if such conditions prevail, people are more likely to grow.

LEADERSHIP PRACTICES THAT SUPPORT GROWTH

It has been our experience, supported also by writers such as Greenleaf (1977) and Collins (2005), that when leaders focus on developing their co-workers' abilities the organizations or communities to which they are responsible get more done and are better able to sustain themselves. If their primary mission is supporting the growth of their co-workers, they will put their energy into activities and practices likely to achieve this end. We have learned from organizational theorists such as Margaret Wheatley (2002), from community activists like Myles Horton (Horton and Freire, 1990), and from our own experience that some practices that are particularly helpful in this regard are listening, staying curious about others, asking constructive questions, learning the stories of co-workers, and championing follower goals. Leaders who publicly model their own commitment to, and engagement in, these activities can have a powerful effect on their communities of practice.

LISTENING

Close, active, attentive listening is the foundation for supporting others' growth and development. Only if we do this can we know what developmental directions will be of greatest benefit to people. When leaders take the time to listen authentically to their co-workers, they are showing that the experiences of followers matter and that time devoted to listening to what others have to say is time well spent. Leaders who listen come to know their organization or community better; they are able to take a movement's pulse and do things that are responsive to what they hear and learn. Community development (Ledwith, 2006), community action (Smock, 2003), participatory research (Park, Brydon-Miller, Hall, and Jackson, 1993), action research (Greenwood and Levin, 2006), and critical teaching (Shor, 1987) are all forms of practice premised on the idea that before action must come prolonged and careful listening. Leaders who listen are better placed to conduct a phenomenography (Marton, 1988) of participants' experiences, to be able to traverse the internal mental and emotional topography of those they serve.

STAYING CURIOUS ABOUT OTHERS

In a recent book about conversation as the glue that holds communities together, Wheatley (2002) urges us to stay curious about each other. Curiosity for her is keeping the focus on other people's experiences and interests, showing that we are eager to learn from them and to find out who they are and what they think. This holds true for leaders who are striving to support people's growth. Such leaders are genuinely curious about others. When they are in conversation with co-workers, they go beyond the idle chit-chat that passes for so much of the communication between people in organizations. Enthusiastically they seek out more information, are excited to get below the superficial level of exchanging pleasantries with their co-workers, and find ways to probe more deeply without being inappropriate or intrusive. Questioning one's own motivations and conduct of projects out loud is a powerful way leaders can model this kind of curiosity.

ASKING CONSTRUCTIVE QUESTIONS

One of the chief strategies that leaders use to deepen their relationships with others is through questioning. For Horton, asking a good question was worth more than a hundred lectures by experts. Constructive questioning tries to balance questions that enlighten with questions that challenge. Such questioning demonstrates respect for colleagues, co-workers, and members by showing them the leader believes she has much to learn from them. Questions that ask about the origins of people's beliefs, about their ideas to make things better, about the concerns that support their passions, and about how they can be supported in doing their best work are questions that signify the leader's respect for what she can learn. Leaders trying to foster everyone's growth ask questions to find out more about a co-worker's special strengths and areas of knowledge that will allow him to come forward to help the organization as a whole. They also are adept at asking difficult questions of themselves in public forums and struggling to find the answers.

LEARNING THE STORIES OF CO-WORKERS

Telling stories has become a credible methodology in the fields of narrative inquiry (Clandinin and Connelly, 2004) and critical race theory (Delgado and Stefancic, 2001). Both these approaches emphasize storytelling and counterstorytelling. Owing to a particularly rich experience in a graduate seminar that was held recently, we have arrived at a new understanding of the role stories play in a true community of learners. Over a four-week period during the summer in which there were relatively few distractions, a group of eleven students working on their dissertations met regularly with two instructors to review their progress on these projects and to compare notes on what they were finding. The more these students met and the more they told their stories about the sense they were making of their topics, the deeper and more substantive their exchanges became. By the end of the four weeks, every member of the group was able to recount in considerable detail the learning trajectory that each dissertator had undergone to produce a dissertation proposal. From this experience we derived a simple principle: the foundation of a learning community is every participant understanding at some deep level the learning/inquiry projects being carried out by all other members of the community. From this, we also concluded that it is important for leaders to develop ways to become aware of the learning paths of the people with whom they are collaborating. Without that knowledge, it is very difficult to support their growth as workers and as persons.

CHAMPIONING CO-WORKER GOALS

One key aspect of leadership is discovering people's passions. If leaders are aware of the passions of their colleagues, they can divert resources and revise goals to feed those passions and spur the intrinsic desire to go on learning. In his wonderful book *From Outrageous to Inspired: How to Build a Community of Leaders in Our Schools*, David Hagstrom (2004) says that once you know people's passions, you have to "pour it on" to maximize the influence of those passions and make the most of what they can contribute to the common good. Of course, we acknowledge that not all passions are equally deserving of support. We would not want to feed the passion some members felt for establishing their racial superiority. But behind most people's desire to live in humane, decent communities are hidden commitments that contribute to furthering this objective. Discovering and then supporting these commitments is one of the distinctive hallmarks of learning as a way of leading.

THE BENEFITS OF SUPPORTING THE GROWTH OF OTHERS

Leaders who believe in promoting the growth of others do so not only because it is a good in itself but also because it leads to community renewal. When people are growing, when they continue to learn and see that their efforts are making a difference for others, the overall effect is positive for the entire community. One of our key leadership assumptions is that leaders should strive to remove the barriers and clear the pathways for each person to make the most of her or his talents. It has been our experience that most people are eager to contribute, excited to participate, and keen to try out new ideas. It has also been our experience that, with relatively few exceptions, workplaces tend to inhibit innovation and discourage creativity. We therefore affirm that a major leadership task is to work to remove the obstructions that limit experimentation, punish risk taking, and curtail exercising the imagination. If such obstructions are removed, people are more satisfied and fulfilled, more motivated to consider a wide range of alternatives, and better equipped to envision new possibilities.

Though there is no doubt that growing individuals lead to a growing community, there is another benefit that emerges when leaders commit themselves to supporting the growth of others. It has something to do with achieving the unexpected, of realizing unseen potential, of reaching an unanticipated height. Growth that continues without limit leads us into unexplored territory and inclines us to accept new challenges. Once the conditions for promoting growth are in place, we are able to face problems and practice finding solutions that were previously unavailable to us. There is no guarantee that we will work through these challenges effectively, but as in almost anything else such practice does tend to breed success. Supporting the growth of others therefore creates the conditions for people to exceed their potential, to try things out and test solutions that can take them to a whole new level of possibility. There is also a selfish pleasure in seeing others learn to exercise agency and become leaders. One of the least acknowledged benefits of leadership is that it allows us to see, and take justifiable pride in, the development in confidence and ability of those we have encouraged.

Developing the capacity to support the growth of others is no easy task, though it helps to have seen it modeled by someone you regard as a mentor. Leaders who seem more interested in your welfare than their own, more intent on drawing you out than impressing you with their accomplishments ... this is the sort of leader we mean. Not surprisingly, one of the first steps in becoming this kind of nurturing, developmental leader is acknowledging that fostering the growth of others comes first. Many leaders simply do not understand the importance of such an acknowledgment. Words are not in themselves sufficient to bring about positive, life-affirming change, but their power should never be underestimated. Until leaders use the language of growth with respect to their followers, the process cannot begin.

But of course, words *are* only the beginning. The real test is the willingness of the leader to use the practice of supporting others as a chief criterion for judging her or his actions. What do co-workers say about the leader in this regard? What do others say in corresponding positions of leadership? When pressed, what does the leader herself say about her ongoing commitment to this practice? How much time is being taken to listen to co-workers, understand their perspectives, and take action on their behalf? What is being done to remove the barriers that prevent co-workers from doing their best work and from performing creatively? How much does the leader really know about co-worker passions? How familiar are leaders with the learning journeys their followers have embarked on? Asking such questions of oneself and assessing one's effectiveness by the responses are the keys to learning leadership.

Where We Have Seen Supporting the Growth of Others Practiced

In *A Tradition That Has No Name*, Belenky, Bond, and Weinstock (1997) note that leaders who support other people's growth do this most successfully through dialogue—by listening, asking constructive questions, responding appropriately and appreciatively, and finding common ground among community members. Ella Baker, the civil rights activist and original director of the Southern Christian Leadership Conference, is often referred to as a prototypical developmental leader who rarely voiced her own views but who went to great lengths to get others engaged and involved. She did this by scouring the group for unheard contributions and, whenever possible, enthusiastically bringing these contributions to the attention of others. She did this too by asking probing questions and by making provocative statements that she knew would stimulate conversation. Her focus was on discovering areas of agreement and accentuating commonality of purpose. In helping individuals grow, she wanted to get the group as a whole to exercise leadership.

Septima Clark, another civil rights activist who taught school for many years and eventually became the Highlander Folk School's director of workshops, maintained a similar commitment to supporting the growth of others through dialogue. Her workshops were planned around the idea that instructors are present to serve participants' needs, and that everything must be done to develop participant knowledge and experience on their own terms. This meant finding out about the participants in depth, exploring the nature of their community challenges, constructing together the content that would be most helpful in addressing their problems, and devoting the last section of the workshop to how participants would use the knowledge they had acquired once they returned to their communities. Clark also believed that workshops must lead to a long-term relationship between the center and participants, and she pledged that she and other Highlander staff would be available with technical advice and other resources to support attainment of their goals.

How We and Others Have Lived This Supporting the Growth of Others

As teachers and as members of communities, we have tried to keep the focus on others, to give people control over their own learning. We have done so by keeping our own participation to a minimum, by encouraging people to interact with each other, by using questions to deepen these interactions, and by trying to create a space for participants to tell their stories. Whenever we teach or meet with people in a variety of other settings, we take time for people to talk about themselves, share pivotal events, and reveal some activity or practice about which they are passionate. We also introduce opportunities for participants to engage in some kind of inquiry project and share the progress being made. As we have indicated, supporting the growth of others requires us to know something about them, to have a feel for their stories and how they unfold over time. We also think it important that all members of a community become familiar with everyone else's story and play an active role in supporting each person's learning journey. We try to model asking good questions that help people think more deeply about their stories, and we bring attention to those issues and experiences that the group in some way holds in common. When we reveal something about ourselves or turn the light on our experiences, we do so, without exception, to provoke further conversation, foster the involvement of reluctant participants, and in general offer incentives for deepening learning.

People Steve P has worked with sometimes comment that they still do not know where he himself stands on some of the controversial issues being discussed. Although he often has strong opinions about many of these issues and occasionally expresses them, he tries to delay the moment he volunteers his perspective. He does this for two primary reasons. First, introducing his own views can bias the rest of the participants and, despite his best efforts, lead some of them to think that they should adopt his point of view. Second, and perhaps more important, all of his efforts are focused on creating conditions for students' growth. He has found that voicing his views is usually an act of ego, an irresistible desire to highlight his position that does little to advance the conversation or support learning. If the goal truly is to develop students' capacities to learn, converse, think critically, and take informed action, then he feels where he stands on a particular issue is irrelevant.

Stephen B differs in emphasis on this matter. He admits that he may be more egotistical (Steve P has often commented how in Stephen B's world it is always about himself), but for him holding back his opinion too long makes it appear as if he is unwilling to model what he is asking others to do. Stephen B's position is that one usually *should* give one's view early on but should then model a vigorous critique of it and invite others to participate in that critique. Otherwise people are left wondering what the leader is thinking and start to second-guess what they think they should say to gain his approval. Stephen B also believes, like Herbert Marcuse, that sometimes he needs to throw his weight—any credibility or authority he has—behind the expression of an unpopular view. This has particularly been the case with his efforts to help White members of groups become aware of their own racial microaggressions (Solorzano, 1998)—that is, the numerous small behaviors and actions (who one makes eye contact with, who one encourages to speak, how one reacts to comments of people of different racial identities, and so on) that accumulate to marginalize people of color. Like Marcuse, he is concerned that the idea of democratic discussion sometimes mistakenly means leaders are reluctant to point out the ideologically skewed nature of particular contributions, let alone say someone is wrong.

What Blocks or Prevents the Practice of Supporting the Growth of Others?

There is so much cultural baggage associated with the concept of leadership that it is easy to fall prey to the idea that leaders command and followers comply. Leaders employ the command-and-control model in part because it is the only model they have ever experienced and also because it yields financial reward, recognition, and power over others. Everyday we hear about another CEO or another political operative who has negotiated some outrageous pay package involving millions of dollars in salary and perquisites. Being a highly visible and overtly powerful administrator pays. But it is not necessarily leadership.

The flip side of the paradigm entails the expectations of followers and co-workers. Because of cultural indoctrination, self-effacing and facilitating leaders who want to support other people's growth are frequently viewed as weak, waffling administrators who cannot make up their mind. In political campaigns a way to defeat opposing candidates is to portray them as flip-flopping on the issues, as if changing one's mind is a sign of fragility. Jimmy Carter and John Kerry are two presidential candidates who suffered from this accusation. Overcoming this prejudice is one of the greatest challenges learning leaders face. Leadership designed to let others lead is neither trusted nor understood, at least at first. In the face of this resistance, a few simple virtues are needed. Patience stands out, along with the willingness to listen actively and keep a meaningful conversation going.

What Are the Perils and Pitfalls of Practicing Supporting the Growth of Others?

As has been suggested, one of the problems associated with the practice of supporting the growth of others is appearing to be weak and indecisive. When you are serious about encouraging people to claim control over the decisions that affect their lives, there are always going to be some who see this as surrendering your responsibility to make the decisions for them. There are others who are going to see such leaders as aimless and directionless. Somehow leaders intent on supporting the growth of others must communicate to people how they are taking action consistently to achieve this. A combination of rhetoric and behavior is needed from the outset.

Two other pitfalls come to mind in following through on this practice of supporting others. One is the appearance of favoring some people over others. The other is neglecting oneself. Even the most well-meaning leader is going to like, admire, and be drawn to some people more than others. The impulse to reward those one admires is understandable, and even in some cases desirable. But we must always remember that those who most need your support are likely to be those you are most likely to neglect. Work hard to avoid this trap. Pay special attention to those who seem to be most challenged, and go out of your way to recognize them for their efforts. Engage them in conversation, get to know them, familiarize yourself with their stories. The goodwill you accumulate and the possibilities you will learn about more than make up for the extra time you take in doing this.

Finally, don't forget yourself. It is easy to do so when you are trying to be a developmental leader. One of the subtlest ways hegemony works is to encourage people to think of their work as vocation. The concept of leadership as vocation—of answering a calling and being in service to members, co-workers, and colleagues—opens leaders to the possibility of exploitation and manipulation. Vocation becomes hegemonic when it is used to justify leaders taking on responsibilities and duties that far exceed their energy or capacities and that destroy their health and personal relationships. In effect their self-destruction serves to keep a system going that is being increasingly starved of resources. If leaders will kill themselves taking on more and more work in response to budgets being cut, and if they learn to take pride in this apparently selfless devotion to community or to organization members, then the system is strengthened. Money can be channeled into corporate tax breaks and war expenditure as leaders gladly give more and more for less and less.

Vocation becomes especially hegemonic when filtered through patriarchy, as is evident in predominantly female professions such as teaching. Again and again, in our time as university teachers we have seen female faculty internalizing the ethic of vocation, and being held to a higher standard regarding its realization than is the case with their male counterparts. Women professors in departments often become cast as the nurturers, known by students for their excellent teaching and advisement. Translated into academic reality, this means that women professors are willing to spend time working with students rather than locking themselves away in their office to write articles and books in an effort to gain tenure. Because dominant ideology presumes men to be less relational, less prone to an ethic of care and compassion (in short, less moved by a sense of vocational calling), they receive less opprobrium for being unavailable to students.

So part of leadership is learning to take care of yourself—learning when to say no, when to draw boundaries, when to insist on decent treatment and adequate resources, and when to take time for your own renewal. Find time to read, exercise, reflect, consider, and reconsider your priorities as a leader. As a leader, you should look for help from everyone in enhancing the workings of the organization or community. But do not expect recognition and do not go looking for it. If you are truly committed to developing the growth of others, it may be a long time before you get the extrinsic recognition you deserve. You have to console yourself with the knowledge that what you are doing is truly what is best for others. This knowledge has to be its own reward.

SEPTIMA CLARK: LEARNING TO SUPPORT THE GROWTH OF OTHERS

As the leader emblematic of learning to support the growth of others, we choose Septima Clark, the lead organizer of the Citizenship schools, created to secure voting rights for disenfranchised African Americans during the Civil Rights Movement. We are not alone in this choice. Charles Payne (1995), in his great book about the Mississippi organizing tradition *I've Got the Light of Freedom*, puts special emphasis on Clark's contribution to the Civil Rights Movement. Payne says that Clark (as well as Ella Baker and Myles Horton) led with great effectiveness by virtue of her collaborative, developmental style of leadership, which "espoused a non-bureaucratic style of work, focusing on local problems, sensitive to the social structure of local communities, appreciative of the culture of those communities" (p. 68). Hers was a relational, collaborative style of leadership that sought to instill "efficacy in those most affected by a problem" by helping them see how their own experience, knowledge, and skill were the most important resources in their struggle for equality.

In Clark's view, new knowledge and deepened understanding were constructed most effectively and lastingly in collaborative groups. She labored tirelessly to ensure that groups were as inclusive and participatory as possible. As Payne (1995) notes, Clark's leadership was "guided by the belief that the oppressed themselves, collectively, already have much of the knowledge needed to produce change" (p. 70). Her view was that "creative leadership is present in any community and only awaits discovery and development" (p. 75). Payne argues that Clark's legacy as a developmental leader was her demonstration of the idea that "ordinary people who learn to believe in themselves are capable of extraordinary acts, or better, acts that seem extraordinary to us precisely because we have such an impoverished sense of the capabilities of ordinary people" (p. 5).

Clark, like Baker and Horton, was a radical democrat by virtue of her insistence on the right of "people to have a voice in the decisions affecting their lives" (Payne, 1995, p. 101), her confidence in the capacity of ordinary men and women to develop a strong and meaningful voice, and her rejection of hierarchically structured organizations in which attention-starved leaders too often held sway. She and her colleagues believed that democracy could not flourish until people have the space to exercise their talents, and that a priority of leadership committed to supporting growth entailed providing such opportunities. Furthermore, like Baker and Horton, Clark held strong beliefs and took strong stands, but remained surprisingly "open to learning from new experiences" (p. 101) and from the wisdom of those both older and younger than she. She was a leader who led effectively because of her complete commitment to her own learning and to creating those conditions necessary to support everyone's continuous growth.

HIGHLANDER AND THE CITIZENSHIP SCHOOLS

Septima Clark joined Highlander in 1956 after being fired from her South Carolina teaching post for refusing to remain quiet about her active membership of the National Association for the Advancement of Colored People (NAACP). Upon hearing this, Myles Horton immediately appointed her the director of workshops, an appointment that soon led to creation of the Citizenship Education Project and one of the Civil Rights Movement's most memorable achievements.

The idea for the Citizen Education Project first emerged when Clark invited Esau Jenkins, one of the pillars of a tiny island community in South Carolina, to a Highlander workshop. At the workshop he painted a powerful picture of the need for effective literacy instruction on Johns Island that would enable islanders to pass the written voter registration test. Highlander offered some financing and technical assistance but most importantly gave Clark, an old friend, the job of working directly with Esau Jenkins.

One of the first things Clark did was to make arrangements for selecting a teacher. She sought someone who was respected and had leadership potential but who was not a professional teacher. Ideally, it would be an instructor open to new methods and strategies and unconstrained by old, ingrained habits. Bernice Robinson, a beautician and dressmaker, was chosen. She had a high school education, was active in the Charleston NAACP, and understood Highlander's approach to adult education. At first Robinson declined, citing her lack of teaching experience. But Clark persisted and convinced her that she had the capacity to inspire the trust of the islanders and encourage them to speak openly about their concerns and needs.

On January 7, 1957, fourteen Johns Island adults showed up outside a building that appeared to be nothing more than a grocery store. Bernice Robinson conducted them into the grocery's back rooms and commenced instruction in reading and writing. The first citizenship school had quietly and unceremoniously begun. Robinson turned to these students and asked them what they wanted to learn. As John Glen (1988) has said in his history of the Highlander Folk School, "It was an inspired question, for the subsequent success of Highlander's Citizenship School program stemmed from its ability to respond to the expressed needs of its students" (p. 162). What the islanders most wanted was to be able to write their names. They sought next to gain the skills to read the newspaper and the Bible, and those portions of the South Carolina constitution that must be decoded to qualify for voter registration. They also asked to learn how to fill out mail-order catalogue forms and money orders. A few of the men requested instruction in arithmetic. Finally, Robinson herself proposed that by the end of their two months together the students would be able to read and understand the United Nations Declaration of Human Rights, which she had tacked up on the wall of their classroom (Horton, 1989).

Clark worked closely with Bernice Robinson, though their wisest course of action was in keeping the curriculum open enough for the learners to shape it themselves. As Aimee Horton (1989) has noted in her history of Highlander, "the curriculum for this first Citizenship School came about almost entirely from its fourteen adult students" (p. 223). The most intense activity, at least at first, entailed learning to write their signatures. At Clark's suggestion, Robinson had them do this kinesthetically, tracing prepared signatures again and again until they could write their names in cursive without a prompt (see Clark, 1962). Using many of the ideas that Clark had developed forty years earlier during her first years as a teacher on Johns Island, Robinson also had the islanders write stories about their daily routines, which they then read aloud back to the whole group. The words that caused difficulty were set aside for further practice and were also used to teach spelling (Clark, 1962). Robinson also found newspaper advertisements that could be used to supplement reading instruction and teach simple arithmetic.

The first test of the program's effectiveness was the ability of the students to become registered voters. All of them, without exception, passed that test with great success. They read the required passages and signed their names so flawlessly that they could hardly be denied their registration certificates. They "were so happy about it that they came back to school fairly shouting" (Clark, 1962, p. 153). It was a great triumph for Clark and Robinson and a landmark in the history of the Civil Rights Movement. It was also a testament to how empowering it can be to learners when leaders and teachers keep their focus on supporting the growth of others.

What stood out for Clark and Robinson, however, was how much they themselves had learned from the experience. Robinson commented enthusiastically how eagerly the students learned and how satisfying it was, given their thirst for knowledge, to teach them. Working with adults in this way became Robinson's new career path. Clark noted that the students themselves must guide what is learned. "You don't tell people what to do," Clark observed. "You let them tell you what they want done" (Wigginton, 1991, p. 243). The experience reaffirmed one of Clark's lifelong convictions: that a good teacher is, above all, a good listener, intent on "always learning herself" (1962, p. 152). One of the hard-won results of all this learning and listening and assertive action was a fourfold increase in the number of Johns Island residents registered to vote by the early 1960s.

THE SCLC AND THE CITIZENSHIP EDUCATION PROJECT

The success at Johns Island spawned many new citizenship schools, first on other islands along the South Carolina coast and later in communities such as Huntsville, Alabama; Savannah, Georgia; and Somerville, Tennessee. In time, Clark spearheaded the effort to transfer responsibility for the project from Highlander to Martin Luther King's organization, the Southern Christian Leadership Conference (SCLC). Clark's chief responsibility was training the teachers who would then fan out to a variety of communities to teach literacy, excite political awareness, and spur organized action. Most of the workshops to conduct this training were held in Liberty County, Georgia, at the Dorchester Cooperative Community Center, which was associated with the United Church of Christ. Andrew Young, who had ties to this church, made the arrangements for securing the center and was responsible for overseeing the Citizen Education Project (CEP), but he deferred to Clark as the center's "undisputed schoolmistress" (Branch,

1988, p. 576). It should be pointed out that although this work of preparing teachers was usually referred to as "training," Clark saw it as drawing out teachers' latent abilities and supporting them in developing talents that the teachers themselves, as well as the "trainers," saw were needed.

The workshops that Clark led tended to follow a format similar to the one she had learned at Highlander. Clark, Young, and their colleague Dorothy Cotton carefully recruited people to spend four weekdays and an evening at the Dorchester Center. On the opening evening, time was spent getting acquainted and figuring out how the workshop could best serve the needs of those in attendance. The following day teaching sessions began in earnest. Music was used to warm up the participants and enliven the proceedings, and then a variety of strategies for teaching reading and introducing basic math were explored. As Taylor Branch (1988) has noted, Clark "taught her pupils how to figure out seed and fertilizer allotments," and when focusing on literacy "worked upward from street signs and newspapers to the portions of the state constitutions required for voter registration" (p. 576). According to Carl Tjerandsen (1980), Clark also used the Socratic method effectively. She asked numerous questions, painstakingly tracked responses that seemed contradictory, and patiently used the colloquy that ensued to impart skills and to deepen understanding of the CEP's larger implications. It was not enough for her that participants learn the processes for teaching literacy and arithmetic; they must also increase their political awareness, learn to think more critically, and gain appreciation for the new leadership role they would be assuming in their communities.

But Clark's real gift, as Branch has also pointed out, was in "recognizing natural leaders among the poorly educated yeomanry" (1988, p. 576) and passing on to them the skills, confidence, and leadership they would need to be effective back in their home communities. Clark always insisted that workshops end with participants demonstrating in specific ways how they proposed to use the knowledge they had gained to make a difference back home. Like Myles Horton, Clark believed that workshop participants should not return to their community without a clear sense of what they had learned and what they intended to do with it.

Despite Clark's best efforts, however, many people felt that the citizenship schools had lost something in the transfer from Highlander to the SCLC. Apparently, King and the other male leaders never fully appreciated the impact of the Citizenship Education Movement. The SCLC failed to supply the funding that Clark always believed was necessary to fully capitalize on the value of the workshops. The number of trainees to be accommodated continued to balloon and sessions were frequently cut short, leaving little time for the all-important "What will we do back home" sessions. Additionally, procedures for following up with participants on problems and successes of their community efforts were never clearly established. Clark also believed that because the CEP was run largely by women, it never got the respect it deserved. She has said quite bluntly that the men on the executive staff of the SCLC "didn't have any faith in women, none whatsoever" (Brown, 1990, p. 77). Reverend Ralph Abernathy repeatedly complained about the presence of Clark on the SCLC's executive council, and Clark felt King himself never took Clark as seriously as she would have liked.

Despite the CEP's limitations, it nevertheless accomplished a great deal. By 1967, the SCLC had trained at least three thousand citizenship teachers. Clark estimated that these teachers taught at least forty-two thousand others. As result of the SCLC programs, voter registration more than doubled in Alabama, and in Clark's native Charleston it more than tripled by 1967 (Tjerandsen, 1980). The impact on voting and on law and social policy was incalculable. Clark was able to retire in 1970 knowing that her contribution to the struggle for social justice had been enormous.

Clark as Developmental Leader

Septima Clark stood out as a developmental leader if we define the term as one committed first and foremost to supporting the growth of others. What she demonstrated during the many residential workshops at Highlander was that Blacks themselves had the capacity to bring about transformation of their own communities. Highlander could give them a taste of the emancipatory possibilities inherent in every local community and offer a few human and financial resources to begin to foster change back home.

Clark added to this a talent for identifying and encouraging potential leaders, particularly those who had never thought of themselves in this way. Her willingness to open herself up to the wisdom of others also sensitized her to what ordinary people could teach her and what they might need from her to develop their potential as leaders. The relationship she cultivated with workshop participants was thus thoroughly mutual. She had much to learn from them just as they had a great deal to learn from her. But Clark's faith in their ability, in their unique capacity to exert the leadership in their own local communities, formed the basis for everything else that transpired between them. Unlike SCLC leaders such as King and Abernathy, who often showed little faith in her ability or in the value of the programs she proposed, her own faith in the people she worked with was unbounded, often allowing them to accomplish things they thought were beyond their capabilities.

Clark's brand of developmental leadership is similar to what Robert Greenleaf (1977) has called servant leadership. Greenleaf stresses that one of the defining qualities of a servant leader is to be a listener first. Certainly, Septima Clark met this criterion. She gradually realized, as she traveled through eleven southern states trying to impart basic reading and writing skills to simple working people, that "I could say nothing . . . and no teacher as a rule could speak to them. We had to let them talk to us and say to us whatever they wanted to say" (quoted in Robnett, 1997, p. 90). She learned that the more she listened and understood what different groups were going through, the more she earned the right to speak up and introduce some new ideas worth hearing. Her attentive patience increased the chances that her response would help the people she was working with realize their potential. But her turn to speak had to be earned, built on an authentic desire to listen and learn from those around her.

Servant leaders, of course, are willing to do almost anything to serve their constituents better. Clark as a young teacher on Johns Island collected dry cleaner bags so that she would have a writing surface on which to record her students' stories and compile their key words. Somewhat later, while attempting to overturn the South Carolina ban on Black teachers being employed in public schools, she almost single-handedly gathered twenty thousand signatures for petitions supporting a new, more progressive statute. As the chief organizer of Highlander's citizenships schools, Clark never hesitated to do whatever was necessary to support Bernice Robinson and other teachers in achieving success. If this meant ordering needed supplies, she would take care of it. If it meant distracting Whites who were suspicious of what was going on in the back of a grocery store on Johns Island, she would do that too. Her goal was always to further the movement for civil rights, never to go out of her way to make herself look good.

Author Belinda Robnett (1997) writes about Clark as an important bridge leader, a view of leadership closely aligned with developmental leadership. By bridge leader Robnett means someone who led quietly and informally in the "unclaimed spaces" of an organization before it had been fully organized. Robnett has also said that bridge leaders, who tended to be women, went largely unrecognized because of a "social construct of exclusion" (p. 20) upheld by many male-dominated groups. But bridge leaders played an absolutely crucial role by bridging the divide between "the public life of the movement's organization and the private spheres of adherents and potential constituents" (p. 19).

Robnett particularly highlights Clark's work with the CEP and her ability to connect with the rural Black masses. When institutional networks failed and national associations performed poorly in attracting the working poor to the Civil Rights Movement, Clark and others used their interpersonal skills and their direct knowledge of local communities to awaken broad interest in literacy, the franchise, and civil rights. Clark's ability as a bridge leader to translate the somewhat erudite goals of Martin Luther King's SCLC into language and practices that made sense to rural and working class Blacks went unheralded but was a key to the movement's success.

A bridge leader is, in Gramsci's terms (1971), an organic intellectual, a leader from the masses who understands their needs and aspirations but who is also familiar with dominant culture. Such a leader has a big picture view of the need for revolutionary change but is able to translate this view in terms that people who are caught within the tight parameters of their own lives can understand. Clark's organic leadership gave people who sought literacy instruction readable accounts of Civil Rights

Movement activity and of the laws that posed barriers for her students. Along with teaching reading and writing, she talked with people honestly and directly about the need for them to give time and effort to a movement that she believed would enhance their freedom and strengthen their rights. As a bridge leader, Clark's initial efforts to further Black literacy and thus fortify Black voting power are even more remarkable for being carried out largely on her own, with little or no support from national organizations or broad social movements. The CEP, which eventually gained renown as an arm of the SCLC, linked ordinary people struggling to secure their basic rights with a well-funded national movement. Clark's leadership made that connection possible.

In the end, Septima Clark was the kind of leader who, as she herself said, completely identified "with the people in the localities where they live and work" (1962, p. 238). Over time, she developed a commitment to democracy that was reflected in everything she did as a teacher and leader, because she defined democracy as a system that allows people to make the most of their talents. This was not simply an espoused commitment but one she struggled to enact in every aspect of her professional and personal life. The conclusion of the statement that she wrote about her faith in democracy while in residence at Highlander is a fitting way to end this chapter. Clark (1962) wrote: "An army of democracy deeply rooted in the lives, struggles and traditions of the American people must be created. By broadening the scope of democracy to include everyone, and deepening the concept to include every relationship, the army of democracy would be so vast and so determined that nothing undemocratic could stand in its way" (p. 198).

CHAPTER FIVE

LEARNING COLLECTIVE LEADERSHIP

Collective leadership directly challenges the individualized model of leadership we believe is most typical in American culture. When leadership is collectively exercised, three things typically happen. First, and most commonly, a group engages in a period of debate and analysis before deciding on a course of action that the majority of its members support. Second, when it comes to selecting who is to speak on its behalf, the group—and not some external authority—decides who that shall be. Third, whoever is selected as a temporary spokesperson can be recalled and replaced at any time; indeed, many groups exercising collective leadership introduce a rotating system in which everyone takes a turn at representing the group in any wider negotiations that take place.

Collective leadership directly counters the traditional concept of leadership we critiqued in Chapter One. Collective leadership challenges the most enduring of American myths: the self-made man and strong, self-sufficient pioneer woman, facing wilderness and danger with only their own fortitude and intelligence to call on, eventually triumphing against insuperable odds and carving out a piece of the world for themselves. Add the power of this myth to the socialistic connotations the word *collective* has for many people (collectivizing the countryside means taking hard-earned goods, services, and property away from the peasantry and destroying private ownership and individual enterprise) and you have a powerful one-two ideological punch ensuring that anything collective is viewed as somehow un-American. Parenthetically, the pharmaceutical, insurance, and medical establishment has successfully demonized socialized medicine as some sort of communistic plot to take health care away from ordinary people, when its whole point is to put decisions back in the hands of citizens rather than in the budget committees of HMOs. In Britain, the prime ministership (some would say presidency) of Margaret Thatcher and then Tony Blair destroyed the idea of collective cabinet responsibility—in other words, of a decision argued, fought over, made, and then publicly defended by a whole group. It is perhaps not surprising that the notion of collective leadership has such a hard time establishing itself when union membership has declined precipitously and where the most successful corporation of all—Wal-Mart—is known for its union-busting practices.

When collective leadership is being authentically practiced, all group members are committed to creating and implementing a shared vision. All assume some leadership responsibility. All have an opportunity to play a leadership role. All are willing to subordinate themselves to the group's goals and interests. When collective leadership prevails, there is no one person everyone else depends on. Rather, work is done interdependently so that everyone is seen as being necessary to the group's success. It should be noted, as Joseph Raelin (2003) has pointed out in *Creating Leaderful Organizations: How to Bring out Leadership in Everyone*, that some people have used the adjective *leaderless* to describe situations where collective leadership is practiced. Raelin argues this term is a misnomer; collective leadership more accurately refers to those contexts where everyone is a leader and is thus better characterized as "leaderful."

Individuals in leaderful groups must alternately learn to lead and follow, must understand when to push things forward and when to wait for others to exert healthy pressure on the group. Such leaders know that everyone cannot lead at once, that there are times to voice a strong opinion or take a strong stand and other times to defer quietly and respectfully to others. In collective leadership, everyone accepts responsibility for outcomes and does everything possible to keep moving the community in a productive and mutually engaging direction. Although there are always going to be disagreements and dissent about what the group is trying to accomplish, collective leadership models do oblige individuals, for the most part, to put self-interest aside and align with the group's sense of the common good.

More than any other model of leadership, collective leadership asks community members to abandon their own individual ambitions in favor of the group's jointly arrived-at aspirations. In this process, half measures are not workable. It is unreasonable to ask community members to give up their own ambitions and support group goals if they have not had significant input into the construction of those goals. Only when the group's aims and decisions are constructed through a process to which everyone has made a contribution can individuals be expected to set aside their self-interest to support the group's communal yearnings and take responsibility for the consequences of their actions. It is critical, then, that groups seeking to lead collectively also ensure that visioning, goal setting, and prioritizing are consciously and conscientiously shared. This is at the heart of Jürgen Habermas's (1996) discourse theory of democracy, which argues that people will commit to decisions that have been arrived at only after full, democratic, public to-ing and fro-ing.

Most of us have had some limited experience with collective leadership in which no one person in a group dominates or pulls rank and everyone actively and freely participates. So-called brainstorming sessions are an example for many people. In these situations, ideas are judged by their intrinsic value, not by who voices them. Position and reputation matter little as participants unselfishly add to the group's thinking and listen closely to what others have to say. Our penchant for individual recognition and reward is happily supplanted by the sense of shared satisfaction that accompanies the process of leading collectively.

Collective leadership is a shared commitment to a set of ideals that are unattainable unless everyone's efforts are included, appreciated, and felt. Because all believe strongly that what the group is striving for transcends individual accomplishment, and because the power of the shared vision demands that each person's contribution be fully supported, there is no designated leader other than the group itself. Functioning as the leader, the group is everyone together doing their best, most selfless work on behalf of a cause that matters deeply to its members. In fact, history shows that collective leadership is most likely to be successfully practiced when the cause is great and people come together to achieve transforming results. The Civil Rights Movement and the United Farm

Workers movement particularly come to mind. Although there were outstanding and well-known leaders associated with these movements, the bulk of the work was done by quiet, self-effacing, behind-the-scenes activists who were satisfied to put their individual identities aside for the sake of a vision of a more humane, inclusive, and just society for everyone. As Martin Luther King reflected after being jailed for leading the illegal Montgomery bus boycott, "The movement couldn't be stopped. Its links were too well bound together in a powerfully effective chain. There is amazing power in unity. When there is true unity, every effort to disunite only serves to strengthen the unity" (1998, p. 88).

THE BENEFITS OF COLLECTIVE LEADERSHIP

Collective leadership rests on the assumption that everyone can and should lead. If this is accepted and practiced, then individual members can innovate without waiting for permission from a designated leader, and the group as a whole can move forward without worrying about a person in authority looking over their shoulder. Collective leadership expresses the notion that people are freed to think, plan, and execute together in an environment where anyone with a good idea can be heard and taken seriously. Under collective leadership, the community opens itself up to the panoply of untapped perspectives that can be found in any group, particularly when those perspectives are meant to help the group attain its mutually arrived-at goals.

When everyone leads and no one dominates, the opportunities for learning are greatly increased. The fears of appearing ignorant or incompetent evaporate in the mix of sharing exciting ideas. The chance to learn from those who have perhaps been reticent in the past is also improved. Questions can be raised, assumptions challenged, errors probed, and new possibilities explored that simply weren't appropriate in an environment dominated by a single leader to whom everyone was expected to defer. When everyone leads, everyone also teaches and learns, meaning that the sites for instruction and enlightenment are enlarged. Whole group instruction is possible, with many people rotating into and out of the role of teacher.

Collective leadership is also a chance for everyone to gain a sense of personal efficacy, to experience what it is like for each person's contribution to make a difference for the whole. There are few things as motivating or as likely to foster ongoing engagement with a community as knowing that one's presence and interaction with others is leaving an indelible impact. It affirms our shared humanity and our continuing commitment to democracy to know that each person is potentially as influential as anyone else.

How Does a Leader Develop the Ability to Practice Collective Leadership?

As with so many of the other discussions in this book, the practice of collective leadership by positional leaders begins with vision and commitment. The vision is one in which everyone contributes substantively to pursuing collectively created goals. The commitment is to the idea that everyone can lead and that each has something valuable to contribute as a leader. Articulating this vision and commitment is the first step toward collective leadership. This is followed by development of dispositions to learn more than teach, listen more than declaim, support more than profess, and focus on the common good more than on individual achievement. Two approaches are productive in developing these dispositions: those in positions of power and authority modeling them publicly for colleagues, and changing an organization's reward structure to embed these dispositions in daily organizational routines.

Where the first of these is concerned, leaders need to pose questions to themselves and to others that heighten people's awareness regarding their interactions within a group. Such questions might include: How much time is set aside for listening, and how actively and attentively do you listen? What have you done recently to contribute to leadership within the group? How are you actively supporting others in being leaders within the group? What is occurring within the group that you are prepared to take responsibility for? For what are you *unwilling* to take responsibility, and what have you done to challenge the direction the group is taking?

What are you willing to abandon personally to pursue the common good? What are the limits on what you are willing to give up in support of the common good? What are some of the things you have recently learned from the group? What are you doing as a teacher or as an expert in some area to support the group's learning?

These questions can then become the basis for job evaluation, performance appraisal, and self-assessment. For example, if a portfolio is being prepared documenting a leader's performance over a period of time it should comprise documented evidence of how she has conducted a careful study of members' concerns, a record of how she has ensured that all had a chance to make their views known in key decisions, examples of how she has stopped a premature rush to judgment to allow the expression of dissenting views, and so on. Particular attention should be paid to how well she seeks to place credit with others rather than claim it herself. In this model, the most effective leaders would be those who claimed the least for themselves—a direct antithesis to most of the performance appraisal systems we know.

WHERE WE HAVE SEEN COLLECTIVE LEADERSHIP

Steve P witnessed a form of collective leadership when he was a teacher in a fairly large social studies department at a junior high school in the early 1970s. (Unfortunately, he wasn't aware of his good fortune until after he had left the institution.) Quietly and effectively, an experienced teacher chaired this department and maintained a particularly strong commitment to discussion-based teaching. He used his skills as a discussion facilitator to promote a shared leadership model within the department. During department meetings, no one teacher, no matter how experienced, dominated the conversation, and each faculty member was able to bring strengths to the table that all the others regarded as beneficial. Occasionally, one colleague would talk about how he used his knowledge of art—an area he loved—to teach world history. During other sessions, a certain member would display his stamp collection and how it facilitated his teaching of American history. Still another would explain how the questions she posed to her students corresponded to Bloom's taxonomy and strengthened their understanding of economics.

In this setting, each person had a special strength or multiple special strengths, all of which, at one time or another, were brought to bear on the department's discussions about teaching. All shared the goal of making social studies the most stimulating subject that junior high students experienced. No one person ever dominated the group or took an inordinate amount of time to feature his or her interests. But gradually all developed a sense that each person had an area of excellence and expertise that all could respect and learn from. Somehow, it even appeared that if any one of those department members left the group (turnover was very low), the group as a whole would be significantly diminished.

How We and Others Have Lived Collective Leadership

Collective leadership is founded on Mary Parker Follett's belief in the strength of power *with* others rather than power *over* others. It is paralleled in the union ideal of solidarity, of strength in unity. In working class culture, in tribal cultures across the globe, in the Africentric ideal (to name just a few examples), leadership is framed as something a group exercises together rather than something observable in only a few talented and charismatic individuals. Collective leadership is premised on the idea that people acting together can exert a power far greater than what any individual can generate alone. It is fueled by a mix of individual humility and undiminished faith in the great things to be accomplished by cohesive groups committed to shared goals.

Most of the individuals we profile later in this book practice collective leadership to a greater or lesser degree. Even the most charismatic leaders profess a commitment to this ideal. Think of Nelson Mandela, Martin Luther King, Jr., and Che Guevara—three iconic leaders whose actions seem to underscore the (now discredited) "Great Man" theory of history in which progress is attributed to the actions of a few powerful men who force the winds of change to blow in the direction they wish. Each of these individuals continuously sought to point out that their individual fate was meaningless compared to the fate of the movements they came to embody. Two of them, of course, were assassinated, while the other spent the greater part of his adult life in prison. Mandela's *Long Walk to Freedom* (1994) presents numerous examples of how he sublimated his own desires and hopes to the needs of the ANC. To take one at random: "I have always believed that to be a freedom fighter one must suppress many of the personal feelings that make one feel like a separate individual rather than part of a mass movement. One is fighting for the liberation of millions of people, not the glory of one individual.... In the same way that a freedom fighter subordinates his own family to the family of the people, he must subordinate his own individual feelings to the movement" (p. 228).

Similarly, the *Autobiography of Martin Luther King* (1998) contains descriptions of his own struggle to keep reminding himself that his growing fame meant nothing compared to the success of the SCLC initiatives and the wider Civil Rights Movement. One of his prayers is to ask God to keep reminding him that chance has placed him as an instrument of a wider movement but in no sense its charismatic creator. Guevara's diaries of the guerrilla warfare campaign to oust the Cuban Batista regime repeatedly stress how his own fate is irrelevant measured against the attempt to rouse the Cuban population to become the chief agents of regime change. Revolutionary leadership was for him the response to a call from the masses, particularly the peasantry. Although the small guerrilla army in which he was a commandant was physically separated from the people for much of the time, Che always viewed it as "very much part of the people. Our leadership role does not isolate us; rather it imposes obligations upon us" (1958/2003, p. 62). All three came to terms with the fact that their commitments could well mean their early death and concluded that the price was worth paying.

Our own lives obviously pale in comparison to these narratives, and our own experiences seem appallingly trite and insignificant. Yet for the great majority of people whose life is measured out in coffee spoons, experiencing collective leadership can be a transformative experience, one that changes them irrevocably, alters fundamentally how they perceive the experience of group membership, opens up new possibilities for their development, and becomes the touchstone by which they measure their future involvements. Steve P continues to search for a professional group like that junior high school social studies department where every member contributed something essential to the whole.

The few times that we have fleetingly been a part of groups living collective leadership we have enjoyed a rare sense of personal satisfaction, of contributing something significant (though modest at an individual level) to a cause far greater than ourselves. In our own feeble way, we have tried to live this commitment not by asking what is in it for us, but by inquiring what we can do to support the group's goals. We have attempted to add our voice to the group's deliberations, but we have also been extremely conscious of our responsibility to let others, less privileged than we, set the agenda for change. We have openly opposed initiatives that violated our own principles, but we have also accepted that some level of compromise is usually necessary, except in those cases when conciliation would mark us as outright hypocrites. We have listened most of the time in such settings, though we also have learned that the responsibility to speak up, at least occasionally, is as strong as the obligation to be a silent witness. We have learned, too, that we can at times lead effectively by following others just as we can follow successfully in some cases by showing others the way. Unless community members are willing to lead and follow, to see these actions as either side of the same coin, then collective leadership cannot reach its potential as a means for making the most of everyone's talents and abilities.

WHAT BLOCKS OR PREVENTS THE PRACTICE OF COLLECTIVE LEADERSHIP?

Just about everything blocks the practice of collective leadership. Ego, the personal difficulty of learning to compromise, traditional leadership models, lack of faith in the ability of people to accomplish great things together, organizational reward systems that encourage individual competition and discourage collaboration, the wider ideological privileging of individuality, the power of myths and mores of the self-made man and pioneer woman, capitalism's emphasis on competition as a natural way of life, bureaucracy's attempt to sift and order people in terms of their specific accomplishments, levels, personality types, learning styles and so on—all of these things stand in the way of collective leadership making a difference.

The sheer difficulty of implementing collective leadership models also presents challenges. As much as we admire community groups and organizations that lead collectively, we also know how unstable and unsustainable collective leadership can be. All that it takes to foil collective leadership is the almost irresistible temptation to hold a single individual responsible for some sort of organizational failure. This leads almost inevitably to a move away from shared leadership approaches and back toward one person taking charge—and responsibility—for what happens. It is also true that when individual leaders do not receive either recognition or reward for quietly guiding the group's accomplishments, some of them begin to wonder if the rewards of collective leadership are worth the lack of career advancement they are experiencing. Isn't it better, they might ask, to return to an individualized model of leadership where their contributions as individuals stand out and are more likely to receive acknowledgment?

Collective leadership takes time, and this can be the most significant barrier of all. To expect results right away is completely contrary to the slow, incremental process endemic to any collective leadership approach. Developing trust in others is the most fragile of all human projects, and the time needed for this cannot be foreshortened past a certain point. People need time to develop faith in themselves and their colleagues. They need to see for themselves in various situations that leading collectively really does result in better work being done by everyone and better overall results for the group. As we have already suggested, positional leaders require evidence that collective leadership is, in some sense, in the best interests of the group and the individuals who make up the group.

Finally, the unconventional nature of collective leadership means it triggers automatic resistance from the forces of tradition and the inertia of entrenched practices. Hierarchy dies hard. The desire to keep the chain of command in place is deeply, systemically, culturally entrenched—and completely contrary to collective leadership's democratic spirit. If everything that someone wants to try has to be sanctioned by the next person in the chain, then collective leadership is doomed to failure. Top-down approaches and giving priority to designated positional leaders have to be abandoned before collective leadership's impact can be felt.

WHAT ARE THE PERILS AND PITFALLS OF PRACTICING COLLECTIVE LEADERSHIP?

Like comedy, collective leadership is hard. In fact, the strain of collective leadership is similar to the struggle to make people laugh. Both take tremendous, creative effort and there is no guarantee with either that anything worthwhile or lasting will ensue. So perhaps the greatest peril associated with collective leadership is the impulse to give up, to label it a failure before it has had a chance to take effect. Collective leadership is so often a losing proposition because it is so rarely given a proper chance. Ironically, positional leaders often espouse commitment to doing business collectively, to involving everyone in decisions. But when pressure builds up around a particularly important issue, the real test of the strength of their commitment occurs. If they give in to this pressure and ignore the group's recommendation, the damage in lost trust is devastating, effectively killing the prospect for such leadership for a long time to come. In this case, the attempt at collective leadership, however well intentioned, has done more harm than good. It stains future attempts at this with a smear of cynicism. We have argued strongly that one of the great strengths of collective leadership is the fact that everyone plays a leadership role; everyone is important. But this is also its greatest point of vulnerability. If anyone lets the group down, if anyone fails to follow through on his or her part of the leadership responsibility, the whole group suffers. If this happens in multiple cases, the group's ability to withstand such a letdown weakens to the breaking point. Unless some members of the group are willing to monitor the group's progress and assess regularly each person's contribution to the whole (though it is preferable and internally more consistent if everyone does this), collective leadership is impossible. A strategy must be in place to identify and repair weak links before they can overwhelm the whole.

How to Address the Tensions, Problems, Perils, and Pitfalls Associated with Collective Leadership

It is a paradox that strong, committed, highly effective leaders are particularly needed when it comes to perpetuating collective leadership. It is true that collective leadership demands leaders who are comfortable being quiet, self-effacing, in-the-background contributors to the common good. But to sustain the long-term practice of collective leadership, such leaders must also remain highly active and deeply engaged with their colleagues. They must be constantly present to show their moral support, offer their appreciation at individual effort, and keep the group focused on its shared goals.

One poorly understood aspect of collective leadership is how different it is from laissez-faire leadership. Collective leadership is always hands-on, always a matter of how to keep people energized around the collective practices and goals that have been mutually identified. People who are responsible for keeping collective leadership models going must be in constant conversation with their co-workers, finding out from them what the group can do better to achieve its goals and acknowledging each person's contribution to the whole. This must be done to keep the group growing and improving and to act on the human need for individual recognition. Leaders associated with the Highlander Folk School such as Septima Clark and Myles Horton learned this practice early on in their life, and it underscored everything they did.

Just as important, leaders who are committed to making change through collective means must help the group stay focused and support the group in keeping its eyes on the prize. The prize may be broadly conceived as universal civil rights, educational equity for all, the end of racist practices; or it may be more specific, such as entry to a boys soccer league, enlivening a school's social studies curriculum, taking back a block decimated by gang warfare, or building a house for low-income people in a high-rent district. Regardless of the focus, it is easy for the group to lose its way. Someone—better yet, multiple people—must assume responsibility for reminding the group of its shared vision and mutually agreed goals while insisting that the group's work remain consistent with that vision and those goals. Conversations about these fundamentals must be a constant, along with regular opportunities for the group as a whole to explore its purpose. It is a truism that the work of collective leaders, genuinely committed to the long-term practice of collective leadership, is never done.

But a final point about all this must also be asserted. Whether it is done through formal professional development or just an ongoing dialogue, shared understanding must develop that collective leadership is unsustainable unless it is truly collective. Until the group understands that everyone is a leader and that this carries with it more responsibility than recognition, more burden than privilege, collective leadership will falter. Whether this means formal processes must be set in place to ensure that key responsibilities are rotated, or that sharing these responsibilities evolves naturally, matters less than the need to pay unremitting attention to how true collective leadership emerges and is maintained.

ELLA BAKER: LEARNING COLLECTIVE LEADERSHIP

In the popular imagination, Dr. Martin Luther King, Jr., is the acknowledged charismatic leader of the Civil Rights Movement. Behind the scenes, however, history has shown Ella Baker to be the movement's most influential theorist of, and practitioner in, collective leadership, or what she often referred to as group-centered leadership. As an unsung leader, Baker worked behind the scenes, partly because that was what she wanted and partly because that was expected of her. But mostly, it was because the nature of collective leadership militates against any one person clearly standing front and center as some sort of leadership figurehead. For Baker, leadership was never about charisma and always about helping people realize the power of collective solidarity.

By collective leadership, Baker (1972) meant exercising influence as part of a community of equals in which every person contributes a distinctive, indispensable voice to the whole, while also standing strong with others in support of mutually agreed goals. Traditional leaders too often make followers dependent, stripping them of the capacity to learn from their experiences and make decisions for themselves; collective leaders encourage self-sufficiency and affirm, as Baker often did, that no one should "look for salvation anywhere but to themselves" (1972, p. 347). At a time when large, impersonal organizations were increasingly the norm, Baker believed that people could have greater collective control over their own lives by being part of small work groups, or by restructuring large organizations for smallness. Baker assumed that organizations should be broken into structures small enough for people to get to know one another as persons, so that a kind of collective ownership of outcomes could emerge. Payne (1995) noted that Baker "envisioned small groups of people working together but also retaining contact in some form with other such groups, so that coordinated action would be possible whenever large groups really were necessary" (p. 369). Only by keeping structures small, she asserted, could both individual and collective growth be nurtured.

Throughout her life, Baker held steadfastly to her belief that leaders are at their best when supporting ordinary people in leading themselves. For her the most effective leaders were self-effacing people, more interested in developing leadership in others than in getting recognition for their individual achievements. When asked by an interviewer to explain how you organize people, she said matter of factly that you don't start with what *you* think. You start with what *they* think. She continued, "You start where the people are. Identification with people.... If you talk down to people, they can sense it. They can feel it. And they know whether you are talking *with* them, or talking *at* them, or talking *about* them" (Cantorow and O'Malley, 1980, pp. 70, 72). She affirmed repeatedly that leaders are teachers who must create opportunities for people to learn from each other and reflect on the best ways to take action collectively. She maintained that leading and learning are part of the same process and that no successful movement can endure unless it has leaders who are intent on learning from those around them.

Leaders were critical to Ella Baker, not as solitary individuals who bask in the reflected glory of group action but as solid and selfless collaborators in the enduring collective struggle for social justice. When she was first organizing the group that became SNCC (Student Nonviolent Coordinating Committee), Baker hesitated to be overly directive. She observed, "Those who had worked closely with me knew that I believed very firmly in the right of the people who were under the heel to be the ones to decide what action they were going to take to get from under their oppression" (Cantarow and O'Malley, 1980, p. 84). She did not seek credit or even much compensation for what she did, but she received enormous gratification from witnessing people who enjoyed little notice from others grow with her support into selfless, collective leaders. As Barbara Ransby shows in her magisterial biography, Baker's approach to leadership was democratic and reciprocal. She saw leaders as both teachers and learners, with learning "based on a fluid and interactive relationship between student and teacher" (Ransby, 2003, p. 359). As Ransby also points out, Baker was in accord with Antonio Gramsci, who observed that "every teacher is always a pupil and every pupil is always a teacher" (1971, p. 239).

Baker's commitment to leadership as partnership and collective endeavor comes through in her description of her work with the NAACP branches:

> If you feel you are part of them and they are part of you, you don't say "I'm-a-part-of-you." What you really do is you point out something. Especially the lower-class people, the people who'd felt the heel of oppression, see they *knew* what you were talking about when you spoke about police brutality. They *knew* what you were speaking about when you talked about working at a job, doing the same work, and getting a differential in pay. And if your sense of being a part of them got over to them, they appreciated that. Somebody would get the point. Somebody would come out and say, "I'm gon' join that darn organization" [Cantarow and O'Malley, 1980, p. 72].

Baker respected people in the classic sense of seeing them discerningly in all their wholeness and uniqueness. Respect means literally to see again, to regard with new, more penetrating eyes. Baker practiced this respect by helping people become more acutely aware of their collective intelligence and power. An important element in this practice was her refusing to make assumptions about the people she endeavored to lead. She strove to find out all she could about them so she could acknowledge and appreciate them in all their complexity and fullness. Not surprisingly, she grew famous among the rank-and-file membership of the NAACP as the leader who seemed to know and understand each branch's special situation and the unique challenges that the branch leader faced. She did this, as Moses and Cobb (2001) pointed out, by quietly working "in out-of-the-way places" and then by really "digging into [life in] local communities" (p. 4). As Ransby (2003) noted, "She met hundreds of ordinary black people and established enduring relationships with many of them. She slept in these people's homes, ate at their tables, spoke in their churches, and earned their trust. And she was never too busy, despite her intense schedule, to send off a batch of thank-you notes, sending regards to those who she did not contact directly and expressing gratitude for the support and hospitality she had received" (p. 136).

Transforming leaders do not hold forth with their knowledge and experience but use them to create opportunities for people to learn together, to become, as Burns (1978) points out, "joint seekers of truth and of mutual actualization" (p. 449). Baker noted that her work as activist and leader did not stress imparting new theories or drawing complex pictures of social relations. She focused her efforts instead on helping people more clearly "see their own ideas" (Ransby, 2003, p. 363). She was famous among the SNCC membership for holding individual side conversations with quieter participants (often women) while group deliberations were going on, and then interrupting the discussion to announce to those assembled that someone had just expressed to her a powerful idea that needed to be heard by everyone. Dallard (1990) reports that Baker would sit down next to a particularly reticent participant, quietly draw that person out, and then grab the attention of the rest of the group by shouting: "Look, here's somebody with something to say about that" (p. 84). In so drawing people out, Baker hoped to make every participant an integral member of the activist community, so that they could join in the collective spirit of these important, often decisive gatherings.

She was also the one inclined to locate areas of agreement or consensus, in the midst of what appeared to be sharp conflict. During a meeting of SNCC when a bitter argument broke out between the partisans of direct action and civil disobedience and those committed to advancing the goal of increasing voter registration, Baker stepped in with unusual directness to show how both goals could be pursued simultaneously. Reflecting on this occasion, Baker noted: "I never intervened . . . if I could avoid it. Most of the youngsters had been trained . . . to follow adults. . . . I felt they ought to have a chance to learn to think things through and to make the decisions. But this was a point at which I did have something to say" (Dallard, 1990, p. 86). Here the lesson that Baker needed to teach was too important not to intervene. She wanted the students to see that creating forums for people to share ideas is an essential element in collective leadership, but there are also times when disagreement should cease and common ground must be identified.

EMPOWERING SNCC AND GROUP-CENTERED LEADERSHIP

In April 1960, with her tenure at King's SCLC coming to an end, Baker welcomed more than two hundred student protesters from nineteen states to Raleigh, North Carolina, to propose an organization to coordinate and support the emerging student protest movement. Baker admired the students' initiative and identified closely with their courageous struggle. She quietly created an atmosphere at the conference that would allow the students to share their experiences freely, learn from each other, and build a foundation for a new student movement. Baker knew that the students' actions were momentous, but she feared that anxious adult leaders, such as King, might slow their progress by urging caution. In organizing the Raleigh meeting, Baker hoped to convene a forum for discussion and learning that would remain student-centered and allow the students to explore creating their own, independent organization. This is, after all, one of the key prerequisites for the emergence of collective leadership: creating free spaces for people to dialogue openly, both to identify ongoing differences and to build new areas of agreement.

When Baker spoke at the conclusion of the student gathering in Raleigh, she touched on a number of these themes. First, she made it clear that the sit-ins symbolized something much more than the right of Black people to be served at a segregated lunch counter. The daring actions of these courageous Black college students were certainly undertaken as part of a struggle for their own emancipation and that of their race. But they were also part of a movement to uphold human freedom that held "moral implications ... for the whole world" (Forman, 1972, p. 218). What they accomplished and how they responded under pressure could inspire freedom lovers across the globe to rise up against their oppressors. Second, because the struggle was so universal and so urgent, Baker noted, a democratic and group-centered focus must be maintained. By deemphasizing the leadership of charismatic individuals, the goal of expanding the sphere of human liberty could be guided by many voices and not detoured by an individual power grab. For Baker, true collective leadership occurs when the individual is stretched to his or her highest potential "for the benefit of the group" (p. 218).

Baker was also adamant that the students should remain independent of adult control and of traditional top-down ways of running organizations. Spurred on by Baker, the students declared they wanted the group as a whole to supply the necessary leadership to advance their cause. Baker also urged the group's leaders to embrace adult education. Although the conference in Raleigh had been a great triumph, she argued that the future success of the student movement depended on the willingness of the organization to create training programs in nonviolence and group dynamics. Again, it was structures and programs to codify and expand people's already developed knowledge and skills that would ensure the success of the movement, not how many in the wider community looked for guidance from a particular person as the embodiment of the struggle. Furthermore, only through organized training could the rage engendered by racism be channeled into efforts for meaningful and lasting social change.

Although Baker was self-effacing and often quiet, the vision she projected was radical. She reminded the students frequently that they needed to "learn to think in radical terms." Baker used "the term *radical* in its original meaning—getting down to and understanding the root cause. It means," she asserted, "facing a system that does not lend itself to your needs and devising means by which you change that system" (Moses and Cobb,

2001, p. 3). Baker was respected as a leader who believed in the Civil Rights Movement as a unitary movement, but who also used the movement as an opportunity to radically alter the structures of the wider unjust system.

Teaching and Learning in the Practice of Collective Leadership

Even as SNCC began to exert a major influence on the Civil Rights Movement, the need for searching and extensive discussions about its mission and structure remained strong. For at least the first two years of its existence, years in which Baker continued to play an active role, SNCC gathered periodically to revisit and explore their collective purposes. The "marathon meetings" that inevitably ensued frequently included Baker's quiet and unobtrusive presence. She rarely contributed a view of her own but participated most often as a listener and occasionally as a questioner. Comparing her to Nelson Mandela, Grant (1998) explained that Baker listened closely and actively to every person and would occasionally refer to a previous speaker's words to lend them added credibility and weight. She regularly paraphrased and synthesized what others had said and taught the young people in SNCC "that everyone had something to give, thus helping them learn to respect each other" (p. 137) and to regard what they were doing as a shared, collective struggle.

Baker also participated by questioning students with a skillful Socratic persistence, an ability she shared with Aldo Leopold. Baker would not tell the students what to do, but she would interrogate participants repeatedly about purpose and mission. As Mary King (1987), an early SNCC volunteer, noted, "Again and again, she would force us to articulate our assumptions" (p. 60). Mary King sometimes felt intimidated by Baker's methods, but she came to see that her questioning was a strategy to combat dogmatism. Only through persistent and sharply worded questioning, King learned, could the temptation to adopt a single, doctrinaire approach be avoided. She attributed to Baker one of the most important lessons of her life: "There are many legitimate and effective avenues for social change and there is no single right way" (Payne, 1995, p. 97). Through such questioning, Baker sought to encourage a new understanding of the nature of shared struggle in which all were encouraged to see that social justice and universal human rights could be achieved only through collective solidarity.

As we have argued, Baker insisted that an organization's members must have control over their own decision making. This was especially true of the SNCC students, who believed that overbearing adults would only hamper efforts to keep the movement energized. But they *would* listen to those rare adults who treated them as equals and who regarded the students as responsible thinkers and doers. This was exactly Baker's stance, which is why the students prized her leadership. As Bob Moses said in recalling Baker's legacy for SNCC:

> It was Ella more than anyone else who gave us the space to operate in. As long as she was sitting there in the meetings, no one else could dare come in and say 'I think you should do this or that,' because no one could pull rank on her. Her stature was such that there wasn't anyone from the NAACP to Dr. King who could get by her. I think that the actual course of the SNCC movement is a testimony to the fact that the students were left free to develop on their own. That was her real contribution [Dallard, 1990, pp. 84-85].

Joanne Grant (1998) points out that although Baker spurned the profession of teaching as a vocational aspiration, her chief role with SNCC turned out to be as teacher. She wanted to develop new leaders, and there was no way to do so except through some form of instruction. Of course, Baker employed a variety of forms to support and guide the students: listening, affirming, questioning, and only rarely asserting. But these were all aspects of her teaching role. Baker was a fount of wisdom and experience for the students of SNCC. As time went on, her ability to teach, facilitate, and redirect the students toward more productive, generous, and humane collective goals grew into legend. It was out of such encounters that her reputation grew.

According to Howard Gardner (1995), leaders tell a recurring story that reveals the identity of the leader, underscores group goals, and highlights the values that the group both espouses and enacts. In a statement to her followers that parallels Gardner's claims about the leader's story, Baker succinctly put forward her own leadership narrative. It brings us full circle by reminding us how she fulfilled her role as the voice of collective leadership during the Civil Rights Movement. She encouraged her followers to foment radical, collective change, but only after cultivating a thorough understanding of the tragedies and triumphs and trials of their collective past:

> In order for us as poor and oppressed people to become a part of a society that is meaningful, the system under which we now exist has to be radically changed. That is easier said than done. But one of the things that has to be faced is . . . to find out who we are, where we have come from and where we are going. . . . I am saying as you must say, too, that in order to see where we are going, we not only must *remember* where we have been, but we must *understand* where we have been [quoted in Moses and Cobb, 2001, p. 3].

CHAPTER SIX

LEARNING TO ANALYZE EXPERIENCE

Learning from experience is often voiced as an unequivocal good, a sign of a leader developing wisdom and maturity. We want to begin this chapter by problematizing this idea before we affirm and explore it further. First, we are wary of any approach that views experience as a unified, monological phenomenon capable of teaching us only one set of lessons. Experience is ambiguous, multifaceted, and open to contradictory readings and interpretations. Events are what happen to us. Experiences are what we construct out of those events. Experience is not a river in which we swim like a fish unaware of its surroundings; it is rather a constructed phenomenon created when we ascribe meaning to events. Second, we argue that experience is not necessarily expansive; it can be restricting. We can analyze our experience in such a way that it teaches us that bigotry is justified, that lighter skinned people are more intelligent than darker skinned people, that power should be kept close to one's chest, or that women are too emotional to think rationally.

Myles Horton famously observed that we don't automatically learn from experience; we learn only from those experiences we learn from. By this he meant that experiences don't teach us anything until we probe deeply into their meaning. To analyze experience is to break it down and examine it in depth so that it is placed in some larger personal and social context. Analyzing experience improves our understanding, helps us make connections, and sometimes leads to alternative means for addressing problems. But it just as likely leads to our asking still more provocative questions: To what extent are our experiences shaped by forces under our control as opposed to forces that transcend our immediate circumstances? How does our understanding of experiences change as we adopt different lenses for examining them? Which experiences stimulate us to repeat them, and which seem to curtail that desire?

Although analyzing experience can take place anywhere and can be done individually or collectively, Horton argued that analyzing experience in groups is especially effective. When people analyze experience together, the diversity of perspectives and histories offered allows them to compare and contrast experiences, thereby drawing out common connections and major differences. As experiences are shared, it often becomes evident that even though each story is unique, there may be striking similarities—recurring themes that unite seemingly disparate experiences. As an example, think of the common themes that emerge when the conversation turns to education. Many people will comment on how their schooling discouraged them or made them doubt their ability. Others will focus on the liability of being the first person in their family to attend college, a circumstance that made the adjustment to higher education particularly challenging. Still others will disclose how lack of economic means forced them to seek out employment during schooling, which in turn disadvantaged them academically. Others will note that the stark contrasts between their home culture and the culture of the educational institution they attended caused them considerable distress, what one of us (Brookfield, 2006) has described as cultural suicide. These experiences, though differing with respect to details, can help people begin to see that virtually all of their experiences are both personal and public, both individually distinctive and powerfully situated within commonly held social contexts.

The starting point for analyzing all experience is the simple act of valuing that experience. There will be plenty of time later on to critique experience, to subject it to sharp questioning and bring out its internal tensions and inconsistencies. But first, people's experiences, so often belittled or discounted in the past, must be acknowledged as a potentially rich wellspring for learning and growth. When it comes to our experiences, we are all experts. This dictum should be reaffirmed often. Questioning others about whether a particular event befell them is almost always inappropriate. How to explain or make sense of that event may be a subject for further analysis and critique, but casting doubt on people's actual experiences is never productive. So the first step in analyzing experience is to offer outlets for people to tell their stories freely. These stories can be about many things: upbringing, schooling, a first encounter with racism or prejudice, cultural traditions, a career turning point, development of hobbies or special interests. Simply allowing people time to share something about themselves, about where they have been or where they think they are going, can be an incredibly eye opening and revealing exercise.

Once people have had this opportunity to tell a story or two, then the process of noting differences and recurring themes—and of connecting them to the speaker's race, class, or gender—can begin. Time to tell and hear stories should not be cut short. People listen closely and learn quickly when the topic touches their lives directly, when the focus is on actual experiences they have had (or know about secondhand). Furthermore, the stories that are told constitute the curriculum that everyone will study together. Asking questions, reframing the experience in light of new information or a relevant piece of literature, begins the process of analysis relatively painlessly. Eventually, as recurring themes are identified, the conversation should turn to how, as C. Wright Mills (1959) said, personal troubles get translated into public problems such as economic injustice, racial prejudice, educational inequity, and cultural imperialism.

Analyzing experience inevitably entails studying issues and conditions that constrain, oppress, and even imprison people. This can be painful. It includes examining privilege and prejudice, power and powerlessness, wealth and poverty. Consideration of such issues can produce tension and lead to conflict. Such conflicts, however, should not be avoided, particularly when they help people see situations more clearly and guide them in understanding issues more deeply. Analyzing experience in this way can, in the short run, uncover individual and collective responsibility, and cause people to become even more divided. The primary purpose is not, of course, to stigmatize a few or alienate people further. It is to create a situation where people really are learning and are seeing their way toward a more constructive, positive, and collaborative future. But such a future will not be realized unless differences are initially recognized.

THE BENEFITS OF LEARNING HOW TO ANALYZE EXPERIENCE

At its most basic level, learning to analyze experience supports the quest for a more satisfying and productive life. It develops self-understanding so that we realize why we keep making the mistakes we do and how we can limit their damage to us. There are limits, of course, to how far our knowing about these barriers can help us overcome them. As we point out in the next section, awareness of the structural barriers to economic democracy, to an antiracist world, or to the end of a pointless war can plunge us deeper into pessimism about the control we can gain over our lives. Yet we both believe that full knowledge of these barriers, no matter how depressing this might temporarily be, is in the long run better for us because we know exactly what we are up against. Fully rounded awareness of these barriers means we are less likely to feel guilty or demoralized if things don't change as fast as we'd like. Additionally, because the process of analyzing experience is best carried out in groups, the sense of collective agency that derives from analyzing experience communally is another benefit that carries over to a whole host of collaborative learning efforts. At the very least, you know that those moments when you feel hopeless are not signs of your personal inadequacy but a predictable response shared by many to facing overwhelming odds.

Stephen B speaks from personal experience about this. He is a well-published author in the field of adult education who has a fulfilling job, a loving family, and a rich avocational life focusing on soccer and music. Objectively, he has absolutely nothing to be depressed about. True, he has suffered predictable life crises—the death of parents, divorce, being fired, and various health problems—but by most people's estimates he lives a life of enormous privilege. For the past decade, however, he has suffered from crippling clinical depression that has overshadowed everything he does. This depression has caused him periodically to remove himself from professional engagements (usually pleading a physical health crisis or other conflicting professional engagement as the cause) and, at its worst, has confined him to his home. Many days he does not know how he will make it through the next fifteen minutes without downing tablets to ensure temporary oblivion. At its worst, he spends the day longing for evening, when he can take sleeping pills and get the five hours of unconsciousness this ensures. His barometer for measuring each day has changed dramatically from "What did I accomplish today?" to "Did I feel suicidal for most of the day?" A day when he doesn't feel suicidal these days is a gift from God, a day to treasure.

But working with family, friends, and professionals to analyze the experience of depression, try to see it from different perspectives, compare one's private hell to the remarkably similar hell so many other people think and write about, is crucial to survival. At its most basic level, analyzing experience helps dispel the debilitating personal shame it induces. As you tell yourself for the hundredth time that day to "snap out of it," yet remain paralyzed by crushing dread and vulnerability, it is easy for feelings of total worthlessness, self-disgust, even, to envelop you. You feel guilty for disappointing those around you who love you, and you are desperate to hide your "weakness" from friends and colleagues.

A crucial step to treating depression is to learn disclosure as a prelude to analysis. One of the benefits of public disclosure is learning just how many others suffer from the same disease. You must learn to talk about this condition to your partner, spouse, friends, parents, siblings, in-laws, children, and colleagues. When you do (at least in Stephen's experience) you are astounded at how many people you discover who either suffer from this themselves or live and work with someone who does. It then becomes much easier to be open to alternative analyses that challenge the perspective that depression is a matter of personal inadequacy that one can overcome with an act of will. For Stephen, being able to analyze the experience of depression through a biochemical lens (with the assistance of professionals) has led him to realize that a mixture of pharmaceutical responses could help. After years of debilitating psychological torture, Stephen finally found a cocktail of tricyclic and tetracyclic antidepressant drugs that keeps him intact. Had he not had help in analyzing his situation through a different frame, he would still be mired in debilitating anxiety, frustration, and depression.

Learning to analyze experience, however, is not solely, or even chiefly, about developing the kind of personal insight described here. It also has a social and political function. Indeed, a major personal barrier to Stephen's treating his depression—his belief that he should be able to fight and defeat it by his own strength of will—is, of course, socially inculcated. In this case, patriarchy taught Stephen that a "real man" should be able to develop an inner strength of will that allows him to reason himself out of depression. So what seem like highly personal inhibitors can usually be understood as sociopolitical phenomena.

Analyzing personal experience usually brings us face to face with needing to understand how power works in society, how people who have power wield it over others who don't, how the exercise of repressive power can usually be subverted (if not fully overcome) in ways power cannot anticipate, and how power as a force moves around a situation permitting its reconfiguration in new and surprising ways. Analyzing experience in groups usually helps those groups understand better how they can organize to increase their power and influence. This is where awareness of the power of collective leadership, of unity, solidarity, and strength in numbers discussed in the previous chapter, comes to the forefront. Groups that take action, reflect on the action, and then take further and more informed action (and so on in a continuous loop of action and reflection) are more likely to exert significant influence on the issues and concerns that matter to them most. Without exception, every activist leader profiled in this book stresses the need to learn from experience. For most of them, the ability to do this well is literally a matter of life and death—the life and death of their colleagues and co-workers as well as themselves.

How a Leader Develops the Ability to Analyze Experience

Like most learning, the ability to analyze experience is honed and refined with practice. Through journaling, dialogue, and the sometimes painful process of interrogating oneself about purposes, actions, and achievements, the habit of systematically analyzing experience gradually becomes routinized. When people work in more individual ways as leaders, a key to this process is regular collection of anonymous data from those one interacts with regarding the effectiveness of one's work. More than most areas of professional practice, leadership is always based on assumptions we hold about how our actions are perceived by those we serve. If there is any power imbalance, lack of trust, skepticism, or resistance felt or perceived by those one works with, asking them to express this face to face will rarely produce an honest response. This is why measures that preserve people's anonymity are so useful. If we are to analyze our experience of leadership effectively, it is crucial that we know as fully as possible exactly what our colleagues are thinking about us.

For some, it is useful to organize analysis of experience around a series of questions. What have I done lately, and how is it linked to past accomplishments? How is my work advancing my goals and the goals of my group? What difference is my work making for the organization or community? Who am I working with, and how are we learning from one another? What factors are limiting our learning and our impact? What constraining factors are within our control and which ones are outside the scope of our influence? What else do I need to be doing to promote knowledge sharing and group growth? These questions can certainly be considered using introspection, through which we conduct an audit of how well we are doing. But we all have mental and emotional blind spots. White leaders, for example, often passionately profess that they work in color-blind ways and that race therefore does not enter into the equation of their work. But to colleagues of color, race and racism are almost always the central feature of their experience and the lens through which they view the world. Only by involving others who see things differently from us can we be nudged (or propelled) into seeing our actions, and our habitual ways of understanding events, in new, useful, and sometimes productively disturbing ways.

Recall our earlier admonition that analyzing experience begins with storytelling. Leaders learning to analyze experience get in the habit of telling stories about their interactions, their decisions, the thinking behind them, and the effects of their work on the communities they are a part of. They try constantly to dig deeper into the issues that stories address so well: Where have we been? What are we are doing now, and why? What obstacles do we face, and what can be done to overcome them? However, as we also noted earlier, all of these questions are connected to the emancipatory possibilities of learning communities. Leaders analyze experience in order to help people individually and collectively realize their potential, continue learning from each other, and further their quest for more just and fulfilling lives. The hope is that accurate analysis will help people equalize the balance of power so that authority and resources do not reside with the few but are exercised by the many. As with so many of the learning tasks of this book, their practice is connected to a powerful vision of what supports human development, human agency, and human happiness.

WHERE WE HAVE SEEN ANALYZING EXPERIENCE PRACTICED

We have witnessed the New Orleans–based People's Institute for Survival and Beyond a number of times as modeling sustained analysis of experience. In an effort to uncover institutional racism in a variety of settings, the People's Institute (as it is known) holds workshops all over the country. They invite diverse groups of citizens to examine how they participate in systems that support White supremacy and racism. Workshop leaders encourage participants to explore their everyday complicity in racism and how unconsciously they legitimize institutions that embody White supremacy. This is a powerful process; to be forced to analyze one's experience (especially believing oneself to be "a good guy") for how one contributes to the persistence of poverty and institutionalized racism is chastening, to say the least. Discussion centers on educational curricula and classroom interactions that foreground White culture and history, banking practices that strongly favor White economic opportunity, legal procedures that penalize people of color, and health care provisions that put the least privileged members of society at constant risk. Participants are encouraged to examine how limited their everyday interactions and experiences with other races are and how much of what they consume about race is inaccurate, stereotyped, or designed to deepen racial hostility. They are also asked to consider how issues of race affect their workplace and how their work practices contribute to the persistence of institutional racism.

Although a huge part of the work of the People's Institute is raising awareness about race and racism, they are also committed to using their analysis of experience to undo racism and advance racial justice. One of the concepts they have participants look at is the role of the benevolent or subversive gatekeeper. How can Whites and others who enjoy privilege expand opportunities for people of color within their workplace and community? This includes creating spaces for discussion of race and for constructing policies that more readily promote a diverse workforce. The institute also facilitates preliminary discussion of how ordinary citizens can begin the process of organizing their neighborhood and community to form multiracial coalitions to confront racism and promote racial equality.

How We and Others Have Lived the Process of Analyzing Experience

It should be clear by now that one of the exemplars we constantly look to for guidance is Highlander Folk School founder Myles Horton. For him, the point of adult education was learning to analyze our own and other people's experiences. Part of the reason this was so important to Horton was that it helped people gain control over their learning. The more effectively you could learn to analyze experience, the more you could expand your learning horizons and take proactive action on your own and other people's behalf. For Horton, the most meaningful curriculum for any form of learning was people's experience. As he said, though, people must learn to mine their individual experience, to make it more generally meaningful by highlighting its universal aspects. For example, each person's experience of perpetuating or fighting racism is his or her own, but the dynamics informing these particular struggles are generalizable. When experience is reframed so that everyone can relate to it, what were seen as individual struggles become shared problems. Then it is but a short step to realizing that if problems are commonly shared, the only way to solve them is through collective action.

For Horton, the project of analyzing shared experience and addressing common problems came out of his desire "to be unlimited" (Horton, 1989, p. 27). He resented anything that hindered his own or other people's fullest possible development. At the same time, he believed without qualification that ordinary people have the capacity to learn how to analyze experience and act on what is learned. As he put it: "People have a potential that is seldom realized, a potential for growth, a potential for love, a potential for knowledge, a potential for wisdom. Those things are only potentials in most people's lives. The potential is there, but it's dormant" (Jacobs, 2003, p. 271). A program that emphasizes analysis of experience "can wake people up, and encourage them by giving them an opportunity to act with this potential; then people can do things, developing the power and strength that goes with unity and solidarity with people against injustice and for justice" (p. 270).

WHAT BLOCKS OR PREVENTS THE PRACTICE OF ANALYZING EXPERIENCE?

As we have implied, a number of things can block this practice. One is the sheer difficulty of sustaining it. Analyzing experience puts demands on people, in particular intense thinking and listening as the general and the particular elements of experiences are unraveled. Sometimes it is painful to recall events or people that have inhibited our development. It can be just as hurtful to think about how our own actions have limited or constrained another person's growth. Because the practice of analysis is best carried out with others, it is sometimes difficult to find the patience to keep such conversation going.

A tendency to judge others inappropriately and quickly can also hinder this practice. Some people are far too ready to take others to task for their flaws and their failures. Others regard the process of analyzing experience as an opportunity to attack fellow participants or take out their rage on others. Although we believe that group gatherings can be a healthy outlet for expression of anger, it is rarely productive for members of the group to personalize their rage by picking on individuals they believe are to blame for their problems. Analyzing experience in groups should focus on how institutions, culture, and ideology, not individuals, exacerbate a problem.

Most important of all, when people analyze experience to find out what is standing in the way of their own and their group's development, this is a direct challenge to the status quo. Such efforts will often be viewed as an attempt to stir up trouble and so are shut down by those in power. Most of the leaders we mention were at one time or another called a traitor to their country, or their race, by the White power structure. Some paid for their commitment with their health, their freedom, or their life. Yet these leaders did not regard themselves as heroes blessed with unusual courage; rather, they felt they had no recourse but to choose activism and organizing as their life's work. Their journey was not spoken of as a conscious choice of any kind but more as a necessity, an imperative, the only way they could live at peace with themselves. In this regard, our exemplars are very similar to the individuals profiled in *Common Fire: Lives of Commitment in a Complex World* (Daloz, Parks, Keen, and Keen, 1997) and *Some Do Care* (Damon and Colby, 1994), two studies of individuals who devoted their lives to activism. Both sets of leaders spoke about their commitment as a natural, almost automatic, life choice that brought them selfish pleasure.

WHAT ARE THE PERILS AND PITFALLS OF ANALYZING EXPERIENCE?

One of the real pitfalls of any serious attempt to analyze experience is the problem of overcoming despair. We have already identified the problem of radical pessimism, of feeling overwhelmed by the social, economic, political, and cultural structures one uncovers as preventing a life of equal fulfillment. As people probe more deeply into their own and others' experiences, they are likely to uncover unfulfilled promise, blocked development, routine inequality of opportunity, and the mean-spiritedness of the human condition. These things make people feel sad and hopeless. A history of greed and disempowerment, the daunting accumulation of injustice, realizing what has to be done to bring about positive change, trying to generate the energy and will to begin . . . when you contemplate what you're up against, it almost seems desirable to soft-peddle some of these past setbacks and future challenges to make the process of moving ahead appear more palatable. Sometimes, what is most depressing is to realize your own contribution to, and collusion in, something you thought you stood against. This is very often what happens with Whites in antiracist work.

Yet, despite the understandable impulse to skip over personal experience that is demoralizing, embarrassing, or shaming, we believe that telling these stories fully and honestly is usually the best way. For one thing, people have been deceived repeatedly about the virulence of injustice. Analyzing experience should not be another venue for deception but an opportunity to face up to the gravity of our problems. Also, there is something potentially empowering about exploring the truth of our shared public problems. The best foundation for any change initiative is clear and comprehensive explication of the problem. Once it is articulated and clarified, we can work to develop the critically tempered hope we explore in Chapter Nine.

Another major problem with the process of analyzing experience is the temptation to play the blame game, to point a finger and never get beyond assigning responsibility. We need to move beyond individual stories and getting stuck in the particulars of each person's narrative. As important as it is to hear and validate those stories, they must eventually be critiqued and interpreted. Idealizing or romanticizing experience through uncritical sharing is not, in and of itself, educational. For the celebration of experience to become educational, it has to be allied to critical analysis. We have to ask how this experience might be understood from different perspectives, what aspects of the experience need questioning and further inquiry, and what parts of the experience have been misapprehended, ignored, or omitted in recollection. Then, perhaps most important, these stories must be reviewed for what they teach us and for what might become the seeds of change.

How to Address the Tensions, Problems, Perils, and Pitfalls Relating to Analyzing Experience

Leaders who are guiding groups through the process of analyzing experience must position it as a strategy for making our organizations and communities more responsive to human need and better able to meet our ethical obligations to promote human wellbeing. Although we emphasize starting by affirming people's experience and giving them the opportunity to tell their stories in their own ways, it must always be made clear that this is just the beginning. Leaders themselves can do a lot in this regard by modeling public critical analysis of their own experience.

Modeling critical reflection seriously would mean that leaders find themselves going public with their own learning. In newsletters, meetings, speeches, and everyday conversation, they would recreate in public the private reasoning behind their decisions and how they understood the problems the community faced. They would pay particular attention to talking about those times when events caused them to rethink their basic assumptions or see things from an entirely different viewpoint. They would invite critique of their actions, and if this critique was not forthcoming (as it would not be at first, given the level of mistrust in most hierarchical institutions) they would play the role of devil's advocate in offering alternative perspectives on what they had done.

Leaders would also take pains to ensure that their words and actions were perceived as being as consistent as possible. They would do this by soliciting regular and anonymous commentary on how they were doing (the anonymity being crucial to make people feel safe in being honest) and then by making this commentary public. Several times a year, employees would receive a written summary of the anonymous comments they had given, and they would be invited to discuss them at a general meeting. Administrators would also do their best to build a case for critical reflection by using their autobiographies to illustrate the benefits of the process in their own lives. They would start professional development days by talking about the role that critical reflection was playing in their own practice. They would invite people from other institutions where critical reflection was valued to come and talk about its importance. A key part of this process is setting aside time for people to tell their stories without interruption or judgment from others. We have tried to do this by using exercises such as the Circle of Voices technique or the Circular Response method, both of which we explain in our earlier book *Discussion as a Way of Teaching* (Brookfield and Preskill, 2005).

Learning to analyze experience requires participants to go beyond merely recounting experiences and probe more deeply into the particulars of the stories told. What else can be said about these stories? What details have been left out? What isn't being said that reflects the larger context of these stories? In this way, the learning task of critical reflection explored in Chapter Three and the task of analyzing experience are two sides of the same coin. When leaders reflect critically, it is often their experiences that are the raw material of their analysis. All the leaders we profile in this book made rigorous critical analysis of their experience a regular part of their practice.

MYLES HORTON AND LEARNING TO ANALYZE EXPERIENCE

Few educational leaders have had such a wide-ranging and enduring influence on others as Myles Horton, the director of the Highlander Folk School and the Highlander Research and Education Center between 1932 and the early 1980s. Few have embodied such a rare combination of humility, passion for justice, and love of humanity. Horton used his position at Highlander to raise the consciousness and transform the educational practices of three generations of social activists. Above all, he taught that people must value and learn from their experiences. The people who visited Highlander were encouraged to dig deeply into their experience and find ways to unloose memories that might be relevant for understanding a particular problem or dilemma confronting them. He sought to convey that the everyday experience of adults deserved attention as a valuable resource for problem solving, but it could not be truly productive without being subjected to systematic analysis. Analyzing experience included validating and appreciating that experience, but it could not end there. Horton insisted that it involved looking at the experience critically and comparing one's own analysis to the meanings drawn from similar experiences by one's peers. In this process errors, gaps, and omissions were identified and important insights were generated. Perhaps most important of all, analyzing experiences collaboratively helped participants identify with each other's situation, leading to a sense of solidarity and aggressive collective action to promote positive social change.

ESTABLISHING HIGHLANDER

In the fall of 1932 in a large house in Grundy County, Tennessee—one of the poorest counties in the United States at that time—Myles Horton and Don West began their experiment in radical community education, the Highlander Folk School. Horton learned quickly, though, that the best way for him to be helpful to others was to learn directly from those whom he was trying to help, paying full and close attention to those he worked with. Of the people he worked with, Horton famously said, "You need to know more about them than they know about themselves" (1998, p. 71). In his view, the reason people didn't know themselves was that they hadn't "learned to analyze their experience and learn from it. When you help them to respect and learn from their own experience, they can know more about themselves than you do" (p. 71). Unless people truly believed that leaders respected their experiences and viewed them as a valuable source of learning, community growth and empowerment could never get off the ground.

Throughout these early experiences, Horton and his staff learned that increased understanding is best achieved through participation in an actual situation, and that conflict and crisis must be seized as opportunities for people to learn how they can effectively resolve their own individual and community problems. It was also about this time that Horton came to understand that "as long as we kept on learning, we could share that learning. When we stopped learning ourselves, then we could no longer help anyone" (Horton, 1998, p. 69). If Horton saw himself as an expert about anything, it was less about the content of what was learned and much more about the process of learning itself. He consistently maintained that the focus at Highlander was "not on how we teach, but with how people learn" (Jacobs, 2003, p. 270). The extent to which education has striven to be "a learning system instead of a teaching system" is the extent to which it remains true to its most essential and enduring purposes (p. 276).

Horton never wavered from the conviction that the firsthand knowledge and experiences participants brought with them to Highlander's workshops must remain the springboard for all learning. "Insofar as I have learned to listen to people," Horton often observed, "and to honor and respect them as individuals, I have been a good teacher" (Adams, 1975, p. 42). One grateful participant in those early years recalled that "the most important thing the people ever learned from Highlander was what we learned then—how we could help ourselves" (p. 38).

Horton felt strongly that the residential experience of Highlander gave people a taste of what it was like to participate in creating a truly humane community. A critical part of Highlander's approach revolved around creating a model community where free and open discussions were encouraged, participants could share and analyze their relevant experiences, and everyone could learn to make collective decisions through consensus. As one Highlander alum put it: "You see, we never took one man's opinion or experience on a subject. Instead, we worked under the theory that it's much more likely that thirty people will be right and the one individual wrong" (Adams, 1975, p. 42). Horton himself argued that students must learn to analyze the world as it is and as it is experienced, with all its injustices, while simultaneously reimagining how the world could be if people were truly empowered.

THE HIGHLANDER EXPERIENCE

In the 1950s, Highlander turned its attention to the problem of racism and racial segregation, and the residential workshops dealing with this problem continued the same approach of focusing on the experiences of participants. One of these workshops, held in 1955 in the wake of the *Brown* v. *Board of Education* decision calling for integration of public schools, quickly coalesced into a highly co-operative and compassionate gathering as participants shared their stories. Esau Jenkins from Johns Island, South Carolina, posed the problem of how to arouse and move to action two thousand Blacks who had lived in an isolated area for decades and had become accustomed to being denied the most basic rights. A White couple from Knoxville talked about the problem of integrating schools in a community with a small Black population and a conservative school board. Rosa Parks described the dismal situation in Montgomery, Alabama, where ingrained patterns of racial segregation in most civic institutions still prevailed and where the Black community according to Parks was "too timid and would not act" (Horton, 1989, p. 206).

After each person detailed the situation in his or her community, the group began the task of analyzing the information given by asking questions, searching out contradictions, looking for sources of strength, and considering starting points for bringing about change. Once all the stories had been told, commonalities were identified that might offer a basis for shedding light on each individual situation and helping each community leader make some larger sense out of his or her dilemma. As the workshop neared its end, each leader was expected to present to the group for comment and critique a plan for dealing with the problem described earlier. In this way, each participant was given the opportunity to be both authority and student, both storyteller and critic. All were experts on their own experience, but all also learned from the thoughtful, constructive feedback given by other participants. As one observer noted, "Participants learn, and learn a remarkable amount in a short time, because they are doing it themselves and because the work stays close to the needs which they feel" (p. 206).

Although information, resources, and networking were prized by Highlander attendees, it was the workshop experience itself that had the most lasting impact on them. Surveys of participants indicated almost unanimously that the cooperative and harmonious spirit of the Highlander discussions meant the most to them in terms of learning about participating as a member of a democratic community. The openness of conversation, the willingness to share and constructively critique experiences, the group collaboration, and the complete absence of competitiveness all impressed participants. Furthermore, the emphasis on the dignity of each individual and the mutual respect evident between organizers and invitees were acclaimed by many as signs that democracy was alive and well at the Highlander Folk School.

Horton said many times that his job was to get people to value their experiences. It couldn't stop there, though; there must be a way to build on those experiences, add to them, and see them in a new light. This was especially true for the poor, oppressed people he chose to work with. In his words: "I had to take into consideration that they'd never been allowed to value their own experience; that they'd been told it was dirt and that only teachers and experts knew what was good for them. I knew it was necessary to do things in the opposite way, to draw out of people their experience, and help them value group experiences and learn from them. It was essential that people learned to make decisions on the basis of analyzing and trusting their own experience, and learning from that what was good and what was bad" (Horton, 1998, p. 57).

THE HIGHLANDER PHILOSOPHY

The philosophy of education practiced at Highlander was both experience-centered and problem-based. Horton did not think learning could be meaningful or sustainable without basing it on real problems that arose from learners' daily experiences. A problem-based approach made the whole process of learning and decision making more authentic and powerful. The problem could be focused on the challenges of organizing a labor union, the difficulties of getting people to go out and register to vote, dealing with an authoritarian boss, or finding ways to restrict the power of wealthy companies to strip-mine the land. But no matter what the problem was, it needed to be articulated carefully and then reframed so as to make it less overwhelming and more manageable.

One way to start this process, Horton quickly learned, was to ask a lot of questions that prompted people to think about their experience with the problem and then question the assumptions they held about how they had dealt with the problem in the past. Opening questions would establish which problems were most on participants' minds, while follow-ups would explore how people wanted things to be different as they visualized a more humane, active, and vital community life. Horton was always intent on starting where learners were. "If you ever lose track of where people are in the process," he observed, "then you have no relationship to them and there's nothing you can do" (Horton, 1998, p. 132). But even as he kept the focus on people's current conditions, he stretched them to reach for something more democratic and humane that would make an important difference in the quality of their lives. For Horton, the process of stretching people to meet and even exceed their potential was an essential part of education, but it was always based on trusting people's ability "to develop their capacity for working collectively to solve their own problems" (p. 132).

What Horton especially liked about questioning was its success in provoking learners to think differently. Questioning could help people examine the underlying reasons for a problem, or why the problem was so persistent, without the facilitator or leader ever having to supply any of the answers. As Horton said, "You can get all your ideas across just by asking questions and at the same time help people to grow and not form a dependency on you" (Horton and Freire, 1990, p. 147). Equally important in preventing teacher dependency was the kind of peer teaching Highlander instituted, in which the participants taught each other how to address the problems posed. Horton frequently declared that ordinary people are the chief experts on their own experiences and problems. Once a facilitator has created a process for people to talk to each other honestly about the challenges and difficulties they face in their hometown, peer teaching and peer learning accelerates. In Horton's words, "The best teachers of poor people are the poor people themselves. The best teachers about Black problems are the Black people. The best teachers about Appalachian problems are Appalachians, and so on" (Jacobs, 2003, p. 13). Once people learn how to learn from their own and other people's experiences, there is virtually no limit to the learning that can happen after they return to their own community.

The point of learning from an analysis of one's own and others' experiences was always to give people more control over the decisions that affect their lives. This is how Horton saw it, anyway. The ability to make decisions arises in part from learning how to analyze experience. But after decisions are made and time is set aside to reflect on the impact and value of those decisions, more opportunities for learning emerge. This was certainly what Ella Baker had in mind when she urged civil rights leaders to hold a discussion after the Montgomery bus boycott was over. It was also seen in the many post mortem conferences that were held at Highlander during the early years of the Civil Rights Movement. At these conferences, lengthy discussions were held about tactics and strategy and consideration of next steps. These were times when the learning that occurred fed future initiatives and brought about new ideas. As Tim Pitkin, an educational innovator and discerning observer of Highlander, pointed out, Highlander offered a complete "physical-emotional-intellectual learning process ... where the adult is free to live, to talk ... to be a live, active human being and not simply an occupant of a seat in a given row" (quoted in Horton, 1989, p. 209).

Myles Horton, like so many of the leaders profiled in our book, believed that democracy hinged on the ability of people to make decisions for themselves on issues that mattered to them. From the beginning, he insisted that learning to do this could only happen experientially, so this had to be the way Highlander ran itself. This is why learning to make decisions and then reflecting on them to improve the decision-making process was, for him, the chief feature of its workshops. Analyzing experiences was certainly central to this task, but such analysis, no matter how focused or incisive, was not enough. If democracy was to be real, people must "participate in crucial, not only peripheral, matters; it means that they must participate in the decision-making process itself and not merely in a supportive or advisory capacity. It means, focally, that they must be taken seriously as persons with a *right* to participate in any and all decisions which affect, even tangentially, their lives" (Jacobs, 2003, pp. 244–245).

In the last analysis, Horton exercised a kind of genius for inspiring downtrodden people to believe they could gain control over their lives. He did this by respecting the people he worked with and encouraging them to analyze their experiences critically and collaboratively so that a new understanding could emerge. He sought to help poor people see that their problems, and the underlying causes, were held in common. He then guided them toward learning decision-making processes that would help them develop solutions that made sense for them. Finally, he enjoined community leaders to recognize that as they acquired more systematic ways to learn from experience they would become increasingly more effective as change agents. Those who became skilled at helping others learn from their experiences were the local, unsung leaders most likely to make a positive difference in their communities. Horton had seen this phenomenon again and again, from Esau Jenkins to Rosa Parks, Septima Clark to Bernice Robinson. In terms of learning leadership, those who had learned how to learn from their experiences were the leaders who left the greatest impact on people's lives.

CHAPTER SEVEN

LEARNING TO QUESTION

Learning how to question is one of the foundational skills of leadership. Without it there is no inquiry, no learning, no movement forward, and no readiness to take stock of where we have come as a guide for where we might go. Leaders who learn must be highly proficient at questioning, skillful at modeling it on themselves as well as with others, and always ready to support it in colleagues and collaborators. Their goal is to make questioning a communitywide practice. *Questioning* is derived from the word *quest*. When we pose questions we initiate a quest, a journey into the unknown or the poorly understood. Through questions we search out the unknown and unfamiliar, but we also reexamine the familiar. Sharp, incisive, focused questioning has a way of pushing people forward to uncover more. So questioning is part of the quest to live more fully and adventurously.

Not all questions, however, are created equal. We are not interested in questions that invite a simple, rote response, but the more complex *how* and *why* questions for which leaders themselves lack ready answers. The point of asking questions is not to elicit information that can be easily located in a book or Website. The point is to get people wondering and encourage them to think in new ways about issues and problems that have no easy answers. Good questions shake people out of their conventional thinking, deepen understanding, and help lead the way toward envisioning new possibilities. Questions that encourage expansiveness and critique can be quite simple. When David Hagstrom, author of *From Outrageous to Inspired* (2004) and then principal at Denali Elementary School in Fairbanks, Alaska, spontaneously asked two parents and two teachers, "What do you want for your children at this school?" he didn't really expect the responses to lead to a complete reconceptualizing of the school's mission. But he knew he was asking people to return to fundamental purposes. As Hagstrom himself recounts, asking this one question opened the floodgates and provoked many additional questions. These parents replied simply that they wanted their children to be explorers and discoverers in school in the same way they were outside of school. Once Hagstrom asked his second question, "How do we make this happen?" there was no turning back.

Learning to ask questions is not an interrogatory project but a way of inviting people to wonder. Wondering, of course, can then lead to all kinds of alternative possibilities being envisioned. Seemingly simple questions like the ones Hagstrom asked help us identify what really matters to us, as well as helping us clarify directions we wish to take. Why are we doing things this way? What might it look like to do things differently? What have we always wanted for this community? How could we make that happen? What are we trying to achieve? These are the first-order questions that frame how we work. Who are we? What do we want to be remembered for? What do we stand for? What are our commitments? What are we becoming? These questions help us gauge how closely our actions and values are aligned.

Asking these questions can be an unsettling, even rebellious act. It disturbs both those being asked (particularly if they're comfortable with the way things are) and those in power (who would rather people did not ask such questions). The edgy, daring side of questioning can also be an antidote to routine, to convention, to automatically pursuing more of the same. Questioning can stir people up in creative ways, tapping into unrealized passions for the novel and innovative. Questioning can also take us to the verge of recreating our world.

Part of the point of questioning is, as Roland Barth suggested in *Learning by Heart* (2001), learning to think otherwise. Asking the right question at the right time can lead to a revolution of thought and action. When Aldo Leopold asked what it would mean if we considered everything in our natural environment—wolves, deer, prairie grass, riverbeds, and so on—to be as precious as human beings, he was raising the question that would lead toward his earth-shaking notion of the land ethic. When Mohandas Gandhi and Martin Luther King, Jr., wondered what the implications would be to meet every act of violence with a peaceful response, they were experimenting with an idea that would lead to social and political transformations on two continents. Every movement toward justice, peace, and righteousness has begun with questions posed by leaders who dared to contemplate the impossible, who risked everything to think otherwise.

THE BENEFITS OF LEARNING HOW TO QUESTION

Clearly, we believe that learning cannot happen without questioning. The more provocative and profound the question, the more lasting and deep the learning is likely to be. Learning to question is one of the ways we learn to think together and become more creative together. As Highlander (which relied on questioning as its chief workshop methodology) showed, it is a necessary precursor to individual and community transformation.

Questioning is also a way we can learn to show our appreciation for one another. In *Turning to One Another*, Margaret Wheatley (2002) said that one of the most important things the members of a community can do is stay curious about each other. There is no better way to show curiosity toward others than to ask them questions. When you ask someone to restate an idea, explain it further, or give an example, you are saying that you care enough about what this other person says and believes to spend energy trying to understand her idea in the way she wishes it to be understood. This is the basic idea of Habermas's theory of communicative action (1984). Humans can reach authentic agreements that are a reliable base for action only if, according to Habermas, they make a sustained effort at intersubjective understanding—at getting inside the other person's head and seeing the world as the other sees and understands it. When we ask someone to describe a thought in greater depth, we convey to her that we believe this thought to be potentially very significant, that it could make a difference for how we think and act. For the person being questioned to know that what she says matters to someone else is both affirming and empowering. Clearly, then, questioning is an important step toward creating community.

Questioning is also a way to critique and assess our shared accomplishments. How well we ask questions indicates how clearly we understand the vision of the community. Some questions can focus on the connections between what we say we stand for and what we actually do. Some are designed to make sense of our reputation, of how others view our role in supporting community learning or making its vision a reality. Such questions benefit the community by exploring whether leadership is true to its professed rhetoric and how well it serves its constituents.

So questions serve multiple purposes. They keep a conversation going about our values, our goals, and our actions. They keep information flowing and ensure knowledge is shared. They help individuals, organizations, and communities learn. Questions help people identify mistakes made and successes enjoyed. As such, they are the engine of knowledge creation. They keep people on the cutting edge, primed for the next new idea and ready for the next creative frontier. The more we question each other constructively and discerningly, the more likely we are to keep our horizons broad and our options open. Good conversation punctuated by frequent and probing questions prevents us from becoming too complacent. It helps people develop the habit of unpacking platitudes and deconstructing conventional wisdom. Questions keep us honest regarding who we really are, where we are really going, and whether we are living up to those fundamental purposes that David Hagstrom so spontaneously uncovered.

HOW A LEADER DEVELOPS THE ABILITY TO LEARN HOW TO QUESTION

As adults, most of us need to relearn the skill of asking questions that came so naturally to us in childhood. But we need to do this bearing some issues in mind. First, we must learn to ask questions sparingly but discerningly. There's no point overloading colleagues and neighbors with a constant barrage of inquiries. Second, those questions we do ask must not be petty or trivial;

they should be asked with the intent of opening up new lines of inquiry and unorthodox ways of seeing. They should invite us to consider unexpected projects and try out challenging styles of learning together. Third, we must recognize and reward leaders who do *not* see their job as having to answer every question or be the master of every relevant field of study. We need leaders who welcome questions they don't have answers to. We must have leaders who organize communities of learners to answer collectively the many challenging and powerful questions that are raised when we examine fundamental purposes. We require leaders to stimulate good questions and have them addressed by individuals and groups eager to face them.

Most emphatically, the last thing we need are leaders who think they must have all the answers, and who, when they inevitably lack knowledge, conceal their ignorance by controlling the flow of information. Instead, we need leaders who are willing to carve out free spaces where a return to fundamental purposes can be contemplated and where challenges to how we structure our organizations and communities can be entertained. Such rethinking of fundamentals cannot go on everywhere or be carried out all the time, but to have occasional spaces to raise such basic and potentially transforming questions is an important outlet for any group, organization, or movement, and a sign of its healthy attitude toward change.

Leaders also need to learn to ask a variety of questions to keep conversation going and stimulate creative thought. Some questions help speakers clarify or explain the origin of their ideas: "Can you put that another way?" "Do you have an example of what you are talking about?" "How do you know what you say is true?" Other questions connect and synthesize a number of contributions: "Is that similar to what was said earlier?" "Were you thinking about what we discussed last week when you made your remark?" "How do you think what you have suggested adds to what we decided at our last meeting?" On still other occasions, we ask questions to push people in new directions: "If we did what you propose, how would things be different?" "What do you think it would take for us to give your idea a try?" "To move ahead on your proposal, what changes would we need to make?"

WHERE WE HAVE SEEN LEARNING HOW TO QUESTION PRACTICED

Myles Horton is the person from whom the two of us have learned the most about questioning. For him, to pose a good question was the ultimate act of pedagogy and leadership. A good question would unite a group of activists in considering how their experiences could be analyzed to help them in their fight for social improvement. At Highlander the chief tool used to help people mine their experiences was questions, and this showed in the practices of many of the women who shaped Highlander's approaches, notably Septima Clark, Ella Baker, and Helen Lewis (De Los Reyes and Gozemba, 2002). Paul Robeson was another who used questions frequently, though his purpose was to encourage people to challenge White supremacy and capitalism, and to force them to consider the links between democracy and the abolition of racism. Questioning for Robeson was an activist tool to challenge the demonizing of the Soviet Union—a project that did not have the effect he hoped for.

In our own work as teachers, we have consistently tried to ask questions that show curiosity, extend our students' thinking, and put the focus of learning on students' issues and concerns. It has been our experience that discussion too often degenerates into an exercise in which one person after another expresses an opinion or offers a perspective without any connections being made. Sometimes instructors seem to be in competition with the rest of the class to wrest as much classroom air time for their ideas as possible.

We have also seen colleagues in community meetings use questions to help focus members on what they share in common, particularly when participants have multiple agendas. Questions that build on already expressed ideas and that show how various contributions have influenced each other change the focus of a meeting from the chair's agenda to the participants' concerns. Such a questioning style does not mean that the chair never ventures an opinion or advances a relevant suggestion, but it does mean that the majority of her interactions are designed to draw the community residents out. As we have noted elsewhere, our own practice as teachers and by extension as leaders centers on the kinds of *questions* we ask, the quality of the active *listening* we engage in, and how closely and attentively we *respond* to our students' observations.

HOW WE AND OTHERS HAVE LIVED THE PRACTICE OF LEARNING HOW TO QUESTION

Aldo Leopold (1949/1969), the groundbreaking ecologist and ethicist, was known for his ability to ask questions that opened up a subject to reveal its many facets. He did this as a teacher, a leader in the environmental movement, and a conservation advocate. With his students, he relied on the tried-and-true Socratic method. Although an effective lecturer, he was best remembered for his pointed and relentless questioning. His tendency to ask seemingly endless questions could exasperate some students, but the questions were never aimless or disjointed. They were carefully designed to pique interest, reframe problems, encourage his students' untapped powers of reason, and help them see the environment in terms of connections and interrelationships. Leopold was only incidentally interested in the identity of plants and animals and such relatively mundane matters as their habits and behaviors. What he was really after, as he pointed out in his essay on natural history, was to understand how everything in nature related to everything else and how to investigate the inner workings of these complex relationships. The questions he posed were designed to help students see these intricate inner workings more deeply and appreciatively, without being overwhelmed by them.

As good as he was in the classroom, Leopold's Socratic effectiveness reached new heights when his students ventured into the field. One friend who often hiked with Leopold said, "He'd stretch your brains until they were tired" (Meine, 1988, p. 397). Once when they were traveling together, the friend recalled, they stopped to observe an intriguing grove of second-growth woods. Questions about what might have happened poured forth from Leopold's lips for the next thirty minutes. The friend commented that Leopold's curiosity was so infectious, so stimulating that you couldn't help but become more curious yourself. Similarly, when Leopold accompanied his students into the field each feature of the land they observed stirred additional questions and prompted a host of collective musings.

Leopold's teaching methods were in part an extension of his own curiosity, his own approach to studying the land. But they were also a reaction against the didactic instruction that focused obsessively on the *what* but never entertained the *how* and *why*. Leopold modeled close observation and accurate data gathering. He was a stickler for exacting exposition of findings and clear interpretation of what the findings meant. Above all, he sought to instill in his students the habit of independent thought, to encourage them to be critics of what they observed so that they might actively address the social causes of environmental deterioration, not merely decry the sad state of environmental education.

As an environmental leader and conservation advocate, the questions Leopold posed challenged the public to see the complexities and interrelationships of the natural world and generate new dilemmas that stretched the bounds of their environmental worldview. The work was never done. Whatever was learned one day was used the next as a bridge to a new set of understandings. In this work, the questions he asked called on ordinary citizens to consider three major issues: What is the relationship between the overall health of the environment and the health of any single aspect of that environment? What are the multiple meanings of usefulness when it comes to any part of the environment? To what extent should aesthetics be considered in allocating resources for conservation? Although Leopold eventually produced answers that were clear, coherent, and even at times uncompromising, it was questions like these that drove his research, writing, teaching, and leadership throughout most of his life.

What Blocks or Prevents the Practice of Learning How to Question?

As we have already indicated, authority figures in our lives often have a tendency to block questioning. They become impatient, fearful of their ignorance being exposed, and unwilling to confront the radical implications of the answers given to provocative questions. Organizations resist change and discourage questions. Power, culture, and history are present in the classroom, the boardroom, and the community center, and they can work to make asking questions seem like a negative act, an impertinent disruption in the conduct of business as usual, or a distraction from the "real" business of the day. Questions do slow us down, do make us examine our assumptions, do make us pause at least for a short while to take a closer look at our routines and habits. For those who believe that action and movement are everything—far more important than thought and reflection—questions truly are an annoying interruption in the headlong rush to get things done.

In part because of the negative connotations of questioning, even the most innocently posed questions are sometimes treated as unnecessarily contentious. Asking questions is seen as a direct challenge, a thinly disguised way of saying "You've got your facts wrong," or "You don't really know what you're talking about." Unfortunately, many people do use questions as one of their main ways to express disagreement. Questions can be skillfully used in a passive-aggressive way to be disputatious without appearing so. Leaders can do a great deal, however, to model publicly their commitment to asking questions as a constructive contribution to community life involving acts of curiosity and affirmation as much as skepticism and doubt.

Ideologically, too, our learned behaviors and instincts—what Raymond Williams (1977) called our structures of feeling—also work to quell questioning. Avoiding dealing with fundamental questions so as not to disrupt "business as usual" is not just a behavior discouraged in public meetings, staff meetings, or team meetings; it is something imbibed with mother's milk. When critical questions are met by rolling eyes, sighs of impatience, or murmurs of annoyance from peers, there is no need to erect any official barrier to nullify the act. We are quite capable of keeping ourselves in line in the mistaken belief that questioning fundamentals only gets in the way of action. Stopping the rush to premature judgment and action just to feel we're accomplishing something is one of the best examples of the exercise of radical patience we can imagine.

What Are the Perils and Pitfalls of Learning How to Question?

Many of the perils of learning to question have already been mentioned. Perhaps the greatest is that in extreme situations the social and political risks of asking uncomfortable questions of authority can get you killed. History is full of activists, politicians, and priests who asked crucial questions about how power was being used and resources distributed and lost their lives as a result. In only slightly less extreme situations, asking public questions can get you thrown in prison. It is not only those in power who exert control over asking questions. When we ask questions about racist, sexist, homophobic, ableist, and ageist practices in our institutions and communities, our peers, workmates, colleagues, families, and friends can punish us. We can lose our livelihood, be beaten up, and see those close to us ridiculed and hurt just because we ask questions that make people uncomfortable and suggest that a wide discrepancy exists between the humane, democratic ideals they express and how they live their lives. In terms of the microdynamics of how we raise questions in specific situations, there is the problem of raising too many questions and the struggle that results in trying to sort out the useful questions from the trivial ones. There is the problem of questions being seen as an accusatory challenge, rather than an expression of curiosity or a desire to know more. There is the problem of relying too much on a narrow range of questions that invite factual knowledge only and that tend to discourage exploration of difficult problems. Then there is the issue of the questioning process becoming a one-way source of privilege in which leaders are designated as the questioners and subordinates as the responders, rather than questioning being treated as a reciprocal dynamic widely practiced by everyone.

At their worst, questions can be used as a bludgeon to punish or humiliate, or as a means of asserting a leader's intellectual superiority. They can degenerate into the habit of driving home a point or showing resistance to an original idea, rather than as a practice that seeks to shed light on an issue or make sense of a shared difficulty. Questions can allow leaders to focus on what is already known or easily grasped as a substitute for investigating challenging problems or probing organizational weaknesses that require everyone's input. When a leader reserves the right to question to himself or herself alone, then questioning is once again being used not to spread wisdom or open up possibilities but to control how information is shared and knowledge is managed.

How to Address the Tensions, Problems, Perils, and Pitfalls Relating to Learning to Question

Our attempt to wrestle with these and other problems forms the bulk of a book we have written on the topic, *Discussion as a Way of Teaching* (Brookfield and Preskill, 2005). Two strategies are prominent for us. The first is for leaders to model questioning approaches toward their own ideas as well as to the contributions of others. Naming and demonstrating how you ask questions that attempt to uncover and research individual and community assumptions is one approach. Talking out loud about the kinds of questions you are employing (ones seeking evidence, or seeking clarification, or exploring a link between two people's ideas, and so on) is another useful tack. This is an approach we have seen modeled well in medical education, where experienced practitioners and preceptors are accompanied on their hospital rounds by residents and relative novices.

The second approach is to experiment with conversational structures that deliberately emphasize equity of participation and the asking of questions that are nonjudgmental and that seek only to gain more information or clarify what's just been said. One example of this is the Critical Conversation Protocol (Brookfield, 1995, pp. 155–158), where participants are allowed to ask only one question at a time and directions are given on how to keep these as nonjudgmental requests for information. Another is the Circular Response exercise in which participants strive to ensure that each comment they make somehow connects to the previous contribution. Still another is the Critical Friends Protocol developed at Brown University to guide collegial conversation.

Recently, in his book *A Hidden Wholeness* (2004), Parker Palmer has written at length about one version of the Quaker practice of the Clearness Committee. This practice assumes that answers to personal problems are to be found deep within the person who is challenged by them and that discerning questioning is the ideal way to bring those answers to the surface. In Palmer's account, a small group of people whom the person affected by the problem trusts is assembled to constitute the Clearness Committee. They listen to the background story behind the problem and then are assigned the task of asking questions that will help the problem poser work her or his way to new understanding. The questions that are asked must not "lead" the problem poser in any way. They must be genuinely open questions, for which the questioner has no ready answer, and the questions must be asked in as self-effacing a way as possible. The opportunity to ask questions is not an opportunity to look good, show off one's knowledge, give advice, or divulge one's own experience with similar problems. It is a time to ask questions that are meant simply and exclusively to help the problem poser think more clearly about the problem at hand. It would serve leaders well to practice taking part in a Clearness Committee. It is a prime example of learning to ask questions that have only one purpose: to serve the needs of another person.

We hope we have established convincingly that when questions are properly used they represent a threshold to organizational and community renewal. They are the irreplaceable foundation for shared wondering and imagining and a valuable way to show each other our mutual curiosity. Questions can also affirm the contributions each person makes to our growing understanding. If questioning is done pointedly, discerningly, and democratically, it helps us make sense of our accomplishments and allows previously unheard voices to come forward. It also helps hold leaders and other authority figures accountable and helps everyone steer the entire community toward a more meaningful future.

Aldo Leopold and Learning to Question

Earlier in this chapter, we mentioned how a major forerunner of the contemporary ecological movement, Aldo Leopold, used public and private questioning of his own, and others', views on the environment as a central element of exercising ecological leadership. His is a story of a leader who never stopped questioning until his untimely death at the age of sixty-one. Throughout his life, his capacity to ask questions in order to acquire new knowledge was the key to his increasing understanding of the environment, to the fundamental shifts he made in this understanding, and to his success in communicating his ideas. Along with his accomplishments as an author, conservationist, game manager, and forester, his success as an exemplary questioner must be included. Leopold's "youthful, inquiring mind, his openness to new ideas and his willingness to move in new directions" (Flader, 1974/1994, p. 28), all attributes noted by his students, were also the chief reasons he became America's best known public intellectual on environmental matters in the midtwentieth century.

Leopold's move to the University of Wisconsin in 1933 set the stage for the most productive and influential period of his life. At least four events around this time prompted Leopold to pose an outpouring of questions to himself and his colleagues and led directly to a reordering of his environmental priorities. The first was his participation at the beginning of 1935 in the founding of the Wilderness Society, a national organization dedicated to preserving and enlarging public land in its natural and untrammeled state. The society represented the tiny minority then championing the preservation of endangered species, even the most predatory. This meant that despite the threat to game that wolves and grizzly bears posed, the society's members favored a policy of noninterference, except when support for endangered animals—including wolves and grizzlies—was warranted.

This was a major departure for Leopold. In the inaugural issue of the Wilderness Society's journal *The Living Wilderness*, he authored an article affirming his commitment to saving threatened animals and arguing that their presence contributed to the overall health of the ecosystem. Indeed, one of the scientific rationales for maintaining wilderness areas was to have the opportunity to study healthy land and use such studies as a basis for understanding other habitats. There were limits to scientific knowledge, however, which the society's founding also symbolized. The society took the position that those who think they fully understand the qualities of healthy land still have much to learn by scrutinizing the balance of nature that is the foundation of wilderness. As Leopold said in the article, some land must be preserved largely untouched as a sign of a new "intellectual humility toward man's place in nature" (Flader, 1974/1994, p. 29).

In the spring of 1935, a second key event occurred that would contribute to Leopold's dramatic shift in thinking and acting. He acquired real estate in south-central Wisconsin that came to be known affectionately as "The Shack." It became his own private nature reserve where he could make close observations of the changing seasons and develop an ever more intimate connection to the land's intricate details and awe-inspiring beauty. These observations became the basis for the first section of his great paean to nature and the land, *A Sand County Almanac* (1949/1969). The short, descriptive, lyrical essays set down in this classic book represent Leopold's remarkable ability to pay attention, listen to the land, and raise questions about everything he saw.

In the fall of that same year, a third incident influenced Leopold's emerging perspective regarding the land. Granted a fellowship to travel to Germany to study forestry and wildlife management, he was stunned to witness the deleterious effects of Germany's highly artificial and intrusive wildlife management practices on the condition of the Germanic ecosystem. With efficiency as their chief goal, the Germans in 1935 ruled the land nearly as harshly as they were administering their society. Predators were almost nonexistent. Spruce trees, overplanted for decades, dominated the forest, leaving decaying topsoil in their wake. The plentiful but seriously compromised deer were artificially fed from straw bales. The Germans appeared to have a lively interest in conservation, but their orchestrated, controlling approach resulted primarily in sick, undifferentiated, domesticated land with little wildness or variety.

Leopold's experience in Germany caused him to doubt the wisdom of the German approach and to raise questions about the implications for America. As he wrote in one of the several articles that resulted from his trip to Germany, "We Americans have not yet experienced a bearless, wolfless, eagleless, catless woods. We yearn for more deer and more pines and we shall probably get them. But do we realize that to get them, as the Germans have, at the expense of their wild environment and their wild enemies, is to get very little indeed" (quoted in Meine, 1988, p. 359). As was common for Leopold, experiences such as his German sojourn prompted more questions than answers, but increasingly the questions he posed pushed him toward a more radical and nonutilitarian outlook with respect to the land.

A fourth experience, his trip to northern Mexico in the fall of 1936, led to even more transformative questions. Encountering the Rio Gavilan in Mexico's Sierra Madre, an area essentially untouched by civilization, was "near to being [at] the cream of creation" and seeing a "picture of ecological health" (p. 367). The vegetation was strong and flourishing, the wildlife remarkably stable and resilient. Predators and game were both surprisingly abundant. He realized that until he visited this part of Mexico "he had never understood what wilderness in the full sense entailed." He characteristically regarded this find as both scientifically and aesthetically significant. From a scientific perspective, he claimed the "Sierra Madre offers us the chance to describe and define, in actual ecological measurements, the lineaments and physiology of an unspoiled mountain landscape" (p. 368).

It was while experiencing the Sierra Madre that Leopold began to ask questions about the land as an organism unto itself and whether the qualities of healthy land could be enumerated, described, and preserved in carefully selected environments. Leopold's questions about the advantages of studying healthy over pathological land also dated from this period. From an aesthetic perspective, Leopold likened the Rio Gavilan to a song in which plants and animals enduringly thrive in "a vast, pulsing harmony" (Leopold, 1949/1969, p. 158). On the Gavilan the imperative was to hear its music. He posed questions about science's capacity to perceive this music and indeed wondered whether science itself might get in the way of preserving such music. He struck an ironic and poetic note in the end, observing that because science had not yet arrived on the Gavilan "the otter plays tag in its pools and riffles and chases the fat rainbows from under its mossy banks with never a thought for the flood that one day will scour the bank into the Pacific, or for the sportsman who will one day dispute his title to the trout" (p. 163). He seemed to be asking, Would science's presence on such land lead almost inevitably to its rapid destruction?

Conservation as Learning

From his trek through Mexico's Sierra Madre Mountains and his encounter with the beauty of the Rio Gavilan region, Leopold returned to Wisconsin in the fall of 1936. His emerging view of the land as not just an organism but a community of living things mutually benefiting one another meant questioning two ideas: that game were more valuable than predators, and that protecting some species over others would not result in harm to the land in its totality. There was no question in his mind, certainly by the late thirties, that conservation endeavoring to preserve the ecosphere's "functional integrity" (Meine, 1988, p. 465), not conservation devoted to specific, detached parts, was the essential foundation for sustaining land health. Articulating the questions and possible answers that would convince his colleagues and the general public of the wisdom of this unified approach to conservation was one of the greatest challenges of his final years.

Leopold's hope was that as people developed into more effective questioners and more knowledgeable appreciators of the land, they also would become increasingly suspicious of policymakers who invariably subordinated aesthetics to economic utility. Despite his own strong opinions, Leopold favored education, formal and informal, that exposed learners to a variety of conservation viewpoints, and teaching people the capacity to question each one so they could understand more clearly the genesis of widely divergent opinions. Most of all he wanted learners to have broad familiarity with the various positions in the conservation debate, enabling them to "formulate their own conservation ethic in response" (Meine, 1988, p. 372). For Leopold, the ability to question thoughtfully, knowledgeably, and persistently was an indispensable part of developing such an ethic. "The only sure conclusion," he declared in a 1939 speech, "is that the biota as a whole is useful, and biota includes not only plants and animals, but soils and waters as well" (p. 394).

This was nothing short of a Copernican shift. Leopold, of course, knew this and believed that the "outstanding discovery of the twentieth century [was] not television, or radio, but rather the complexity of the land organism" (Leopold, 1949/1969,

p. 190). He also knew that as the ecological revolution took hold, a whole new attitude toward conservation would have to follow: viewing conservation as "a state of harmony between men and land" (p. 189). Leopold was not naïve and did not believe that such an ideal could ever be fully achieved, but he was convinced great progress must be made toward it, not only for the land's sake but to further the growth of human civilization as well. His unrelenting questions led him toward the view that how human beings think about land affects virtually everything else they contemplate and enact. In a speech given in 1940, Leopold exclaimed, "To change ideas about what land is for is to change ideas about what anything is for" (quoted in Meine, 1988, p. 408). With this change, virtually everything was productively subject to questioning.

WRITING AND ADVOCACY

As Leopold's shift accelerated and ecology became the root idea of his final years, he committed himself irreversibly to two projects. One was the book that would become *A Sand County Almanac*. As Leopold wrote and assembled the essays that would make up the book, he regularly corresponded with respected friends, sharing what he had so far composed. One of his closest colleagues, Albert Hochbaum, was a fellow naturalist who had agreed to do some preliminary sketches for the book. Hochbaum liked what he read but questioned Leopold sharply for scolding those who lacked an ecological conscience without acknowledging his own previous errors and misconceptions. He wanted the book, in some small way, to document Leopold's growth over time, to show how significantly his own perspective had changed through the years.

Characteristically, Leopold lauded Hochbaum for his constructive criticism, declaring that he wished he received more letters that used questions in such a personally instructive way. He tentatively agreed with Hochbaum's conclusion, writing that "the essays collectively should make clear that everybody, including myself, goes through the points of view which are deplored in the essays" (quoted in Meine, 1988, p. 455). But soon Leopold was backtracking again. Hochbaum wrote a follow-up letter, first praising the essays so far crafted, but lamenting the absence of any hint that the environmental views he now advanced were the result of hard-won questioning, numerous wrong turns, and many misguided assumptions. Hochbaum urged Leopold to include an essay that incorporated his former views about wolves and other predators.

As a result, Leopold went to work on the article that eventually became "Thinking Like a Mountain." This became one of the most celebrated essays in *A Sand County Almanac*, a tribute to the persistence of Albert Hochbaum and a symbol of Aldo Leopold's willingness to question and his capacity to grow. In the essay, Leopold describes an incident in his early career as a forester in the southwest. The story goes that one day Leopold and his forester colleagues were eating lunch on a ledge above the whitewater of a raging river when they spotted an older wolf frolicking with its grown pups. Without hesitation, Leopold and the others in the group grabbed their rifles and attempted to gun down the pack. As Leopold (1949/1969) said, "In those days we had never heard of passing up a chance to kill a wolf" (p. 138).

More agitated than precise, the rangers allowed the pups to escape, though one was seen dragging a shattered leg into the brush. The mother wolf was down, however, and expiring quickly. As Leopold remembered the scene, "We reached the old wolf in time to watch a fierce green fire dying in her eyes. I realized then, and have known ever since, that there was something new to me in those eyes—something known only to her and the mountain. I was young then, and full of trigger-itch; I thought that because fewer wolves meant more deer, that no wolves would mean hunters' paradise. But after seeing the green fire die, I sensed that neither the wolf nor the mountain agreed with such a view" (pp. 138–139). After this incident, his questions about the wisdom of the rarely questioned practice of killing predatory wolves only grew and would over time turn into a skepticism so strong that by the 1930s he could no longer countenance something so cruel and antithetical to what he saw as the land's overall health.

The second major project of his last years was his appointment to the Wisconsin Conservation Commission in 1943. Most of his efforts focused on educating the public about predators. His vocal opponents continued to promote, without question, two long-held, hunter-friendly tenets: it was necessary both to eliminate wolves and to increase the number of available deer. In frustration, Leopold retorted: "Those who assume that we would be better off without any wolves are assuming more knowledge of how nature works than I can claim to possess" (quoted in Flader, 1974/1994, p. 215). For Leopold, scientists, almost by definition, are forced consistently to recognize the limits of their understanding. As he says in *A Sand County Almanac*, "the biotic mechanism is so complex that its workings may never be fully understood" (Leopold, 1949/1969, p. 241). Such complexity demands humility and a critical attitude toward the facile claims of those who think their knowledge is definitive. But the public officials he confronted had vested interests in more deer and fewer wolves and professed little patience for such musings. They seized every opportunity they could to condemn Leopold.

THE LAND ETHIC

It is probably true that Leopold's most far-reaching influence stems from the central essay of "The Upshot" section of *A Sand County Almanac*, "The Land Ethic." In this piece he subjected the primacy of the human species to the most severe questioning and argued that the land ethic demanded that people change their conception of themselves, from environmental conquerors to respectful members of the land community. He also questioned those who viewed the land and its component parts solely through an economic lens. Birds should not be preserved or extinguished on the basis of some scale of economic benefits. Such claims were the result of a breakdown of ecological education, which too often eschewed the habit of thoughtful, assertive questioning. People must be helped at least to consider the possibility that each member of the land community is an indispensable and integral element of the biota, not a commodity to be added to the bookkeeper's tally sheet. Leopold concluded that an overemphasis on economics tended "to ignore, and thus eventually to eliminate, many elements in the land community that lack commercial value, but that are (as far as we know) essential to its healthy functioning" (Leopold, 1949/1969, p. 251).

In the end, Leopold urged his readers to give ethics and aesthetics as much credence as economics in considering land-use questions. He argued famously: "A thing is right when it tends to preserve the integrity, stability, and beauty of the biotic community. It is wrong when it tends otherwise" (p. 262). Leopold did not completely reject economic utility as a necessary criterion in reaching environmental judgments. What he rejected most strongly was the unquestioned assumption that "economics determines *all* land-use" (p. 263).

One of the last things Leopold wrote before his death was the Foreword to *A Sand County Almanac*. In it he indicated how strongly he questioned the tendency to commodify environmental questions. Placing himself within a small but vocal minority, he doubted whether economic growth was worth the environmental costs and worried that so-called economic progress brings only diminishing returns. He attributed the tendency to abuse land with the inclination to see it as a commodity, and he contended that it is only when land is regarded as part of a community to which we all belong that we will begin to love and respect it. The revolution in values he called for was nothing less than a shift from the economic to the ecological, from an obsession with material blessings to an increased reverence for things "natural, wild, and free" (p. xix). It was the final analysis of a radical conservationist, a conscientious ethicist, a leader who led by virtue of his enormous capacity for critically reflective questioning.

When it came to questioning and posing problems, Leopold knew no peer. Because conservation science was new and so little knowledge in the field was confirmed, he believed that almost everything must be questioned. He subjected what he *thought* he knew to what one historian has called a "pattern of investigative questions" (Newton, 2006, p. 98) that included how current conditions differed from previous periods and what occurred to bring about those changes. More generally, though, he was never satisfied with final answers and held fast to the view that nature was too complex to be fully understood. Willing to venture "shrewd guesses" (p. 337) when necessary, he found himself questioning those guesses more often than he relied on them.

Leopold also used his marked skill as a listener to raise better questions. People often commented on his attentive listening and how he used what he heard to pose the next logical or needed question. Even his opponents were struck by how carefully he listened to their arguments, learned from them, and then, building on what they had said, found ways to ask the questions that needed to be asked, questions that went directly to the weaknesses in their own arguments. Out of such questions would arise a new and more comprehensive synthesis of the issue under consideration. Similarly, by listening closely to the natural environment, hearing things and perceiving things that few others could discern, Leopold used what he heard to ask the most incisive questions.

Of all Leopold's leadership characteristics, we have focused on his unrelenting persistence as a questioner. As a tireless advocate for the environment, he wrote, spoke, goaded, cajoled, and questioned until others in power would, at least to a degree, concede the wisdom of the position he championed. Whenever he was in the wild, he continued to raise questions until he could explain what he observed. He was noted for "digging into things," for going deeper and probing more thoroughly than most people were willing to do. Leopold was hardly ever impulsive. He would carefully think things through before acting, and rarely did he offer an opinion until he had had time to weigh it judiciously. He was a prudent man who valued deliberation and relentless rounds of questioning and who sought out associates who were similarly thoughtful, deliberate, and wondering. At the same time, however, his passion for his cause and his calculation of its urgency often led him to take risks that might threaten his livelihood or undermine his professional reputation. But for him, commitment to rigorous and continuous questioning of accepted environmental wisdom was the only way to lead the nation to a more inclusive, ethical, and just set of attitudes and actions toward the wilderness he so dearly loved.

CHAPTER EIGHT

LEARNING DEMOCRACY

Democracy is the most venerated of American ideas, the one for which wars are fought and people die. So most people would probably agree that leaders should be able to lead well in a democratic society. Yet genuinely democratic leadership, at least in our experience, is a relative rarity. Why is this the case? At root we believe it boils down to an unwillingness to trust people to know what's best for them. This unwillingness is evident on the left and the right. On the left is the view that the majority of people live in false consciousness as dupes of capitalism, patriarchy, and White supremacy, and that consequently the needs they mistakenly feel as their own are in fact implanted in them by dominant ideology. On the right is the view that the masses are less intelligent than the elites, regularly exercise poor judgment, and must either pay the consequences for their poor choices or forgo the right to make those choices when they are regarded as immoral (for example, to have an abortion or to marry a same-sex partner). Put this lack of trust in ordinary people in the context of a political system dominated by corporate interests, global capitalism, heightened surveillance, and deliberate suppression of dissent and you have a situation in which expecting much democracy is clearly naïve.

Defining democracy is not an easy task, but it is one we obviously need to address. For us, a democratic system exhibits three core elements. First, its members engage in a continuous, ever-widening conversation about how to organize social and interpersonal affairs. To be democratic, this conversation must be as inclusive and broad as possible involving diverse groups and perspectives. Second, we see democracy as an economic arrangement.

Democracy is not just a political form involving voting procedures and structures of representation, but an economic one requiring abolition of vast disparities in wealth, equalization of income, and placement of all forms of resources under common control. This is why, for one of us, democracy and socialism are intertwined. Important elements of democracy for us include many of the things that FDR called for in his 1944 State of the Union Address, sometimes dubbed the Second Bill of Rights (Sunstein, 2006). They include the right to a decent job and livable wage, adequate food and clothing, acceptable medical care, some protection from the ravages of old age, and good education. One of us views a socialist economy in which the populace as a whole controls the production and distribution of goods and services (as against control by an unrepresentative, privileged elite) as the most democratic economic arrangement possible.

Third, we see democracy as a struggle against ideologies that exclude disenfranchised groups from full and equal participation in social life—ideologies of White supremacy, class superiority, patriarchy, homophobia, ableism, and so on. Western industrial societies purport to be completely open democracies in which all have equal opportunity to flourish, yet they are actually highly unequal societies in which economic inequity, racism, and class discrimination are empirical realities. The way this state of affairs is reproduced as seeming to be normal, natural, and inevitable (thereby heading off potential challenges to the system) is through dissemination of dominant ideologies; our form of democracy can flourish only if these ideologies are challenged and then replaced.

From a leadership perspective, leading democratically includes two specific, indispensable, and inseparable notions. First, everyone has a *responsibility* to lead, to put their energies and talents at the service of the group, and to be held accountable for their actions to the group. Second, everyone has a *right* to lead, to participate fully and have an equal opportunity to influence the outcome of deliberations regarding how we are to share resources and ensure all have equal life chances. Without faith in the ultimate ability of everyone to exercise leadership, democracy cannot last. Without avenues for everyone's voice to be heard, democracy withers. Leaders committed to a genuine democracy do not hesitate to lament publicly how grievously people's talents have been wasted in the past. They do this not to make trouble or to accentuate the negative but to bring attention to the everyday wisdom that historically has been so tragically underused. Most of all, they study the destructive and exclusionary patterns of the past closely to avoid repeating them in the present, and to emphasize how much richer our society would be if everyone's capacity for leadership were fully developed.

The animating metaphor for democracy is dialogue, people in constant and meaningful communication with each other. Through dialogue people learn to listen as well as speak, learn as well as teach, follow as well as lead, and collaborate more readily than labor in solitude. The democratic dialogue supports a shared existence that is responsive to each community member's voiced needs and concerns. As with any good dialogue, time is set aside to pose questions, prioritize issues, and solve problems. Dialogue helps us know our neighbors better and learn how to create, out of the disparate elements of any diverse community, a workable consensus. Dialogue also helps us become more than an individual with private interests. In its give and take, we learn how to be members of a public group looking after our shared interests.

Democratic faith rests on the idea that ordinary people are more likely than isolated elites or narrowly trained experts to make decisions that are in the broad interests of the majority of people. In Mary Parker Follett's terms (1924), expert knowledge must always be democratized, its application guided by the working majority. Democratic power is power that is broadly distributed to serve the common good. An important dimension of this shared power is the community knowing its members well enough to understand how they can serve and lead from their strengths as empowered members of the community. This is the approach that the Industrial Areas Foundations (www.industrialareasfoundation.org/) has taken for many years. Democracy for IAF, established by Chicago organizer Saul Alinsky some sixty-five years ago, begins with relationship building. Through relationships, both private and public, IAF builds its democratic base and learns how each individual participant can contribute her or his distinct strengths to promoting a shared and common good. For Ed Chambers, IAF's current executive director, there is nothing inherently sinister about power. It can be employed for good or ill. It can be practiced in a limited, one-way, unilateral manner, or it can be as unlimited and reciprocal as any set of meaningful relationships. Power, collectively and authentically exercised, is after all the basis of empowerment.

Learning to lead democratically in the cause of empowerment entails learning to distinguish each distinctive voice in the sometimes overwhelming cacophony of democratic deliberations. Who each community member is, what each person most needs, how each individual can best contribute to the group's well-being are all concerns that democratic leaders—which means, potentially, everyone—must learn to address.

As James Baldwin noted in the opening pages of *Notes of a Native Son* (1955), leaders can easily lose sight of the individual, glossing over rich differences and astounding distinctiveness, in their haste to draw the sort of generalizations that shape social policy. For Baldwin, this meant there was much danger in attempting to draw any meaningful and valid conclusions about the "Black experience." To illustrate, for a Native American leader who is keenly aware of the five hundred plus highly diverse tribes that are federally recognized, reaching useful generalizations about the American Indian would seem a perilous exercise indeed.

Generalizations about racial group membership or cultural identity, though well meaning, discount how people specifically and concretely relate to each other and form communities together. They omit all the gritty, messy details of individual lives. The strength of democracy lies in these details, particularly in the mix of traditions, cultures, and languages. Democratic leaders view these as strengths, not liabilities. The more people can use what they know best, not just to adapt to the dominant culture but to transform what is meant by dominant culture, the closer we can come to democracy's ideal of a rich, diverse, endlessly inclusive community. People are often discouraged from foregrounding their cultures and traditions on the assumption that this will lead to a divisive separatism, but as Boyte points out, democratic communities "cannot build a future if they don't bring their past with them" (2006, p. 105).

THE BENEFITS OF LEARNING DEMOCRACY

As with so many other learning tasks of leadership, learning democracy supports the realization of human potential. It focuses on developing each person's abilities and assets, not for the sake of individual growth but to allow the community as a whole to flourish. The belief is that ultimately this flourishing will be for the benefit of all. To paraphrase John Dewey (1916), democracy makes possible the highest quality of human experience by offering a forum for self-expression as people learn from one another. Democracy affords the chance for people to relate their experience to the experiences of the many others who make up democratic communities. Leaders committed to learning democracy know that the more points of contact people have with each other the more they will develop their capacities for understanding and appreciation.

If democracy is viewed as creation of a system to benefit all, it follows that every person must enjoy all of the basic necessities: affordable education, satisfying employment, adequate medical coverage, social security. Only when people are ensured of these things can they make the most of their abilities. This, in turn, helps every member of the community. This is why democracy always has an economic dimension, as stressed earlier. Democracy's central project is how to promote human wellbeing. As such it is simultaneously both an end and a means. In its ideal form, democracy stands against shortcuts taken in the face of apparently irresolvable differences. The democratic project requires, again and again, that we keep the conversation going in the hope that eventually we discover our common interests.

HOW A LEADER DEVELOPS THE ABILITY TO LEARN DEMOCRACY AND DEMOCRATIC PROCESSES

Learning democracy can happen only in the doing of democracy. The first step in this process is for leaders to make a public commitment to working democratically as communicators, learners, and collaborators. This means acknowledging that anyone is as likely to make a valuable contribution to the community as anyone else, including the designated leader. One of the main learning projects of democracy therefore is how to create communication channels that are open enough to invite those contributions and allow them to have the fullest possible impact on thinking and action within the group.

One provocative discussion of what learning democracy looks like is the model of leadership that political theorist Benjamin Barber (2000) introduced originally in a tribute to James Mac-Gregor Burns. According to Barber, a democratic leader helps people see the connections within a group that build community. Democratic leaders keep a stimulating conversation going that incorporates many voices, supports fruitful collaborations, and allows everyone in the group to get practice as both leader and follower. One of the most important ways democracy is learned is through intentional creation of open and inclusive systems of communication.

Even something as quotidian as a weekly staff or board meeting becomes an opportunity to lead democratically. For example, the CIQ (Critical Incident Questionnaire) can be adapted to become a formative assessment tool that is administered at the end of weekly staff meetings with the results being reported as the first order of business at the next meeting. An organizational consequence that one of us experienced when he did this was the decision of the work unit to start each meeting with "any other business," which until then had always been relegated to the last item on the meeting agenda. The CIQs had revealed that when the chair called "any other business" as the last item on the agenda, for many people it was treated as a sign to start putting on coats, packing up briefcases, and moving toward the door. Those who had been waiting to raise their concern under this agenda item then had to battle the din and distraction of people getting ready to leave. Not surprisingly, this was reported to be highly distancing. Changing the meeting format to begin with any other business demonstrated to members that their concerns were the most important ones, not those defined by the institution.

Leaders learning democracy think relatively little about their own individual contributions and a great deal about the best ways for others to add value. Such leaders encourage others to share their experiences and ideas, develop their community building skills, and become effective advocates for causes that matter. These leaders are learning how to make the most of the community's many strengths for everyone's benefit. Their job, in other words, is to make the group look good and do good. When democracy works, it makes the group more inventive and creative than it otherwise would be.

WHERE WE HAVE SEEN LEARNING DEMOCRACY PRACTICED

Neither of us can point to many settings where we have experienced someone leading democratically to its fullest possible extent. On the other hand, both of us have many experiences where it has been a partially realized ideal. Stephen B's proudest moment came in his adolescence when a soccer team being run as a cooperative by the twenty or so boys who started it, the Easington Boys football club, elected him to be captain. This team was formed because the school Stephen attended had pretensions to gentility and would not allow soccer to be played because of its working-class associations. So a group of fifteen-year-old English boys researched local soccer leagues, filed an application to join one of them, chose and purchased its own strip, coached itself, booked a local playing field for Saturday afternoon home matches, and traveled together on public transport to away matches (road games, in the United States). When the team was told by the league that it required a captain to be appointed (an appointment usually made by whoever the adult coach of the team was), the group of boys met, talked, and collectively asked Stephen to do it. As he looks at his belly in the autumn of his life, in his mind Stephen is still captain of Easington Boys First Eleven.

Another example is the case we discussed in Chapter Two of a college in which the dean's chief motivation was to remove the barriers to allow people to do their best work. Here the person leading the faculty began from the starting point that everyone employed there had unique talents and that if they were allowed to flourish it would be for the benefit of all. Crucial to allowing these talents to flourish, in this dean's opinion, was providing a democratic space for people to express what conditions they needed to be in place for them to do their best work.

How We and Others Have Lived the Practice of Learning Democracy

We have both been involved in doctoral programs designed to work democratically in which curriculum and learning processes are continuously negotiated and renegotiated between the cohort of students and the faculty (Baptiste and Brookfield, 1997; Avila, 2000; Colin and Heaney, 2001). One of us has been a musician in various rock bands in which leadership was exercised, in turn, by each member. We have tried as parents to turn the family dining table into an arena of democratic decision making. One of us also coached little league soccer on strictly democratic lines, rotating every player with equal time in every position rather than playing only the most talented in positions that most suited them. This was a practice strongly and loudly resented by parents but one much appreciated by players.

In community settings, we have both been involved in community councils, tenants' associations, autonomous learning groups, and neighborhood groups that pursued their activities democratically. One of us is a long-time union member and can point to many meetings where decisions were reached democratically–in direct contradiction to the popular demonizing of labor unions as Stalinist and authoritarian. We have both been members of various editorial collectives in which decisions were reached democratically and the talents of each member were deliberately used for the good of all. One of us participates in an annual professional gathering, the adult education research conference, distinguished by democratic elements, particularly the fact that all substantive executive decisions are made by all members of the conference.

We have also both been members of academic departments in which democracy was learned as leadership rotated around the department depending on the match between the task needing accomplishment and the talents available. Even when a clear hierarchy existed, it was still the case that the views of all were sought and status differences deliberately blurred. For example, the opinions and preferences of short-term clerical and support staff were sought as assiduously and granted the same airtime as the opinions of the most senior faculty members. Another experience we have shared is membership of teacher reflection groups, both within and outside our institutions, in which the agendas and activities were decided democratically. Finally, we have both participated in larger social movements—antiapartheid and antiwar movements in particular—in which local affiliates of wider movements reached their decisions regarding the movement's directions and tactics, and the affiliate's own involvement, in a democratic way.

Although we work in different parts of the country, we have managed to co-teach a two-course sequence and community building experience that was part of a doctoral degree program in critical pedagogy. The course was only a modest, small-scale success, but we planned it and carried it out with democratic principles and a commitment to development of democratic leadership constantly in mind. The content of the courses, which focused on the history of democratic experiments in education and on the practice of adult learning supported by democratic processes, clearly helped us in our effort. Not to teach them democratically would have been such a contradiction that it would have completely invalidated our efforts. We began by sharing with students our general vision for these courses but keeping the specifics of the courses completely open and as subject to their input as possible. Long before the courses were scheduled to begin, we distributed annotated bibliographies of materials that we found helpful but asked students themselves to nominate books that would be the course texts. We also offered some thoughts about activities to be tried and some guidelines for conducting these classes in a democratic manner, together with an invitation to students to suggest materials and topics and take the lead in deciding what would actually happen.

Although the silence was deafening at first, we were adamant that these courses must be constructed bit by bit by the students themselves. We knew how easy it would be to give into the habit of having the instructors set the goals, choose the reading, and decide which activities and assignments to pursue, but we refused to relent. Gradually, we began to hear from the students, and the more they proposed ideas, and the more warmly the instructors welcomed these ideas, the more they put forward additional suggestions. Consequently, not long before the courses were scheduled to begin, syllabi had been constructed for the two courses that were largely the result of student preferences.

The students remained skeptical about our commitment to democratic practice even after the courses actually began, but as time went on they could see that our chief interest was in having their ideas explored through a format that was primarily dialogic. We kept our own participation relatively brief, offering our perspectives on the issues discussed only when asked. What we tried to do was model the kind of leadership we have described in this chapter. That is, our participation was confined to accentuating each class member's voice (about twenty students); constructively questioning those voices to promote clarity, elaboration, and depth; making connections among those often disparate voices to highlight the sense of community; and relating what was shared to actions students planned to take in their own work at the conclusion of these classes. This "hands-off" approach frustrated some members of the group and often meant that conversations were longer and more dragged out than they would ordinarily be. But our unremitting commitment to democratic practices and shared leadership was also appreciated by many of the students, giving them a feeling of empowerment and raising new hopes about the possibilities inherent in learning and practicing democracy. At the end of the course, the anonymous student evaluations of our teaching were some of the best we have ever received, which is why we mention the experience here.

WHAT BLOCKS OR PREVENTS THE PRACTICE OF LEARNING DEMOCRACY

As we argued at the beginning of this chapter, the thing that most consistently blocks democracy is lack of faith in the ability of people to control their own affairs. The impulse for advantaged elites to see so-called ordinary people as irresponsible, hopelessly distracted, ideologically hoodwinked, and even dumb is very strong.

Overcoming this impulse requires what Myles Horton (Horton and Freire, 1990) viewed as a democratic trust in people's good judgment. This in turn requires leaders who are not afraid to unleash their followers' and co-workers' energies and who are willing to take a chance with shared, interdependent models of community leadership. Our experience supports Horton's; when people's ability to run their own organizations and communities is taken seriously, they are highly effective, even inspiring, in demonstrating their individual and collective commitment.

More problematic still is the enduring attraction we all have to what Mary Parker Follett (1919/1998) called *power-over* leadership. People in hierarchical leadership positions often like being in charge and all that it entails: being on top, telling people what to do, controlling the flow of information, and enjoying the prestige that accompanies such loftiness. Consequently, they tend to focus on consolidating their power, as opposed to doing what is best for the community as a whole. Wresting control from such power-over leaders is hugely challenging; it appears to be in their interest to keep a tight rein on everything. Like many of the leaders profiled in this book, people have been known to risk their lives in the effort to democratize power. Less dramatically, they lose jobs, freedom of movement, prestige, or economic security in this effort.

Hierarchies generally get in the way of democratic processes. They are admittedly not always a problem; indeed, emergency rooms, union organizing, freedom movements, and guerrilla (as well as conventional) armies depend on them to accomplish their objectives. But because hierarchies tend to limit participation, concentrate power in a few people, and discourage opposing ideas, there must be a democratic presumption against their constituting the preferred pattern of organization. Those favoring hierarchies that also claim to support democracy must be prepared to show why they are advantageous to every member of the community, as well as the community as a whole (Shapiro, 2001).

Finally, we would be remiss if we did not observe that the mass of community, movement, or organizational members themselves could sometimes present the biggest obstacle in trying to move toward more democratic practices. People raised in hierarchical cultures (including the so-called open democracies of the West) and unaccustomed to democratic processes in their organizations and communities assume that decision making is not part of their responsibilities, and that open, democratic leaders are weak and indecisive. Getting people to participate, to assume leadership roles after decades of being told that their experience is meaningless and that their opinions don't count for anything, can be overcome only by stubbornly sticking to democratic practices.

Furthermore, experience has taught many of us not to trust leaders to share power for the good of all. We can imagine scenarios in which we are urged to take the lead on important projects, only to have the rug pulled out from under us just as we begin to feel comfortable with leading. Both of us have repeated experiences of avowals of democratic process being an excuse for leaders to dump on our shoulders the bulk of the work and responsibilities that leaders themselves should be exercising. We have also experienced the injuries of counterfeit democracy, of participating in a supposedly open, democratically determined process that is manipulated by leaders to support their own purposes and agendas. The very real histories that give people little reason to trust their supervisors require leaders to exercise almost superhuman persistence in the face of resistance born of disappointment and disillusionment. This disillusionment is almost entirely the result of dishonest, inauthentic leaders who claim to want democracy but in the end really cannot tolerate it or understand how to make it real.

WHAT ARE THE PERILS AND PITFALLS OF LEARNING DEMOCRACY?

The tyranny of the majority is a danger to democracy identified by liberals and critical theorists alike. From J. S. Mill to Herbert Marcuse, the tendency of the majority to reach a premature foreclosure of necessary dissent has been recognized as the major trap to democratic process. Another peril of learning democracy is believing that it must be extended to every trivial nook and crevice of organizational and community life. Leaders who haven't really thought through the value of democracy for promoting learning and fostering human growth think that even when it comes to the number of reams of paper to be ordered, when to call a coffee break, or what kind of cookies to serve, a vote must be taken or the people must be extensively consulted. This is a grave mistake.

The often excruciating deliberations that accompany democracy must be reserved for those issues and decisions that will empower people meaningfully and that have the potential to alter the quality of group existence. Using democratic processes every time a decision must be made, no matter how unimportant, is a surefire way to exhaust both the process and the people who keep it going. Good judgment about which issues to bring to the group as a whole, periodically monitored by small subcommittees, is an essential part of learning and leading democracy. Also, as Albert's work (2004, 2006) on participatory economics ("parecon") explains, different models of decision making are appropriate for different situations. As a general rule, those most affected by a decision should have a greater say in its outcome.

A related peril is the problem of permitting interminable discussion. Leaders of all kinds do have a responsibility to put a limit on the amount of time set aside to exchange views on an issue and to reach a decision. Again, if too much time is allotted for discussion and closure is put off for too long, frustration, exhaustion, and eventually hostility set in. Although it is always difficult to know how long a conversation should go on, democracy will be defeated if the group begins to develop the feeling that decisions are constantly sidestepped and discussion never leads to anything worthwhile.

Also perilous is the tendency of democratic leaders to quell honest and reasonable opposition to decisions, particularly when the vast majority of community members support those decisions. Opposition to and dissent from the prevailing views and practices of any community is basic to democracy. Dissent allows alternative perspectives to be heard that may, in time, become widely accepted practice. It also helps community members to see issues in a new light that, even if it may not result in reversing decisions, nevertheless leads to subsequent decisions that are sounder and wiser.

How to Address the Tensions, Problems, Perils, and Pitfalls Relating to Learning Democracy

Despite all the potential problems associated with learning and leading democracy, we are convinced that it is the best setting for people to talk, think, and act together. In its commitment to hearing every voice, honoring every person's experience, making the most of everyone's strengths, and turning the strengths of the many into a powerful force for positive change, democracy knows no peer. Less a way of governing ourselves and more a way of learning to use our diversity to live and lead together, democracy—more than any other set of processes—helps us answer questions about who we are and where we should go. It asserts that each of us is worthy of full inclusion and that no one lacks the capacity to guide others. It poignantly reminds us of how much is lost when some are cast aside and others are denied what they need if they are to become their best selves. It demands of us that we do more—for our neighbors, for our nearby communities, for distant unknown others—always in pursuit of a shared good and in quest of those things that promote social justice and human flourishing.

In a real sense, democracy is self-interest writ large. It is the environment, the processes, the commitments, the goals that we would want for ourselves and our families extended to everyone, known and unknown, alike and unlike. Democracy is how Myles Horton lived his life. As he put it: "I do think if I have an idea, if I believe something, I've got to believe it's good for everybody. It can't be just good for me. [Similarly], you can't have an individual right. It has to be a universal right. I have no rights that everybody else doesn't have. There's no right I could claim that anybody else in the world can't claim, and I have to fight for their exercising that right just like I have to fight for my own" (Horton and Freire, 1990, pp. 105–106). Like Horton, we view democracy as a struggle not just for others but even more fundamentally for our own humanity.

MARY PARKER FOLLETT AND DEMOCRATIC LEADERSHIP

Mary Parker Follett, who was born in 1868, came to develop as deep an understanding of the democratic process and the role leaders can play in sustaining such a process as anyone of her time. Like so many women of her generation, her efforts to share what she had learned were constantly opposed by a patriarchal society that at first trivialized her contributions. Over time, however, she won fame not only as a discerning analyst of democratic processes but as a consultant to corporate managers searching for new, more inclusive ways to run their organizations. Follett was no ivory tower intellectual; she spent the two decades before America's entry into World War I (in 1917) working closely with a variety of school, community, and political associations in Boston. In all these involvements, her overriding concern was to create opportunities in neighborhood settings for ordinary people to gather to debate and learn about the most pressing issues of the day. The more she did this work, the more convinced she became that when simple, everyday people have a chance to think and talk through problems together, they are able to grasp the complexities of these problems and act on solutions that work.

Through the last half of her life, owing primarily to the experiences she enjoyed in the community associations of Boston, Follett contended that virtually every issue was better served through democratization, that is, by ensuring that the people most affected by an issue have frequent opportunities to air their ideas, concerns, and differences and take actions that are consistent with their deliberations. The idea that those most affected by decisions are those who should have the greatest say in framing them is not just a democratic ideal; it is also at the heart of socialism and central to contemporary reinventions such as parecon (Albert, 2004, 2006). Of course, Follett was definitely no socialist and could be naïve in the extreme in seeing capital and labor, stockholders and workers, as operating on a level playing field. But Follett for us is a learning leader because of the way she constantly applied her learning about democratic dynamics to the communities and organizations in which she worked.

Follett and Creative Experience

Creative Experience (Follett, 1924) is by many accounts probably Mary Parker Follett at her best and worst. At her best, she deepened her analysis of the psychology of group interactions and demonstrated more firmly than ever that integration—a process of painstakingly synthesizing differences of opinion—is one of the surest routes to creative and collaborative democratic living. At her worst, however, she occasionally used examples that offended more than they informed. Particularly offensive was her claim that Harvard University's decision to adopt new entrance tests would make quotas unnecessary as a means to reduce its large proportion of Jewish students. Although the practice of restricting Jewish attendance at Ivy League colleges was widespread at that time, it is alarming that Follett did not question this prevailing view. Also disturbing was her assumption that in the many conflicts between management and labor the two adversaries had been rough equals. She referred often to their disagreements over wages and hours and believed that fully airing their differences afforded an excellent opportunity to achieve real progress. But she seemed ignorant of the fact that throughout capital and labor's tumultuous history, capital again and again asserted its superiority, often by ruthlessly inflicting violence.

Still, the chief thrust of Follett's view (1924) remains illuminating and relevant. She repeated her claim that democracy demands, more than anything else, the participation of all, and that conditions must be established at every turn to encourage such full and uninhibited participation. One of the most famous ideas from *Creative Experience* is Follett's notion of "power-with" decision-making processes as opposed to "power-over" management. By introducing this distinction, she was seeking a means for people to create and wield power together, not by one prevailing over another but by one joining strength and experience with others. Her idea of power-with requires the fullest possible participation of people. The more that each one contributes something of herself or himself to the group, the more likely it is that the group as a whole will benefit and thus grow more empowered. In fact, Follett's notion of power-with is the germ of the current understanding of empowerment and of the notion that empowerment's meaning is fully realized in groups of people working together for change, never simply as individuals.

Yet it is also true that Follett particularly sought situations in which the full power and presence of each individual could influence the deliberations of groups. In embracing what she referred to as integration as distinct from, and preferable to, compromise, she was rejecting the idea that one's individuality must inevitably be suppressed in the search for common ground. She did not hold that what one person desires must always be sacrificed for some greater and final good. Instead, she wanted each person's distinctiveness recognized and celebrated. She wanted the differences between people to emerge as fully and consequentially as possible in group outcomes. Only in this way could people learn from one another.

Follett challenged her readers in *Creative Experience* to find common ground, create new ideas in common, and build more comprehensive and representative syntheses. This was possible, she warned, only if sufficient time was taken to air those differences and "evolve" the power that grows from genuine collaboration and mutual respect. Through the "slower process of education" a more constructive "power-with" situation is created in which each person adds his or her power to the community and thereby empowers all. Follett's analysis constitutes an early analysis of how democracy can be realized even in an increasingly diverse and fractured society. It also prefigures Ella Baker's fostering of collective leadership and Myles Horton's oft-quoted distinction between organizing (which sometimes required fast action without consultation of community members) and education (which always took more time than planned and could not be foreshortened).

Follett developed the concept of circular response to describe how multiple agendas, expectations, backgrounds, and community features constantly intersect to inform and transform community life. Joan Tonn (2003), in the only comprehensive biography of Follett's life, defines it as a "process in which the various factors in a situation not only are constantly evolving but also are continually influencing each other" (p. 326). In a precursor to contemporary postmodernism, Follett's circular response reminds us that in highly complex and participatory democratic environments people create, recreate, and co-create themselves. Hence, "I never react to you but to you-plus-me; or to be more accurate, it is I-plus-you reacting to you-plus-me" (Follett, 1924, p. 62). By this Follett meant we are constantly influencing each other in a mutual and cumulative process of relating. One person may seem to stimulate you, but it is also true that something in you has called forth something in her, which makes possible her stimulating effect on you.

The democratic implication of this is the need for people in a democratic group to be open to being changed, to accept, in some degree, the possibility of being "recreated" and "co-created" with those around them. For Follett, the "integrations"—or the synthesizing of differences of opinion—that result from healthy democratic conversations are progressive, reflecting the growth of the group as a whole and the individuals who constitute it. In contemporary terms, this is one of the keys to building democracy in a diverse society. Hence, in the interplay of group discussion, "I can only free you and you me. This is the essence, the meaning, of all relation" (p. 130). This reciprocal feeling, this calling forth of one from the other, this constant evocation, is the truth of "stimulus and response" (p. 130), the raison d'être of democracy, a living and breathing project model of democratic liberation.

Follett insisted that the central problem of democracy was not only "how to get collective action that is socially valid, that is satisfying by the criteria of enlightened living" (p. 211), but also "how to maintain vigor and creativeness in the thinking of everybody, not merely of chosen spirits" (p. 211). Such vigor and creativity are stimulated and perpetuated by a release of energy that, in Follett's view, can only be liberated when people are prepared to confront one another with their differences, to engage willingly in fierce but constructive conflict. To reduce conflict, Follett proclaimed, "is to reduce life" (p. 262). The process of articulating, understanding, and working through differences called for application of creative powers, for finding thoughtful ways to fashion common interests and common goods. Her view was that controversy and conflict remain the normal processes by which "socially valuable differences register themselves for the enrichment of all concerned" (p. 301). These processes of controversy and conflict are not just the engine of democracy, not just the road to a greater synthesis; they are the dynamo of lifelong education. Without them growth is stalled, development stunted. With them, the chance to "free the energies of the human spirit" and realize "the high potentiality of all human association" (p. 303) is within reach.

FOLLETT ON DEMOCRATIC LEADERSHIP

After the publication of *Creative Experience*, Follett's life shifted again. More than ever, she began working closely with corporations and with other organizations interested in applying her group process theories to business operations. Follett spoke and wrote widely during these years, though she never completed another book. The essays that she composed were eventually gathered and incorporated into two edited volumes: *Dynamic Administration* (Metcalf and Urwick, 1941) and *Freedom and Coordination* (Urwick, 1949). On the basis of these writings, Follett is today regarded as an original and enduring influence on organizational and management thought. Yet what she wrote was merely an organizational extension of the democratic theorizing she had been doing since at least 1918. But then, for Follett, as Pauline Graham (1996) has noted, "a business was not merely an economic unit but a social agency that was a significant part of society. She placed the functions of business and management within the total social framework and emphasized their essential importance in making society fairer—her constant endeavor" (p. 19). Of course, the only way in which fairness could be assumed and counted on was via democracy.

Follett was far ahead of her time in claiming that the leadership influence is not a one-way relationship, from designated leader to designated follower. Rather, leader and follower influence each other in a continuous and mutually beneficial way, making it difficult to determine at any one point in time who is leading and who is following. To put it another way, the leader has as much to learn from the follower as the follower does from the leader. Even the terms *leader* and *follower* can be misleading, as everyone collaborates, sometimes taking the lead, sometimes taking the lead from others. This is a relational, *I and Thou* (Buber, 1971), circular response theory of leadership distinguished by the constant interplay of a group's or movement's constituent personalities and changing external factors.

Where the leader's function may stand out is in organizing the experience of the group in order to get, as Follett said, "the full power of the group" (Fox and Urwick, 1973, p. 223). Part of this work is in skillfully articulating common purposes, not by imposing them but by expressing what the group's members have together already created and defined. Follett captured this leadership role well in *The New State* (1919/1998) when she said that the leader "stimulates what is best in us," uniting and concentrating "what we feel only gropingly and scatteringly" giving "form to the inchoate energy in every" person (p. 230). Again anticipating much later thinking that leadership is primarily a function, as opposed to a person, Follett observed that leadership keeps the focus on developing a partnership in which the object is "not so much to locate authority as to increase capacity," not so much to share power as "to seek the methods by which power can be increased in all" (quoted in Tonn, 2003, p. 419).

Leaders are learners, Follett affirmed, skilled at learning from everyone around them. They also possess the ability to make the most of what the people around them have to teach and to put it to use for the sake of the whole, be it neighborhood, school, organization, or nation. They encourage, and even reward, dissent, as Warren Bennis (1996) observes in a commentary about Follett's ideas, and they understand "that whatever momentary discomfort they experience as a result of being told from time to time that they are wrong is more than offset by the fact that 'reflective back talk' increases a leader's ability to make good decisions" (p. 180). The best leaders, Follett found, create spaces for expressing disagreement and regard those disagreements with the utmost seriousness. For Follett, however, it was not enough to accept those ongoing differences and move on. Leaders must foster a means by which those differences could become the basis for a deeper and more enduring democratic unity. For Follett, this was the democratic leader's most vital role, one bordering on a sacred and indissoluble trust.

Since Follett's time, organizational analysts, community activists, and peace advocates have continued to draw on her wisdom regarding the process by which differences are integrated and transformed into more democratic and representative wholes. Some refer to this process as conflict mediation; others refer to it as the art of mutually advantageous negotiations; still more see it as a win-win approach to relating to others. However it is labeled, Follett's influence continues to be felt anytime people come together and reach an understanding that is less a compromise and more an awareness of common ground. For example, in their book on negotiation, Fisher, Patton, and Ury (1992) acknowledge a substantial debt to Mary Parker Follett, who, they feel, showed there are humane ways to reach a wise agreement that "meets the legitimate interests of each side ... resolves conflicting interests fairly, is durable, and takes community interests into account" (p. 4), all the while *improving* the relationship between contending parties and allowing some degree of mutual enlightenment.

At a time when xenophobia reigned in America, Follett supported democratic structures and democratic processes to encourage neighbors, in all their diversity, to confront and learn from one another. She implored people not to shrink from controversy and conflict, but to seek it out actively, learn from it, and build on what was shared. The new idea that arises from these apparent differences, the idea that cannot emerge until divergent opinions have a setting in which to clash, was for her the great fruit of the democratic project.

CHAPTER NINE

LEARNING TO SUSTAIN HOPE IN THE FACE OF STRUGGLE

It may be useful to begin this chapter by distinguishing optimism from hope and critical hope from naïve hope. Optimism is a positive outlook, a tendency to look on the bright side. It is an unearned given, a way of thinking that seems to come automatically and naturally. Hope, on the other hand, is more sober and thoughtful, the necessary result of trying to face struggle while wallowing in despair. In *Democracy Matters* (2004), Cornel West refers repeatedly to authentic hope as being critically tempered, smelted in the fires of experience, realistic about the dangers it confronts, and committed to its perpetuation.

Naïve hope, a weak form of hope, is inattentive to how disorienting despair can be and unappreciative of how much must be done to overcome injustice. Naïve hope announces that change will come, but it does not divulge how hard it will be, how great the challenges are, or the fact that hope by itself is not nearly enough. Critical hope, a much stronger, even fierce form of hope, acknowledges how destructive the absence of hope can be, but it also comprehends at a profound level how complex and multifaceted is the fight for social justice. Those who practice critical hope, furthermore, know deep in their hearts that the fight for justice can never be anything but a never-ending struggle, a long revolution in Raymond Williams's terms (1961).

Leaders learning to sustain hope in the face of struggle are purveyors of critically tempered hope. They hold no illusions about how difficult the struggle is that they face and remain unpersuaded by simplistic slogans and easy sentiment. Their hope is born of the unyielding day-to-day work that ordinary people do to make their communities better. These learning leaders constantly remind their sometimes despairing co-workers to look about them for evidence of how much can be accomplished by everyday activists. They urge colleagues to gain a new measure of hope from what they see and what they can learn to do in collaboration with other practitioners of hope.

Paulo Freire (1994) declared, "I don't understand human existence, and the struggle needed to improve it, apart from hope and dream" (p. 8). By this, he does not mean that hope alone can bring about needed changes. In fact, Freire regards such a view as naïve, a formula for negativism and disillusionment. He sees hope nonetheless as a necessary precondition for the social justice struggle. Without it, there is little that can be done. Hopelessness and despair, Freire warns, can bring only failure and ruin. Asserting that hope must be paired with criticism, Freire envisions an informed, clear-sighted, thoughtful hope that is based on an effective critique and a workable strategy to bring about transformation. Like West, Freire believes that energy in the face of massive resistance is a limited resource that must be husbanded carefully. A naïve optimism expressed in the face of deep entrenched stasis quickly sours to the point that it reinforces despair. In this regard, naïve hope actually becomes a major cause of hopelessness. Freire further contends that critical hope does not necessarily come naturally; there is a need "for a kind of education in hope" (p. 9).

In his long autobiographical essay *The Discipline of Hope* (1998), Herb Kohl explores what such an education might comprise. Kohl defines hope as "the refusal to accept limits on what your students can learn or on what you, as a teacher, can do to facilitate learning" (p. 9). Like Freire, he observes that hope cannot ensure human thriving, or basic survival, but that it is a precondition for living well. He also insists that teaching, his chosen profession, can be a powerful source of hope. In Kohl's view, teachers who teach freely and openly, without thought of limits or deficits, instill hope in their students, which can in turn stimulate an epidemic of hope in the larger society. In this sense, Kohl continues Freire's theme that hope does not simply happen but needs education and nurturing.

In other words, we need evidence for hope, reasons to believe that hope is warranted. One source of hope comes from working with seemingly ordinary people whose abilities often go unappreciated but who, when aroused, can accomplish great things by joining with others to make change for the better. The thousands of communities all over the United States supported by the Industrial Areas Foundation, for instance, who have empowered themselves to improve social and educational services offer abundant testament to the power of ordinary people working together for change. Understanding the basis for the IAF's successes is also one recipe for dismantling despair.

Critical hope is not just a remote concept or a nice turn of phrase. It has a concrete reality that is hard, practical, and angry. In his analysis of social and educational activism, *Teaching Defiance* (2006) Australian Mike Newman writes of angry hope as both fuel and flamé of purposeful action. Hatred of, and anger at, injustice are positive catalysts for change. Newman writes vividly of the mass anger evident in Australia at the 2003 U.S. invasion of Iraq and how this ignited mass protest. Angry hope grows out of love for people and hatred of the injustice and poverty so many people must face. Most of all, it is a hope that rejects all limits on learning, affirms everyone's capacity to grow, and demands that hard questions be asked and that the most troubling issues be confronted. Critical hope demands that leaders take up the most difficult challenges, explore the most sensitive subjects, and raise the most daring questions. Hope begins with an effective critique of the present and is sustained by a powerful, unifying vision for the future.

The capacity to express dissent is a carrier of critical hope. In his great posthumously published essay *A Testament of Hope* (1986), Martin Luther King, Jr., declared, in the wake of the demonstrations and marches that sustained the Civil Rights Movement, that "dissent is America's hope" (p. 328). Those who dissent, King went on to say, "tell the complacent majority that the time has come when further evasion of social responsibility in a turbulent world will court disaster and death" (p. 328). Dissent points to our shortcomings and the terrible consequences that can ensue when those shortcomings are ignored. Dissent illuminates the contradictions between rhetoric and reality and enjoins us to live up to our ideals. In this way, dissent engenders hope and imparts an education in the continuing creation of hope.

During our writing of this book, the attempt by the Bush administration to equate dissent over the war with Iraq with a lack of patriotism—treason, even—is the exact opposite of King's argument. In the face of the mainstream media's timidity regarding the war, the nurturing of dissent is, in our view, the most profoundly patriotic act. After all, those who love their country are duty bound to ensure that it does not become hated by those who are its natural allies and that it risks the lives of its citizens only in the face of genuine threat. West's book *Democracy Matters* (2004) and Amy Goodman's daily Pacifica Radio show *Democracy Now* are two flickering candles of democratic, hopeful, patriotic dissent that represent what we mean.

Interestingly, there is wide agreement that abstract speculations about hope don't seem to help much. Studs Terkel in *Hope Dies Last* (2003), Mary Zournazi in *Hope: New Philosophies for Change* (2003), and Rebecca Solnit in *Hope in the Dark* (2004) all argue that such abstractions on the importance of hope can quickly turn to despair, disappointment, and frustration. What fuels hope is frequent contact with ordinary people out in the community who are committed to making a difference. This kind of interaction invariably seems to yield new hope, to revitalize an emboldened sense of purpose. This is one reason mass demonstrations are so crucial. Even if they fail to lead to an immediate and desired change, they remind us that we are not alone, that thousands, even millions, of others share our outrage and dissent. Encountering the thousands of dedicated people deeply engaged in the work of trying to create a more just, more egalitarian, more democratic society powerfully supports hope.

It follows, too, that leaders who are interested in understanding hope and how to employ hope to keep good work going must spend a great deal of time in the community talking to a variety of people and becoming immersed in everyday, hope-inducing activities. In Terkel's *Hope Dies Last*, many of the people who speak of hope agree that it is best secured by a slow, incremental chipping away process that often results in no perceptible change at all. Hope is an everyday phenomenon, says Catholic priest Robert Oldershaw. It is "parents really struggling to get their kids raised and through schools, who take on two or three jobs to do that. Hope is people of my parish going through terminal illnesses but staying above it, not letting it dominate them. Hope is the people who minister to them.... Hope has a human face. Sure, I'm worried, but as long as we have people who are speaking out loud and clear, and holding our leaders accountable, I'm hopeful" (Terkel, 2003, p. 9).

Ken Paff, on the other hand, founder of the Teamsters for a Democratic Union, believes that hope is sustainable only when you show results, when you can demonstrate you are making progress. Most of all, hope is powered by faith in people. You have to believe, Paff declares, "that ordinary people can do extraordinary things." He has seen it happen. He adds that critics have suggested that union members only care about an increase in their paycheck. But he has found again and again that "working people do care about having a say in their work, a say in their union. And they'll fight for it" (p. 112).

All of these ideas about the connections between leadership and hope are reinforced by Solnit's *Hope in the Dark*, which examines the myriad everyday ways in which all of us can touch and positively influence the future. Solnit comments that an important source of hope is the conviction that each of us can, in some small way, change the world. To know "that the current state of affairs is not inevitable, that all trajectories are not downhill" (p. 16) is in itself a powerful realization. Allying oneself with others who share such optimism, who live such possibilities, is a key part of keeping the faith. Myles Horton, the founder of the Highlander Folk School, used to say that his school was a place where people could come together openly and creatively, and where, however temporarily, limits did not have to be accepted. It was a place, one former participant famously noted, where "we can live freedom" (Adams, 1975, p. 143).

The Benefits of Learning to Sustain Hope

Hope will not make change happen, but without hope change is impossible. Without a sense that ordinary people working together are potentially limitless, the journey toward justice cannot even begin. As the philosophers of science would say, hope is not a *sufficient* condition to bring about humane, positive change, but it is a *necessary* precondition for so doing. Leaders learning hope and, in turn, learning to bring hopefulness to others create a climate of possibility, an atmosphere that anything can happen. This thrilling, expectant feeling that is in part fueled by hope can infect any organization, movement, or community group that is free to explore new ideas and experiment with innovations. When the constraints are removed and the limits are lifted, a kind of buoyancy prevails that can lead to previously unimagined changes.

There is no question that sustaining hope motivates people and increases their enthusiasm for work and their creativity. Hope includes the possibility of making a difference, of doing something that can produce a worthwhile, even transforming change. Leaders have a responsibility to help create settings where this sense of possibility is conveyed in conversation and in practice. They need to refer to specific examples of how co-workers have actively made a difference. There is nothing so galvanizing as being able to offer regular evidence that groups are actually bringing about tangible, meaningful results. The more leaders can do this, the more their organizations will be the beneficiaries of leadership and learning nurtured by hope.

How a Leader Learns to Sustain Hope

When you have lived where hope has died, you quickly learn how much better it is to reside in a place where hope is alive. So one of the best ways to develop the ability to learn to sustain hope is to witness how its absence can wound the human spirit. When Stephen B was convinced his depression was permanent, his spirit was deeply wounded. One of the most important things that kept him hopeful about the prospect of living with this was hearing others speak of their success in addressing their depression. So leaders who learn realize how necessary it is to talk about things that breed hope. This is one reason Stephen decided to make his struggle public and use himself as an autobiographical model of living in, and learning about, depression.

At all times, there must be a sense that however daunting the obstacles, however challenging the problems, there are things people can do here and now to make little dents in the wall of injustice. Sometimes, preventing actual harm or limiting abuse of power is the most we can achieve. At other times, helping people live with the reality of failure, and of not letting this lead to a demoralizing radical pessimism, is a positive act. There are also times when the most valuable thing you can do is conduct a realistic audit of the perils of the territory ahead. These are not inconsequential achievements. Without them the hopelessness that is the inevitable consequence of naïve hope sets in.

Leaders also learn that how they talk about the shared work in which they are participants can have a powerful impact on the sense of hope. Speaking affirmatively and enthusiastically about the assets the community enjoys as they face the challenges ahead is crucial. Treating each day as another opportunity to move forward meaningfully and powerfully cannot be overestimated. Leaders have a responsibility to learn what postures they can strike and what emotions they can stir to keep the momentum pointed toward hopefulness.

As we have said, leaders learn how essential it is to be able to point to evidence that people's efforts are making a difference. Summative evaluations and assessments are one way of presenting important objective evidence of what is being accomplished by any organization, but formative evaluations are even more valuable as indicators of what is happening for good on a regular basis. Such evaluations, whether they are based on informal interviews, on-the-spot observations, CIQs, or quick reviews of daily logs, can be a convincing sign that however incremental it might be, real and steady change is occurring.

WHERE WE HAVE SEEN LEARNING TO SUSTAIN HOPE PRACTICED

One of the leaders we have observed practicing critical hope is Sam Howarth, a New Mexico parent, advocate, and state administrator who is also the father of a boy with multiple disabilities. To his dismay, Howarth frequently found that his son was not welcome in public school classrooms, and that his efforts to lobby for his son's welfare were too often ignored or greeted with hostility by the schools. Further, he found it difficult to find support and allies.

A student of critical theory as well, he found the views of Foucault and Freire illuminating, yet also silent regarding how to address the issues he was facing.

He concluded that once he had analyzed the problem theoretically, he still needed help finding a positive, hopeful perspective that would inspire him to take action within the community. He initially took action by joining a parent advocacy group called Parents Reaching Out, part of New Mexico's federally funded Parent Training and Information center working to assist families of children with disabilities better support and advocate for their children. Here he found a community of practice, one that helped better translate his theoretical and critical understandings into positive actions on behalf of his son and other students with disabilities. He eventually became the state director of special education for New Mexico. In this position he was further able to break through the ice of resistance that he encountered so frequently to students receiving a "free appropriate public education" in the "least restrictive environment." He also aspired quite consciously to become a leader who practiced a version of critical hope.

He did this most notably by getting to know the people in New Mexico and throughout the nation who were already doing a particularly exemplary job of serving public school students with disabilities. He asked hard and persistent questions about what they were doing on the ground to serve students. What strategies were they specifically employing? How did they continue to learn? Who did they talk to? How well did they listen to parents and other community members? He worked with people who were compiling best practices. He visited schools constantly to find out how outstanding teachers were conducting their classrooms. He read widely and brought his increasing knowledge to bear on how New Mexico's statewide professional development effort was attempting to transform attitudes and practices with respect to students with disabilities. He created processes for recognizing outstanding schools and for using them as resources to help other, less advanced schools.

Howarth found that these ideas and policies not only fueled other people's hope but also accelerated his own sense of hope that something truly substantive was finally being done on a statewide level to educate students with disabilities in the least restrictive environment. As he toured the state, observed classroom teachers, allied himself with disability advocates in the community, and collaborated with committed faculty from university programs and national experts, he learned about how hard people were willing and able to work. He also developed an appreciation for how ingenious they could be (given appropriate resources and guidance) not just in providing support for students with disabilities but also in supporting everyone's education. Almost everywhere he went, he discovered inspiring, undeniable, and inexhaustible wellsprings of hope.

Sam Howarth still believes in the power of theory, in its value for clarifying and illuminating social problems. But unless that theory also opens a path to practice, to getting to know and being a part of groups of people trying to do things differently, then it will always fall short. Like all true critical theorists, he believed the purpose of theory is to animate us to create meaningful, concrete, transforming practices, and hence to be an effective and ongoing carrier of hope toward critically informed positive changes.

How We and Others Have Lived the Practice of Sustaining Hope

For Jessie De La Cruz, one of the unsung leaders of the United Farm Workers movement who so famously declared "*La esperanza meure ultima*" (Hope dies last), remaining active in La Causa became her elixir of hope. La Causa meant not just securing better wages and working conditions for downtrodden Mexican Americans but a *movimiento*—a social and economic movement to advance nonviolently the human wellbeing of oppressed peoples everywhere. Through La Causa, De La Cruz pinned her hopes on an unending struggle to promote racial dignity, ensure social justice, and affirm her people's deeply embedded cultural traditions.

The challenges that people such as Cesar Chavez and Jessie De La Cruz faced in creating a lasting union were staggering. The power of the growers and their willingness to use violence to maintain their dominance over the farm workers was potentially deadening. Also, the workers often spoke little English, and to stay employed they moved frequently. These conditions posed special problems for organizers trying to bring about sustainable change. It became clear, however, that the leaders who would be most effective were those who had themselves performed farm work, were bilingual, and understood the culture of the largely Chicano workers.

Chavez and De La Cruz fit this description well, just as their spirit and vision and their inextinguishable hope were also crucial. They were eager and apt learners who believed that forming a lasting union transcended the politics and economics of union organizing and that combating racism and preserving cultural dignity were critical parts of the movement. De La Cruz has commented: "I was well known in the small towns around Fresno. Wherever I went to speak to them, they listened." She would describe the horrible conditions faced by farm workers, which would stir angry memories and reactions. This in turn would fuel her indignation with the growers: "Well! Do you think we should not be putting up with this in this modern age? You know, we're not back in the twenties. We can stand up! We can talk back! This country is very rich, and we want a share of the money these growers make of our sweat and our work by exploiting us and our children" (quoted in Cantarow, 1983, p. 135).

It is probable, though, that De La Cruz's greatest contribution to the movement was as head of the Hiring Hall for the farm workers. Here she was in charge of one of the nerve centers of the movement where many abuses had occurred in the past. Previously, when the growers ran the Hiring Hall, older workers were ignored, fees were exacted before wages could be paid, and sometimes wages were withheld altogether. De La Cruz made the Hiring Hall a hospitable meeting place where people could socialize and share the latest news and where the workers knew they would get not only a fair deal but one that looked after their best interests. She saw to it that older workers were often the first ones hired, and she helped others in getting food stamps and other government support needed just to subsist. Eventually, her work extended out into the community, allowing her to speak frequently before city councils and other public forums on behalf of workers. She promoted bilingual education in the schools, and she supported legislation and governmental policies designed to help the families of workers. Although not an activist until late in life, her experience as a farm worker and as a wife and mother to her five children prepared her for the caring support she gave and for the hope she kept alive among farm working families.

Like De La Cruz, others have found that hope most readily springs from joining with people in taking daily action to make their lives better. Deborah Bayly, a teacher and principal at a small alternative school for students who have failed everywhere else, considers her school's mission to be restoration of hope. Having served perhaps five hundred students over a period of thirty years, Bayly often finds herself responding to the question, Why work in such a small and confined environment when you could be serving thousands of learners every year? Because, Bayly explains proudly, her school is a great source of satisfaction for herself, her staff, and the students who attend, and it is also a powerful symbol of hope, a place that welcomes those who have not found success anywhere else. As Bayly has said, people know the school is there and that it is able and willing to support those who need it most: "Even if it doesn't provide service to massive numbers of people, the *message* reaches massive numbers of people that no matter how bad things get a school like Lakeville is there eager to reach out" (Terkel, 2003, p. 179).

What Blocks or Prevents the Practice of Sustaining Hope

Hope is blocked by structures and ideologies created to keep people in line and by the penalties endured by its practice. It is blocked too by cultural factors, negative attitudes and words, experiences that have too often resulted in failure, and dead-end theories that leave little room for taking action. It is also prevented by the pervasive sense that we are only going through the motions to get a reliable salary or get through the day, that in the end our work is not producing a meaningful difference.

It is easy enough to see the paraphernalia of structured hope-lessness: laws penalizing dissent; prisons full of political prisoners;

paramilitary vigilantes who beat up, kidnap, or kill those practicing hope; and so on. But on an interpersonal level leaders can also unwittingly kill hope. It is surprising how easy it is to steal hope away from people with a harsh word, a skeptical tone, or a dour look. As leaders working to sustain hope, we have to monitor our own behavior carefully. Staying upbeat, recognizing real achievement, appreciating strong efforts, and connecting with people in affirming ways are all things that can be done to avoid behavior and dispositions that lead to despair.

Similarly, we need to engage people in projects that have a healthy chance of being successful. Barack Obama's autobiography *Dreams from My Father* (2004) vividly recounts how his early impulse to change the world through community activism in Chicago quickly foundered for lack of a specific achievable project that people could see would make a difference in their lives. If our efforts are not successful in the terms we have set for ourselves, we need to reframe outcomes as partial successes and build on the parts that show improvement and strength. Hope will be extinguished without evidence that some movement is occurring, that improvement of some kind can be demonstrated. It is another burden of leaders to play a role in helping co-workers see that even the most dismal failure includes elements of success. Outstanding individual and collective performances often accompany efforts that do not produce hoped-for results. Concretely acknowledging those performances is a critical part of forestalling despair.

Finally, to bring hope alive people must have the sense that their work, however mundane or routine it may seem, is part of a long-term vision that is purposefully focused, in some sense, on enhancing human wellbeing. This is a hugely important role for leaders. Sometimes inaccurately called the vision keepers, leaders nevertheless must constantly remind people what they are working and fighting for. They must regularly engage people in conversation about purpose and meaning and direct their attention to how their work is supporting the overall purpose, or if it is not, then what can be done to sharpen the connections between their work and this purpose. Either way, hope truly is the thing with purpose and meaning. Leaders sustaining hope must persistently reconnect us to these concerns.

What Are the Perils and Pitfalls of Learning to Sustain Hope in the Face of Struggle?

Perhaps the most important peril is the possibility of introducing false, insubstantial hope. In our understandable desire to sustain hope, we sometimes inspire hope inappropriately when there really is none to be had. In his book on hope in cancer victims *The Anatomy of Hope*, Jerome Groopman (2005) refers to false hope as giving patients reason to think they may live even when all the weight of the evidence contradicts this assertion. False hope results from ignorance and misinformation. What Groopman calls true hope is founded on knowledge, analysis, and clear-eyed emotions that allow a person to face and deal with even the most alarming diagnosis. Underplaying the obstacles facing us, fooling ourselves into thinking that regardless of what we do everything will turn out all right because it always has in the past is what Groopman calls false hope.

False hope even undermines our sense of agency because it implies that our efforts, our actions, and our comprehension of the difficult challenges ahead do not really matter. In contrast to this is what Groopman regards as true hope, "the elevating feeling we experience when we see—in the mind's eye—a path to a better future. True hope acknowledges the significant obstacles and deep pitfalls along the path. It has no room for delusion. Clear-eyed hope gives the courage to confront our circumstances and the capacity to surmount them" (2005, p. xiv). The knowledge and courage that constitute true hope also have the underestimated effect of empowering us.

How to Address the Tensions, Problems, Perils, and Pitfalls Related to Learning to Sustain Hope

Joining with others in the ongoing struggle for social justice and witnessing their commitment, self-sacrifice, and strategic intelligence is the best way to learn how to sustain hope in the face of struggle. Seeing firsthand how much is accomplished by ordinary people possessing little more than a healthy dose of critical hope remains the surest antidote against despair. Grounded in solid knowledge of past injustices, these leaders of hope keep their eyes on the prize and remain determined and undeterred.

Learning to sustain hope in the face of struggle involves nothing less than the conviction that by joining with others anything can be accomplished, any restriction can be overcome, and any limit can be eliminated. Leaders must model this authentic sense of hopefulness. It includes a clear-sighted view of how great the obstacles are, how daunting the challenges continue to be, but also an attainable strategic vision of what can be done to create communities where everyone has a fair chance of becoming their best selves as learners, active participants, and leaders. Learning and leading with hope includes honest assessment of how far we have to go, and deep faith that with the necessary resources and support people can develop the capacity to get us there.

Paul Robeson and Sustaining Hope

Paul Robeson is the learning leader we choose to exemplify the practice of hope. Robeson was one of the towering Black public intellectuals of the twentieth century. His biographer claims that at one point in his life he was the most well-known Black man alive (Duberman, 1988). But he was also one of those rare examples of a successful, admired and feted leader who sees through the sham of ideological manipulation and risks everything to move to the left. The more success he gained, the more he realized that the White supremacist power structure was using his success as evidence of the lack of racism in the United States. Once aware of this, Robeson turned the ideological tables and learned to use his success to fight that same supremacy. In contemporary terms, this would be as if Michael Jordan or Michael Jackson—at the height of their fame and their ability to secure millions of dollars in contracts and lucrative sponsorships—had announced they were devoting their talents and energies to forging a mass movement between Blacks and labor unions to fight White capitalism, or to sponsoring the Black Panther Party as a mass movement.

As government and popular pressure on him mounted, and as he saw his earnings plummet and how his family was affected by his principled stand, it would have been easy for Robeson to lower his profile, even if he didn't change his private political stance. This he refused to do. He maintained a radical hope in movements, countries, and people, often when history screamed at him that such hope was misplaced. Even after Khrushchev's 1956 speech detailing the horrors of Stalinist repression, Robeson clung steadfastly to his hope that the Soviet Union could remain a global actor in the struggle against colonization. For Robeson, socialism was a vision full of hope for creating a society that had as its priority meeting humans' needs, not creating profit.

The Hope of Popular Culture

His work with popular culture is probably the area of his life that is known to the broadest number of people. Beginning as a singer, Robeson expanded his activities to include film and theater, starring as Othello at Stratford on Avon in the United Kingdom once the U.S. State Department returned his passport to him. For him art was always politically charged; he famously declared at a rally in support of the anti-fascist forces in the Spanish Civil War that "the artist must take sides. He must elect to fight for freedom or slavery. I have made my choice. I had no alternative" (Robeson, 1978, p. 119). He tried to work in the commercial studio system to develop race pride by providing historically accurate representations of Africans in films such as *Sanders of the River*. His hope was founded on his belief that film "is the medium through which to express the creative abilities of the masses" and that "only on the screen can the Negro's real place in the building of the United States be properly shown" (p. 39).

As he became disillusioned with Hollywood's White bankrollers, he gradually moved away from commercial films and ceased to target his appeal to a broad audience. Increasingly, he aimed his acting at members of labor unions, believing that art could help demonstrate the common economic interests of poor working-class Whites and Blacks and thus play a part in creating a viable mass, working-class movement. (The film *The Proud Valley* is probably the best example of this.) His hopeful commitment to popular culture became channeled in a strategic, targeted way. First, he proposed an alternative system for financing, producing, and distributing films that totally bypassed the major studios. Such films would be financed by unions, cultural associations (such as the Council on African Affairs), or wealthy independent backers, which would allow him to make films on such topics as the life of a Black commander of the Lincoln Brigade in the Spanish Civil War (a project he was never to realize).

Second, he suggested that African Americans, union members, and progressive Whites boycott studio-produced films, hoping that such a stand would inspire similar boycotts in international markets. It was his conviction that "the mounting of the right kind of campaign could shake Hollywood to its foundations" (1978, p. 126), seriously affecting its members. Consistent with his internationalism, he argued that if elements of the American public took the lead "help would be forthcoming from all over the world" (p. 126). This reconfiguring of his efforts was typical of Robeson's stubborn hope in the power to effect change. If the Hollywood system wouldn't promote justice, then his hope led him to work for subverting the system from within while simultaneously developing alternative, popularly controlled media.

RACE PRIDE

For Robeson, a precondition of hope was self-respect. Until people believed themselves worthy of respect from others, there was little likelihood they would exercise a sturdy, critically tempered hope to improve their communities. This led him to a second leadership task of developing race pride among African Americans by educating them about the richness of the African cultural heritage. Like DuBois, Robeson believed that a commitment to Pan-Africanism and to socialism were compatible. While in London he studied at the School of Oriental Languages and learned a number of African languages (Swahili, Yoruba, Efik, Benin, Ashanti, and Tivi). Indeed, he often said that it was in England that he became an African, partly as a result of his language studies and partly through his conversations with African seamen in London, Liverpool, and Cardiff.

Increasingly he became a passionate advocate of African Americans learning about the rich heritage of African culture, believing that a lack of knowledge of their culture meant they were denied a potent source of race pride. As early as 1934 he declared that "in my music, my plays, my films I want to carry always this central idea: to be African" (1978, p. 91). The next year, he declared that "for the rest of my life I am going to think and feel as an African—not as a white man.... To me it seems the most momentous thing in my life" (p. 91). Anticipating the contemporary Africentric turn away from Eurocentrism (Asante, 1998a, 1998b), he maintained "it is not as imitation Europeans, but as Africans, that we have a value" (Robeson, 1978, p. 92).

The heritage Robeson sought to educate people about was that of Africa's "great philosophy and epics of poetry" (p. 352), which he maintained were comparable to the achievements of Greek and Chinese poetry. He celebrated what he felt was the "great precision and subtlety of intonational structure" to be found in African languages, the "rich oral folklore ... distinctive decorative art (especially culture)" of African culture, and the "highly developed and original musical art distinguished by an extraordinary wealth of rhythm" (p. 352) he found in his studies of Africa. Yet, he lamented, none of these were evident in the "savage and cannibalistic" images of half-naked Black people presented as examples of Africans "as the newspapers, radio, book and lecture propagandists would make them" (p. 228).

As Robeson conducted this educational project he became more and more aware of the political underpinnings of the opposition he faced. As he put it, "There was a logic to this cultural struggle, and the powers-that-be realized it before I did. The British Intelligence came one day to caution me about the political meanings of my activities. For the question loomed of itself: If African culture was what I insisted it was, what happens to the claim that it would take a thousand years for Africans to be capable of self-rule? Yes, culture and politics were actually inseparable here as always" (p. 352). This analysis led him to switch his emphasis to placing cultural education as a central political component in the Black liberation struggle.

What was particularly frustrating for Robeson was the fact that American Negroes shared the White supremacist stereotypes of Africa, which viewed Africans as uncultured savages lacking even language. Hence the major purpose of his studies of African language and folk music was "to dispel this regrettable and abysmal ignorance of the value of its own heritage in the negro race itself" (p. 87). His decision to sing only Negro spirituals in concert, to charge low admission prices to his concerts, and to make independent films financed outside the studio system were all manifestations of this project. These were political statements, not just cultural choices. As his career evolved, he learned more and more the importance of integrating the cultural and political dimensions of educating people about African culture. This became reframed as an important element in the anticolonial struggle rather than an act of purely aesthetic or anthropological education.

COLLECTIVE LEADERSHIP

As his political commitment hardened, Robeson focused more and more on reframing his practice within a collective movement. In 1953, at the Peace Arch on the Canadian border, he declared that he would spend his "day-to-day struggle down among the masses of the people, not even as any great artist on top somewhere—but right here in this park, in many other picket lines, wherever I could be to help the struggle of the people. And I will never apologize for that. I shall continue to fight, as I see the truth.... there is no force on earth that will make me go backward one-thousandth part of one little inch" (pp. 365–366). Here we have a fiery radicalism voiced even as Senator Joe McCarthy's investigations had caused the state department to confiscate Robeson's passport, but a defiantly hopeful radicalism expressed in the service of collective, not individual, struggle. Declaring himself to feel "a part of a tremendous collective strength and power" (p. 272), Robeson moved to advocating the sort of collective leadership we explored in Chapter Five.

For Robeson, the hope of collective leadership was in helping African Americans realize the tremendous collective power they could exercise through mass action. Much in the manner of Septima Clark and Ella Baker, he urged that Blacks should build on the already tremendous organizing spirit alive in Black churches to form mass organizations that could exert political pressure. Writing in his autobiography *Here I Stand* in 1958, he declared "For Negro action to be effective—to be decisive, as I think it can be—it must be mass action. Mass action—in political life and elsewhere—is Negro power in motion; and it is the way to win" (Robeson, 1958, p. 107).

The hope of collective leadership could be realized, in Robeson's opinion, only if it was exercised in the context of a working class movement led by racially integrated trade unions. Again and again, he urged African Americans to join labor unions, and for Negro unions to affiliate with the CIO. For him the struggles of African Americans and the struggles of the White workers were one, with far more uniting these two groups than dividing them. In the trenches of the Spanish civil war, in the Welsh coalmines, and on the New Jersey docks, Robeson consistently emphasized the power of the union. In particular, he identified Negro leaders within unions as the vanguard of African Americans' interests.

SOCIALIST PERSUASION

Robeson's sturdy and hopeful independence of thought is perhaps seen most dramatically in his commitment to socialism, a commitment that included loyalty to the Soviet Union that never weakened, even in the darkest days of anti-Soviet hysteria and McCarthyism. In adult life, Robeson became a fervent socialist, an unwavering commitment that alienated him from much of mainstream American opinion (and the NAACP leadership) in the 1950s and until his death in 1976. As a result of his frequent travels to the Soviet Union, he came to believe that only in a socialist state could true antiracism flourish. He constantly cited the Soviet Union as a hopeful example of a nonracist society that people of color the world over should look to as a model. For him, Socialism represented "an advance to a higher stage of life ... a form of society which is economically, socially, culturally, and ethically superior to a system based on production for private profit" (Robeson, 1978, p. 39).

Two dimensions of his commitment to socialism are of particular interest. First is his commitment to the need for a political party to advance progressive interests. Although he constantly urged Negro unity, integration of African American leaders into leadership positions within the union movement, and the importance of Black leadership of multiracial alliances, he equally consistently urged that these must all go hand in hand with membership in a political party. This explains his support for the Progressive party in 1948. Second, Robeson remained to the end of his life a steadfast supporter of the Soviet Union, refusing to abandon his faith in that country's ability to fight colonialist expansion across the globe. He frequently contrasted favorably the respectful personal treatment he received in the Soviet Union with that received in the United States and sent his own son Paul to school in the Soviet Union.

In the midst of World War II, his statements supporting the Soviet Union were well in the mainstream of progressive opinion. As the chilly winds of the cold war began to blow, Robeson regarded the turn against the Soviet Union as a clear instance of ideological manipulation. In his view, the campaign against the Soviet Union was emblematic of a wider campaign to keep colonial peoples, and African Americans, in a state of subjection. For him, "the 'Stop Russia' cry really means—stop the advance of the colonial peoples of Asia and Africa toward independence; stop the organized workers of America from trying to hold their ground against their profit greedy employers; stop the Negro people from voting, and joining trade unions in the South. 'Stop Russia' means—*stop progress*—maintain the status quo. It means—let the privileged few continue to rule and thrive at the expense of the masses" (1978, p. 170).

Robeson is an unjustifiably neglected learning leader who deserves our attention. As a leader, he constantly learned about other cultures, other languages, other ideologies, and about the tactics and strategy of fighting White supremacy. He held steadfast to a lifelong hope that through a broad-based alliance of Blacks and Whites, united in collective organizations such as trade unions and channeling political demands through the Progressive Party, an international nonracist world could be created. His life was framed as an educational project to build hope by educating Blacks and Whites about their common interests, educating African Americans about the storehouse of art, music, dance, and poetry that African culture represented, and alerting people to the ideological manipulation endemic to the maintenance of White supremacy in the United States and White colonialism abroad. Finally, socialism in its theory and in its practice (as he saw it on his visits to the USSR) was for him a beacon of hope, an ideal enshrining a vision of a more humane world. The project of his life became convincing people that hope for such a vision to be realized was clear-eyed and realistic—a learning leader indeed.

CHAPTER TEN

LEARNING TO CREATE COMMUNITY

This is our final learning task. We deal with it last because the capacity to create community depends on the practice of all the other learning tasks already discussed. In thinking about how this process incorporates all these tasks, one should recall the concept's root words: *communication, commune,* and *common.* First, community is impossible without ongoing communication. Part of the rationale for building community is to provide a setting for exchanging experiences, knowledge, and ideas, a setting where competing visions of what people desire can be hashed out. Continuing communication among the members of a community helps bring them closer together and bind them to a shared purpose. Second, people who are part of a community give up some of their individual identity to identify with the whole. They literally commune or join with others in pursuit of something that is greater than themselves. They do this because they know that community can accomplish goals and impart new meanings to experience in ways that cannot be achieved individually. Part of this communing process requires that everyone be willing to come forward to play a leadership role when necessary. No one person is treated as a stand-alone, designated leader. All lead, all follow. Third, any common vision that is developed is designed to promote the common good of all. Community brings us back to the idea that whatever benefits an individual should be regarded as something for all to enjoy. When we learn to create community, then, we keep a good conversation going about our joint purposes, we identify with others at least as much as with ourselves, and we do all we can to define and promote a mutually advantageous common good.

Creating community requires leaders to engage in the learning tasks already discussed in Chapters Two through Nine. For example, community as we understand it cannot happen without openness. To create an environment in which everyone is invited to make a distinct contribution to the whole requires that people remain open to the group's broad and often disorienting diversity. Only when there is a kind of radical openness to the full panoply of perspectives it contains can a community achieve its full potential. This openness is particularly important with respect to immediate others. We are sometimes more likely to be open to viewpoints from outside "experts" we see as possessing specialized knowledge. Leaders must make a special effort to stay open to community insiders—the people they see everyday—and treat them with the kind of deference usually reserved for experts. This is a major step toward creation of community; it informed everything Myles Horton did at the Highlander Folk School.

Similarly, a strong and sustainable community is impossible in the absence of attention to every person's growth. Getting to know people well enough to learn their strengths and passions and find out what it takes to continue supporting them are central leadership tasks. This is especially true when we define community as a group of mutually supportive, interdependent individuals. If it is in everyone's interests for each member of the community to be in the best possible position to make a worthwhile contribution to the group as a whole, then promoting each person's growth is a must.

We also know that unless people learn to analyze their problems critically their growth will be stunted. Consequently, leaders must model critical reflection on their own assumptions and create frequent opportunities for colleagues to practice this skill. People also need to learn how they can analyze experience as a means to gain control over their own development and contribute to a redistribution of power. Creating a sustainable community without learning to analyze experience and reflect critically (to paraphrase Thomas Jefferson) is something that never was and never will be. Thoughtful, discerning questioning initiates and sustains these forms of inquiry and is therefore an essential ingredient in any recipe for community building.

But critical reflection of experience cannot proceed meaningfully in a vacuum; it always springs from a vision regarding how a community functions to help all involved live the fullest, most creative lives possible. So creating community demands that some animating vision for what the community stands for be collectively fashioned. This is why creating community is closely aligned with leading collectively. Many of the same assumptions inform the two learning tasks. In both cases, people are willing to sacrifice their identity as individuals, at least to an extent, to promote the group's agenda. Paradoxically, leading collectively and participating in community also mean that all are willing, at different times and under different conditions, to assume responsibility for leadership. People accept the need to step forward periodically to redirect the group's work, facilitate reconceptualization of their vision, and even represent the collective at important gatherings. When we lead collectively as part of creating community, seeking credit for leading has no place.

Of course, creating community means nothing without the freedom of each individual to contribute a proposal or idea and to know that it has as much of a chance of affecting the community's progress as any other. This is the foundation for learning and practicing democracy and so is integral to the building of community. A community's great strength, as Freire suggested, is its unity through diversity, its commitment to a set of principles arrived at after rich and varied deliberations. Neither unity nor diversity can be fully exploited without attention to the participatory virtues of democracy.

Finally, communities are founded on hope—the hope that together we can identify the most important problems that face us, pose the most generative questions to explore them, think more clearly and deeply in solving them, and take meaningful action that makes a difference. As we have said, such hope must be clear-eyed, never underestimating the challenges facing us, or understating how entrenched injustice has been historically. Still, a sense must be retained that in learning to create community and realize solidarity we are stronger and wiser in confronting injustices.

THE BENEFITS OF CREATING COMMUNITY

In shaping community, people create what Belenky, Bond, and Weinstock (1997) call a public homeplace and Habermas (1984) calls a public sphere. These are spaces beyond one's immediate family, where diverse people come together to deliberate about issues they see affecting the quality of their lives. Those involved in these conversations feel welcomed and develop affiliations with others that enhance their commitment to the community. They feel free to take a strong stance, listen intently without speaking, express opposition to a popular view, or work toward consensus on a new social policy. Such public homeplaces are sites not only for conducting stimulating conversation or lobbying for change but also for wondering, questioning, and learning. When we create community, we create a location for our individual and collective growth. Even though we may disagree sharply with other group members, we share with them a similar commitment to our mutual development.

Community is about the power of collective thought and action, demonstrating how much more can be accomplished in a cohesive group than can be done by a lone individual. We learn to create community because of its potential for stimulating actions that can transform the balance of power within the larger society. By virtue of numbers and collective strength, community solidarity enables people to exert pressure on the powerful few to redistribute resources, share authority, and actualize democracy. Without broad agreement on things that are most important, the community's power to make a difference is diminished. With this agreement, there is virtually no limit to the influence it can have. One of the greatest challenges facing leaders learning and supporting community is making the most of the strength of solidarity without letting the need for unity overpower the group and short-circuit healthy dissent.

HOW LEADERS DEVELOP THE ABILITY TO CREATE COMMUNITY

Leaders learning to create community are, in part, teaching themselves and others the value of surrendering a measure of individuality for the sake of group strength and solidarity.

Committing to group objectives and putting one's own preferences aside are habits not easily acquired in this individual-istic culture, but they are basic to creation of community. There is a very real sense, though, in which we can learn community only through community. We must engage in continuous conversation with others for community to be forged. Only in this way, too, does one experience the satisfaction of contributing to a whole that is wiser, more inclusive, and more comprehensive than anything that could be conceived alone.

Leaders who are learners invariably have wide experience with communities of learners and the processes that promote inclusiveness. They learn processes that foster the community's capacity to rally behind a decision. These processes include sus-taining communication and long-term relationships, identifying deliberative processes that bring about the transition from dia-logue to action, and using procedures for achieving consensus on key issues. Finally, learning leaders consider the specific ends that the community should be striving for. Without attention to the quality of those ends, the most outrageous demagogue could be regarded as a successful community leader. For Ryan (2005), the most important of these ends is inclusion.

WHERE WE HAVE SEEN CREATING COMMUNITY PRACTICED

One year, Stephen P participated in a University of New Mex-ico initiative called the Institute for Educational and Community Leadership. Run by Michael Morris, a highly experienced com-munity educator and leader, this institute modeled many of the principles of community leadership already explored. What made it work specifically was Morris's commitment to engaging every participant in the institute's work and his skill in ensuring that each participant's involvement in the institute was meaningful and substantive.

The people who participated in this institute were an incredi-bly diverse group, but all were in one or way or another attempting to support youth development in poor neighborhoods. Some had experience counseling gang members, others were involved in programming for after school programs, and still others were certified teachers in pocket-of-poverty schools or working with underachieving Native American students. All of these community leaders would gather regularly for discussion facilitated by Morris. Over time, they created community projects designed to enhance their leadership skills and develop their inquiry abilities.

What was particularly striking about these gatherings was Morris's own leadership in highlighting every participant's experience. He did this by virtue of his relationships with these participants and his increasing knowledge about their community work. At each session, he would draw attention in a highly concrete way to a dilemma facing one of the participants. He would invite the participant in question to talk about the problem and then ask the rest of the group to think out loud about how to address or resolve this issue. In the process, he drew parallels to other people's work and helped the group as a whole see how similar many of their challenges were.

The leadership that Morris exercised was not easily accomplished, however. He made frequent visits to all of the participants' community sites and spoke to them often by phone or in person to stay in touch about their progress. It was his persistent relationship building, his thorough knowledge of the community challenges people faced, and his desire to make connections and draw parallels that made this such a memorable community learning experience for everyone. Morris's efforts to foster more effective community leadership were animated by his own unremitting commitment to teaching and creating community.

As with most community builders, Morris wasn't helping to develop these community relationships for their own sake. He was intentionally trying to build a network of collaborative leaders to promote positive change in the community. Through such a network, he believed that these community leaders could better solve and engage their particular problems if they saw each other as resources and allies. An important indicator of his long-term success in achieving this goal is the fact that most of the members of this original group continue to consult with each other and in many cases have become highly regarded activists and policy makers. Many, as well, are now helping to mentor the next generation of community leadership.

How We and Others Have Lived the Practice of Creating Community

One of the unlikeliest practitioners of community learning and leadership was Eleanor Roosevelt, who, even while her husband served as president during the darkest days of the Great Depression, continued to serve as a teacher and mentor at the Todhunter School in New York City. One of the classes she taught for Todhunter was a course on current events called "Happenings." There was no set curriculum, no text, rarely any lectures. Topical accounts from newspapers and magazines of the day's most pressing issues were used in place of books. The primary pedagogies were discussion and fully exploiting New York City as a vital, "living" classroom. Visits to such places as Ellis Island, settlement houses, tenement buildings, and courthouses were common. The strategy was to give the students vivid, firsthand urban encounters that could be dissected and analyzed within the context of an expanding community of learners. The program's purpose was to hone each student's critical sensibilities by giving the person the experience of being a part of a questioning, inquiring community of urban learners and leaders.

Exposing the students to a range of possible lives was critically important to her. She insisted that their time in school be devoted, at least in part, to transcending their narrow privileged backgrounds by moving outside the school—often literally—to see how others lived and understand how severe were the limits on most people's opportunities to aspire for more. She urged the seniors to do community service and introduced them to the accomplishments of the Henry Street Settlement, the Neighborhood Playhouse, and the Women's Trade Union League. She even taught a course for recent Todhunter graduates in order to support and direct their continued involvement in the larger community and encourage them to be leaders in the community for the sake of creating more livable and intellectually lively neighborhoods.

Everything she did as a teacher built on her students' everyday experiences and challenged them to look again on that everyday world with new, more critical and discerning eyes.

What Blocks or Prevents Creation of Community

One of the most daunting enemies of community building is lack of time. It takes a great deal of time and energy to bring people together regularly enough for long-term relationships to form. It takes even more time and energy to hold recurring discussions that go deep enough to allow many viewpoints to be explored and a meaningful consensus to emerge. The testimony of those who have participated in such time-intensive efforts should persuade us of their worth, but it requires leaders with vision and a readiness to take risks to make it work. Because vision and risk taking tend to be in short supply, such opportunities rarely materialize.

Another issue that can block creation of community relates to leaders who do not understand their role as community brokers, enablers, or facilitators. They may employ a traditional leadership model in shaping consensus, using top-down tactics and authoritarian strategies. Instead of giving community members the time and space they need to allow agreement to emerge, they may impose a vision around which everyone is supposed to rally. Or instead of imposing agreement they may require that consensus be reached within an unreasonably short timeline. Either way, such approaches misunderstand the value of sustained consideration of challenging issues in forming an enduring community of active learners and leaders.

Still another obstacle to learning and leading community is the historical commitment to individuality. As we have indicated repeatedly, community building does require individuals to give up something of themselves to promote the community's goals. Part of the struggle of being in community is to recognize that although dissent and disagreement should be encouraged, one of the community's strengths derives from the kind of shared vision that is impossible without a degree of individual compromise. Particularly problematic are those situations where community learning and leadership are imposed on people as some kind of organizational initiative. Unless there is a voluntary decision to make the compromises and sacrifices necessary to support community building, disgruntled community members who resist the process of shared decision making will undermine the group's development. It should be noted that the kind of community leadership we are exploring here obliges everyone at some point to play some kind of leadership role. If community is imposed on people or they fail to understand that leadership is entailed in their work as a member of the group, the strengths that grow out of initiatives in which everyone assumes some responsibility for the outcome are lost.

Finally, community is made difficult by social and technological developments that force us further and further apart into a chaotic assemblage of fractured individual existences. Cyberspace; video games; multiple satellite TV channels; transportation systems that remove public transport in favor of individual car ownership; testing and assessment legislation that requires individual students, individual teachers, and individual schools to compete with each other in pursuit of test scores that will bring them greater resources and create opportunities for them ... all these factors and more conspire to separate people into their own individual enclaves. Although David Riesman's *The Lonely Crowd* (1965) is more than forty years old, its thesis—that as we live in closer and closer association in urban agglomerations we feel further and further apart—has never been more apposite. No wonder Margaret Thatcher repeatedly asserted during her time as British prime minister that there is no such thing as community, and the trickle-down economics of the influential Milton Friedman is founded on the assumption that "society" is no more than the intersecting economic decisions of individual actors.

WHAT ARE THE PERILS AND PITFALLS ASSOCIATED WITH CREATING COMMUNITY?

One of the greatest problems with learning and developing community is maintaining a balance between the needs of individuals and the needs of the community itself. It has not been sufficiently explored here, but a large group can become a tyrannical enterprise, neglecting individual concerns and eliminating opportunities to express dissenting perspectives. Individuals who constitute a community must have time and space to hash out their differences, to allow many diverse voices to come forward, and to create avenues for disagreement and opposition. Communities must be wary of bringing the deliberative and decision-making process to premature closure.

At the same time, one of the distinct advantages of community is the strength in solidarity that derives from a shared vision or carefully constructed consensus. Steady movement toward some kind of mutual agreement or understanding is essential, the conceptual glue that holds community together. Only gradually, then, should a shared vision or consensus on a key issue be permitted to form. Even after this vision or consensus is expressed and acted on, openings to register dissent should be maintained. Yet it must also be understood that the community's identity depends on its shared mission. Holding these two notions in balance—the value of the individual dissenter and the power of group solidarity—is one of the great, enduring challenges of community leadership.

How Can Leaders Address the Pitfalls, Perils, and Other Problems Associated with Creating Community?

The delicate balancing act that is a central part of effective community leadership makes this a particularly difficult practice. How to optimize the solidarity that is one of community's greatest potential assets, while keeping the door open to a variety of further viewpoints and perspectives, is bewilderingly contradictory. But we believe there is a way out: through the developmental dynamic we referred to in the previous section. This can be expressed as the Ecclesiastes Approach—in other words, the idea that a time for every purpose under heaven must be acknowledged. The central idea is that there is a season for consensus and a season for dissent, a time for outward solidarity and a time to resolve internally the group's festering disagreements. Leaders must work patiently with their co-workers to create a workable and authentic consensus. This can never be the result of railroading, coercion, or artificially engineered agreement. But once genuine consensus is forged there must be an understanding within the group that everyone will stand behind it, that everyone will do all they can to make it work. Simultaneously, there must also be an understanding shared by all that this consensus will be revisited periodically and that at specific times concerns and dissenting views may be fully aired and explored. In this way, the advantages of community learning and leadership can be fully realized.

CHAVEZ AND CREATING COMMUNITY

Although he became known around the world for his personal charisma, by vocation Cesar Chavez was a *community* organizer. Like all the leaders we profile, he believed that the most intractable problems of people were best addressed through activating the collective power and shared resources of the entire community. Central to such organizing was learning: learning about power, about how best to mobilize people, about using conflict to galvanize energies, and about how to recognize embryonic leaders. Chavez knew too that a sense of community does not emerge naturally; it must be carefully nurtured in the face of flagging energy. Leaders therefore need to learn what it takes to keep a sense of community vital and strong. For Chavez, the union community that he created to secure rights for farm workers was important, but so was the larger community of millions who boycotted nonunion products and donated money to support the farm workers' cause. In the end, though, Chavez's effort to forge a community had one central and unified purpose: "To overthrow a system that treats farm workers ... as if they are not important human beings" (quoted in Dalton, 2003, p. 9). Those who joined the community that Chavez fashioned were united and inspired by this one simple and yet incredibly daunting goal.

In his quest to restore the human dignity of the farm workers, Chavez saw community building as his most important leadership task. In fact, as Dalton points out, Chavez's vision included the idea that "our humanity is verified by joining together in communities of solidarity characterized by sacrificial service, voluntary poverty, and nonviolent action" (2003, p. 164). Chavez never supported communities that were in any way exclusive or concerned only with the welfare of the farm workers. His community leadership always entailed commitment to mutual service, to every member being held in some way responsible for the welfare of others no matter what any individual's relative power might be. Although his leadership was most visibly exercised on behalf of farm workers,

Chavez viewed it as being in pursuit of a society in which no one goes hungry, no one is kept out of work, and everyone is accorded respect as a valued human being. In the process of building the farm workers union, Chavez made sure that this organization was more than just a union designed to secure steady work and fair wages for its members, but truly a community of people who looked after each other across many realms, including health services, child care, education, and immigration.

With great sacrifice to himself and his family, Chavez helped to create out of virtually nothing an influential union that not only won better working conditions for thousands of people but also greatly accelerated empowerment of the Chicano community. His accomplishments were attributable in part to irrepressible persistence and unparalleled courage. But as Chavez himself was quick to affirm, his success in building a community of farm workers also arose out of a burning desire to learn. Even as a young boy, he listened closely to the stories his relatives told about the exploitation that Mexican farm workers had faced and of the efforts of Mexican patriots to bring about economic and political justice. He also witnessed his relatives stand up for the rights of others and learned that it was his duty to do the same. He was taught that he would disappoint others if he was fired for failing to do a job well, but he also learned that "if somebody was fired for standing up for a person's rights, it was quite honorable" (Levy, 1975, p. 33). For Chavez, a commitment to gaining rights for others that one enjoyed oneself was at the core of what it meant to live in and for community. His mother, in particular, taught him about the responsibilities of peace and nonviolence, without actually using these words. It was only much later, after he had read about the lives of people such as Gandhi and St. Francis, that Chavez realized how closely aligned his mother was with this tradition of nonviolence.

MASTERING THE ART OF COMMUNITY ORGANIZING, 1958–1962

Chavez's skills as a community organizer were developed in the Community Service Organization (CSO). Funded by Saul Alinsky's Industrial Areas Foundation (IAF), the CSO was launched in

1947 to increase the political power of Latinos in poor and working-class neighborhoods, first in East Los Angeles and later in other parts of California. Recruited by Fred Ross, the CSO's founder, Chavez began as a volunteer for the CSO canvassing the Chicano neighborhoods of San Jose to rally and register new voters. Chavez contributed to this effort so unstintingly that he was named the chairman of what turned out to be a highly successful voter registration drive. From there he helped Ross set up CSO chapters in many of the towns of Central and Northern California. Soon he was working for the CSO full-time and became one of the few paid IAF organizers on the West Coast. During his time with the CSO, Chavez helped to register half a million Chicano voters, contributed to efforts to secure citizenship and retirement pensions for some fifty thousand Mexican immigrants, and fought tirelessly for the "installation of paved streets, sidewalks, traffic signals, recreational facilities, and clinics, and forced a drastic curb on police brutality" (Ross, 1989, p. 4). All of these specific efforts were aspects of his overarching concern to organize Mexican Americans to heighten their awareness of their common interests, and their interests in creating a common future.

In 1958, Chavez settled with his family in the damp, sleepy town of Oxnard, California, about fifty miles north of Los Angeles. What he discovered as he attended small house meetings was the complaint that because of the *bracero* program, which brought in low-paid workers from Mexico, the residents of Oxnard were prevented from securing work harvesting fruit and vegetables. Seizing on the situation as a wonderful opportunity to improve life in Oxnard and empower the local citizenry, Chavez and his associates temporarily broke the back of the bracero system by creating a clearinghouse whereby local workers could secure jobs at decent wages before anyone else. It was in Oxnard that Chavez began employing the organizing strategies that would play such a large role in his subsequent efforts to unionize the farm workers. He insisted that Oxnard residents who wanted to work apply each day at the Farm Placement Service and that careful records of these applications be kept. He staged boycotts of local merchants to protest their endorsement of the bracero system, and he directly challenged the continued hiring of braceros by encouraging field workers to engage in sit-down strikes. Led by Chavez, Oxnard workers lobbied the California legislature, directed hundreds of complaints against the Farm Placement Service, and picketed the secretary of labor when he visited the Oxnard area.

Finally, succumbing to the pressure applied by Chavez and his associates, the director of the Farm Placement Service was replaced, along with many of his staff. The hundreds of Oxnard workers who lined up each day outside its office to secure employment were finally getting hired. It was in the wake of this success that Chavez wanted to use his CSO connections to organize the local farm workers. The CSO board of directors rejected the idea, claiming that the CSO was strictly a civic organization and not prepared to support a labor union. Not long after Chavez left Oxnard for East Los Angeles, the braceros were once again the first choice of the growers.

In 1959, Chavez was named executive director of the CSO and was assigned to the East Los Angeles area to continue his organizing efforts and work with other organizers throughout California. However, the idea of organizing farm workers never died. The more he witnessed the plight of his own people being exploited by the owners of the farmers, the more convinced he became that a union must be created. In March 1962, Cesar Estrada Chavez decided he needed to take a radically different professional path.

When members at the 1962 CSO national convention in Calexico, California, voted against Chavez's request to launch a pilot project to organize farm workers, he resigned his post.

LEADING THE FARM WORKERS, 1962–1966

Chavez's efforts to serve the farm workers were set against a history of 125 years of exploitation and violence. The growers had always been in control and had always been backed by California's leading institutions, from the police to the courts to the banks. Chavez had come to know this history well and was thus aware of just how difficult his task would be. But as he said, sometimes the only way to overcome such daunting odds is to pursue your goal as if nothing else mattered, even if it meant coming across as a fanatic, a fanatic for basic rights, a fanatic for community, a fanatic for human dignity. One of the ways dominant power controls threats to its dominance is by naming those who challenge it as fanatics. In response to this labeling Chavez said, "There's nothing wrong with being a fanatic. Those are the only ones that get things done" (Levy, 1975, p. 161).

His fanaticism was most evident in the inexhaustible energy he expended talking to people and getting them interested in a union. He moved to Delano, California, a central location for many of the farm workers. His method was simple, a variation on the house system developed by IAF founder Alinsky. You visited poor people's homes in their own neighborhoods and you asked questions about what they thought was needed to make life in these neighborhoods better. You also asked them about a union and whether they thought it could be one of the solutions to their problems. You did this night after night after night, even if it meant you were talking to only a half dozen people at a time. You listened mostly, but you also made sure there was time to talk about your own vision about how to improve life in the community. You wrote down names and phone numbers, and you were happy if one person out of twenty was interested enough to continue to work with you, to help mold a community of like-minded leaders.

One of Chavez's early allies, a Protestant minister named Jim Drake, noted that everybody thought Chavez was crazy. "They had so many children and so little to eat," Drake observed, "and that old 1953 Mercury station wagon gobbled up gas and oil. Everything he wanted to do seemed impossible. He used his tiny garage as his headquarters, but it was so hot in there, all the ink melted down in the mimeograph machine I lent him" (quoted in Levy, 1975, p. 162). But as time went on, the feeling that Chavez was crazy turned into a different, much more complicated and profound characterization. For one thing, despite his desperate straits Chavez didn't want any money, for fear that it might compromise him and his mission. Second, his perseverance was legendary. "Building the union was a slow, plodding thing based on hard work and very personal relationships," Reverend Drake continued. "The growers didn't know he was in town, but the workers knew. After a while, they were coming to his house day and night for help" (p. 162).

Drake became intimately familiar with the way Chavez organized the workers. He didn't do it in dramatic, all-encompassing flourishes but one by one, another reminder that community building is always painstakingly incremental and intensely personal. Sometimes Chavez would attempt to recruit a new worker during a drive to a labor hearing or en route to an organizational gathering. "While the new member drove, Cesar talked," Drake recalled. "He talked clearly and carefully, and the plan was set forth. The trips were not futile either, for a growing number of farm workers passed the word, 'If you have trouble, go to Delano, Chavez can help'" (p. 162).

By the fall of 1962, Chavez had engendered enough interest in a union among the workers around Delano to call a convention. About 150 "delegates" attended. Before that first meeting was over, a flag was chosen, a motto for the union was adopted ("Viva La Causa"), and dues were set at $3.50 a month.

Chavez believed that the only way to prevail over the growers, to put the necessary pressure on them so they would yield to the workers, was to go on strike. But he also believed that a strike would be suicidal until the union was strong. As a community, the union needed to steward its assets carefully and develop a shared sense of how best to use its power. He thus meticulously built up the union's strength. He did what he could to serve the workers' needs, defending them when they ran into trouble with the police, supporting them in workmen's compensation cases, and advocating for them when employers refused to pay wages for completed work. All this time he continued to listen to their concerns, talk to them about his vision for the union, and recruit them in any way he could. Slowly, the National Farm Workers Association (NFWA) acquired the fortitude it would need to endure a strike. Through Chavez's leadership, the organization he built looked less like a labor union and more like a community of people working hard to support one another in improving all aspects of their lives.

On September 16, 1965, the National Farm Workers Association voted to go on strike. They gathered on the picket line, expecting a terrible fight. Many brought guns, knives, or anything that might inflict damage. Chavez told them to leave these things behind, that this strike would be different. As Consuelo Rodriguez (1991) has noted, Chavez knew that the union lacked the money or the physical might to hold off the growers. A show of force would only end in tragedy and would produce no gain. Chavez shrewdly understood that, "along with the courage of his people his greatest asset could be the conscience of the American people" (Rodriguez, 1991, p. 59). He also believed with great conviction that the only right way to conduct the strike was to do so nonviolently.

On the strike's first day, twelve hundred workers participated. They formed long picket lines and held signs that read *huelga*, the Spanish word for strike. The growers often reacted with violence, but the workers refused to be budged from their nonviolent posture. In the meantime, Chavez attempted to draw on the sympathies of possible supporters and build the larger national community that would end up delivering such an important measure of support to the cause. He traveled across the country attempting to rally backers for the strike. He enlisted college students and civil rights workers and even won the support of the Longshoreman's Union. As the strike dragged on, Chavez did not relent from his commitment to nonviolence, though he did exert new pressure on the growers by initiating a successful boycott of grapes. The AFL-CIO and United Auto Workers eventually endorsed the boycott and also supplied much needed financial support.

The culminating event of the strike was a dramatic twenty-five-day march from Delano to the state capital of Sacramento. Chavez had learned about the almost "mystical power" of the march from other organizing efforts, and now he once again witnessed its magic at work. Each day brought more favorable publicity for the marchers and the strike. By the end of the march, at least one major grower was prepared to sign a contract with the NFWA. It was a huge victory, however short-lived. There would be many more struggles with other growers to come. But the progress that was made and the powerful, unifying community that Chavez helped to create simply could not be overestimated.

CHAVEZ AS A LEARNER

In the context of our book, the most striking and significant aspects of Chavez's work as a community builder was his openness to new learning—learning about the dynamics of power, the incremental nature of mobilization, and the need to develop organic leaders grounded firmly in the community. When Fred Ross first approached him about helping the CSO to organize San Jose, Ross recognized something special about Chavez's commitment. For one thing, he asked questions that showed how interested he was and how much he wanted to learn. But there was something else. It was what Ross called "a kind of burning interest rather than one of those inflammatory things that lasts the night and is then forgotten" (Levy, 1975, p. 102). Ross discerned early on that, like Ross himself, Chavez would persevere to achieve his goals. He would not give up easily. Ross also appreciated Chavez's quick, absorbent mind. Chavez may not have had much formal education, but he understood with surprising rapidity that it was necessary to consolidate the power of the Chicano community to make change. Ross noted, "He made the connections very quickly between the civic weakness of the group and the social neglect of the barrio, and also conversely, what could be done about that social neglect once the power was developed" (p. 102).

Chavez did learn quickly about power. Without an understanding of power and without knowing how to use it, the work of building community was rendered nearly impossible. When he was at the height of his influence as a union leader in California, he stressed that power formation was the key ingredient of change. In dealing with his adversaries, Chavez found it was best to have some power, some influence over them before actually staging a meeting. He knew as well that such power did not come easily, that to generate it required an enormous amount of work, a huge commitment to organizing people. Although he was realistic about the necessity of accumulating power, he was actually rather distressed that wielding power was the only way to bring about real change. He attributed this to the flawed nature of humans and noted often, like so many before him, that as important as power was, excessive power could corrupt even the most righteous movement. He was quick to add, however, that his own work was rarely if ever plagued by such a dilemma, as the farm workers' movement hardly suffered from a surfeit of power.

What Chavez learned about power in the most concrete sense was that it could be developed only one person and one house meeting at a time. Every time he held a meeting of perhaps a dozen people in a person's home, he hoped to gain one solid ally, one person whom he could help and who in return would support the farm workers. As Chavez said, "helping people was an organizing technique.... I was willing to work day and night and go to hell and back for people—provided they did something for the CSO in return" (Levy, 1975, p. 111). In other words, you organize and you build a power base slowly and painstakingly by establishing relationships with individual people. You get to know them by listening to them, by expressing a genuine interest in their situation, and by doing what you can to improve their lot and address their problems. Slowly, but inexorably, you build a community of people who have been helped by the organization, and who in turn want to be of some service to others. Chavez expresses it simply but powerfully: "The only way to build solid groups is through problem solving with them around the situations that most drain their energies. In the process of doing this you not only learn how to solve people's problems, you learn 'how to help people by making them responsible'" (p. 111).

The lessons about community power, problem solving, and encouraging communities to take responsibility were related to another lesson that Chavez never forgot. When dealing with the problems faced by poor people, you never go to the established leadership. You go to the grassroots, to the communities who are struggling on an everyday basis with a lack of power. There you develop leaders out of the rank and file, out of the people who know directly what it means to be poor and what it feels like to be exploited. In such a manner, community leadership is always embedded in the desires and concerns of the least advantaged. This is a direct implementation of what Gramsci (1971) meant when he described organic intellectuals as directors and persuaders of a movement that arose out of an oppressed group.

Chavez himself was living in the barrio and barely scraping by when Ross recruited him for the CSO. Chavez subsequently looked for similar organic intellectuals, people who were treated as expendable laborers but who were eager to learn about what could be done to change a system that was neglecting them. He also learned that the people who made the best leaders were those who had the least to lose, who were unlikely to act conservatively because of a concern about protecting their self-interest. He would later state it quite explicitly. He welcomed leadership from many groups, but he learned from experience that the movement must avoid overreliance on middle-class leaders. They simply could not be counted on to promote, without hesitation, the rights of the poor and working class. They had too much to lose.

For many poor and working people in California, Cesar Chavez was that rare, selfless leader who sought only to make other people's lives better. He was a fanatic—for rights, for justice, for decency, for love. Through some thirty years of organizing, he maintained a deep and abiding affection for his followers. For him, the power of community always lay in the extraordinary untapped talents of so-called ordinary people. As Griswold del Castillo and Garcia (1995) have noted, Chavez "believed in everyone—regardless of race or color," especially the least well off and the least advantaged. For Chavez, "everyone was equal and deserved respect, dignity and love" (p. 176). As these same authors have pointed out, Chavez always remained as well a model of persistence, a beacon of hope. He agreed wholeheartedly with the Spanish words so often chanted on marches: *se puede; sí se puede* (it can be done, yes it can be done).

Chavez also stood out as someone for whom community building was made possible only through constant learning. He became an avid reader in adulthood and a close student of the history of unionism, as well as the vast literature on the politics of nonviolence. He also learned a great deal from the labor organizers who preceded him. But he probably learned most from the seemingly ordinary people who surrounded him: his family, his neighbors, and the many farm workers for whom he became a chief advocate and whom he always viewed as the community's greatest asset. He listened to them with great interest and great care. He came to know them one by one and acquired an understanding of what mattered to them most: dignity, respect, and a decent livelihood. Out of what he learned he fashioned a union, a community, really, that not only won for the workers a decent wage but also gave them a forum to experience and reflect on the labor struggles in their midst. In this forum, they could also gain new insight into the value of collaboratively and nonviolently resisting those conditions inhibiting their growth as workers and as human beings.

Finally, Chavez's leadership helped his followers learn that they could develop the capacity to transform, however fleetingly, the power relations in one small part of the world. He learned that building community was a lifelong learning project, one that leaders and followers alike could never regard as finished. Community died as soon as it was viewed as completed. True community leadership relied on constantly staying alert to the talents and concerns of the community's least advantaged but best-informed members. By that credo Chavez lived his life.

CHAPTER ELEVEN

APPRAISING AND MODELING LEARNING LEADERSHIP

Our journey in this book has been a long and arduous one. We recaptured small, unheralded moments from the American Civil Rights Movement and remembered the grand, persevering, courageous leadership that turned the South African anti-apartheid campaign into a worldwide crusade. We sat in on heated exchanges among the women of Hull House and overheard the participants at Highlander consider how to apply what they had learned back home in their own communities. We overheard reflections on the democratic strategies needed to bring every viewpoint, however dissenting, to the fore, and we eavesdropped on beleaguered but hopeful farm workers pleading for simple respect. In every case, we encountered humble, self-effacing leaders who showered credit on others but rarely, if ever, sought to bring attention to themselves, and whose energy, enthusiasm, and faith in their own highly principled cause never seemed to waver.

WHAT MAKES LEARNING LEADERS?

As diverse as the leaders profiled in this book were, a single purpose ultimately united them. They all stayed committed to creating environments for healthy, fully realized human beings by ensuring that relationships were inclusive, empowering, and respectful. These conditions offered their collaborators the chance, rarely experienced in other settings, to become creative, unconstrained agents of morally purposeful change. All of these leaders sought to give people a say in what happened to them so that those at every level could feel ownership of the result. For these leaders, the means and ends were the same: justice, freedom, and self-realization for all. How people were treated on an everyday basis mattered as much as the far-reaching goal of creating a more equitable and just society.

These leaders were also conscious role models. Treating immediate others with kindness, patience, and compassion was no less important than building organizations to register more voters, defeat segregation, or empower workers. They shared Reinhold Niebuhr's belief that democracy is made possible by a human capacity for justice and made necessary by the human tendency toward injustice. Democracy is at its best when it is self-correcting and self-sustaining and when it calls on varied perspectives within a community. All of these leaders knew that motivating people to stay engaged in the quest for democracy was crucial; hence, giving people reasons to stay involved in the struggle was a key part of leadership.

These leaders led as equals to their followers. They were as ready to be guided as to guide, as willing to listen as to speak, as eager to be part of the group as to stand out from it. In fact, for these leaders it didn't matter much at all whether they were seen as leaders or not. What mattered is that healthy, positive changes occurred and that people were supported in doing their best, most life-affirming work. Often it was just a matter of galvanizing people, helping them see possible responses to their problems, and then getting out of the way so that energetic, enthusiastic people could get on with the reforms to which they were so deeply committed. Other times, it meant reorganizing a group from the inside out so that many voices could be heard instead of only one and so that the better angels of people's natures could prevail.

Central to these leaders' work was the constant search for colleagues who could fashion organizational conditions that allowed people to flourish as learners and as human beings. This meant keeping lines of communication fluid and staying open to new ideas and perspectives. It meant, too, finding time for people to reflect on their experiences so that new learning could be applied to the next challenge in a spirit of continuous improvement. Of course, it followed as well that inquiry of all kinds was embraced and consistently rewarded. Questioners would be welcomed, critical thinkers appreciated, highly collaborative researchers praised. Anything supporting the quest to know more, understand better, explain more satisfactorily would be encouraged.

Moreover, the leaders we have examined gave priority to seeking answers to questions from the unacknowledged many instead of privileging the high-and-mighty few. They viewed people traditionally omitted from decision-making authority as the experts on the decisions that affected their lives. These leaders, who included socialists as well as democrats, met on this common ground. All believed that the core to any just social organization was the basic principle that the people most affected by decisions should have the chief say in making those decisions. For example, Paul Robeson (himself a lifelong socialist) constantly stressed the essentially democratic nature of socialism, and the way it mandated that decisions be made collectively by those most affected by them. The two of us also meet on this common ground, and it is why we view the ongoing capacity to learn to be such a critical part of effective leadership. The more voices leaders hear, the more everyday wisdom they can soak up, and the more able they are to facilitate social change that promotes the interests of ordinary people.

We have also discovered that learning to lead collectively and democratically depends in part on the leader's ability to absorb the stories of co-workers. Knowing where those co-workers have come from, what challenges and obstacles they have encountered, what talents they have developed, and what commitments they have formed all should influence the kind of leader one will be. It is only through an exchange of narratives—an exchange of life experiences, really—that a leader can get in touch with where people are and use what is learned to decide where to go next as a group. Such exchanges oblige the leader to hear out the diverse stories of followers in all their multiplicity and complexity, sort out the differences and commonalities, and sculpt a vision that reflects the group's breadth. Leaders such as Ella Baker, Mary Parker Follett, and Jane Addams all saw it as part of their function to take in these stories, learn from them, and emerge from that learning with a more inclusive and yet sharply delineated purpose.

THE POWER OF STORIES

In his recent book on how leaders use storytelling to inspire action, Stephen Denning (2007) observes that leaders need to initiate conversations with their co-workers in which stories are exchanged in order to stimulate the "co-creation of innovation" (p. 206). It is through the sharing of stories that leaders and followers get to know each other's strengths, interests, and vulnerabilities, and thereby know best how to create new ideas that matter for people. Denning says that leaders must take the lead in this process by asking questions, leveling with people, showing vulnerability (when appropriate), building on the inputs of others, sharing stories, encouraging others to share their stories, and having participants tell one another's stories.

As Denning indicates, this process requires leaders to be curious about others, be open and honest, admit the need for help from others, listen attentively to others, be willing to tell their own stories first, and create a culture in which the telling of stories is widely and habitually shared. These qualities, closely aligned with many of the learning tasks we have identified, contribute to community learning and thus help to strengthen the sense of community that so many of our leaders were after. The higher level of intimacy this entails enables the organization or community to be innovative.

LEADING FROM COLLECTIVE STRENGTHS

Juana Bordas's recent book *Salsa, Soul, and Spirit: Leadership for a Multicultural Age* (2007) builds beautifully on this point about leading from our collective strengths. Bordas comments that leaders who embrace diversity derive their authority from the group. She further notes that such "leaders are expected to reflect the group's behavior and values. By listening and gathering people's opinions, the leader integrates the group wisdom. The leader must find unanimity in the group *first*, and then act in concert with it. Like a battery, leaders charge people up, facilitate their working together, and assist them in solving problems. Through empowering others, a community of leaders evolves. Standing out too far from others or calling too much attention to oneself can damage the group cohesion that is central to collectivist cultures" (p. 84). What Bordas has found in collectivist cultures strikingly parallels what we have found in our leadership profiles. The leaders we were most attracted to, whether hailing from a collectivist environment or not, understood at some deep level that democracy and authentic empowerment demanded this kind of collectivist, "lead by being led" orientation.

Yet we admit to being daunted by the possibility of true group-centered leadership. Ella Baker is probably our greatest progenitor of this approach, though even she, we think, would admit that she advocated it more than she practiced it, idealized it more than she realized it. Even the organizing scheme for this book, in which individual leaders are profiled, militates against the quest for authentic group-centered, collective leadership. This is an enduring contradiction in leadership studies. No matter how much we profess a commitment to collective leadership, it is always the individual stories, the particular struggles against the odds, that capture our attention.

A particularly compelling tale of collective leadership is documented in a book called *Leadership Ensemble* (Seifter and Economy, 2001) about the Orpheus Chamber Orchestra, said to be the world's only "conductorless" orchestra. Totally committed to a "leaderful" (Raelin, 2003) approach to making music, the authors explore the eight Orpheus principles that they believe ground their collective approach. These principles include many of the themes we have identified as integral to learning leadership, among them the need to clarify roles, rotate leadership, learn to listen as well as learn to talk, seek consensus, and passionately dedicate oneself and the collective to the mission. What they describe seems to capture at least one way to get things done in an organizational context without the need for any permanent positional leader. For anyone interested in understanding how to create a truly democratic group, in which the spirit and practice of shared leadership are taken seriously, their book is an excellent place to begin.

Leading in a group-centered fashion is very difficult, but certain things make it more likely. Such leadership is facilitated by humble, self-effacing leader-followers who willingly defer to others, are skilled at drawing people out, and enthusiastically invite stories from throughout the group. These leaders establish early on in the group's life specific processes for decision making that occur at many levels and involve many people. They make a special effort to discern and appreciate each group member's special strengths and find ways to develop leadership throughout the group. This is done by offering multiple opportunities for people to lead on specific tasks, and constantly affirming that by pooling their experiences and talents groups are more likely to have an enduring impact. Such leaders are rare fruit in the weed-clogged orchard of daily practice. When the rubber of good leadership intentions meets the road of organizational politics, the skid marks are far clearer and frequent than the smooth trails people forge.

THE INTERPERSONAL DIMENSION OF LEARNING LEADERSHIP

Leadership done in the way we have profiled is difficult when intense interpersonal conflicts exist, when generally negative attitudes prevail in a community, and when leadership is exercised only in extremely large groups. None of these problems is insurmountable, but anyone who has spent time in any kind of organization knows how challenging such situations can be. We think it is worth noting, particularly in the context of this book, that when people are extremely passionate about the mission of the group they are in, when they see the fulfillment of that mission as the most important issue, at least some of these challenges tend to be subordinated to other more pressing concerns. Struggles for social and economic justice, for environmental responsibility, for civil rights, or for self-determination and democracy are less likely to be derailed by these challenges, particularly if those who are the designated positional leaders (and for us this is absolutely decisive) affirm that a collective leadership approach is best.

It is our sense that leaders give leadership a bad name. The people designated as the leaders of groups, organizations, and movements (executive director, chairperson, founder, and the like) are often the very ones who are most likely to get in the way of leading collectively. This is why appointment decisions are so crucial and why they must involve everyone at every level in an organization. Obviously it is unrealistic to expect that all members of an organization or movement be on a search committee (though both of us have been candidates for positions where this seemed to be the case!). But a way must be found to have representatives from every corner of the movement, every unit in the organization, represented on such a committee. It then becomes absolutely decisive that the leaders putting themselves forward to lead such groups be questioned relentlessly about their leadership philosophy and the practices that they believe are consonant with this philosophy. A decision must be made by the group as a whole (as in the case of the Orpheus Chamber Orchestra) that no permanent position leader be appointed and that responsibilities for leading be thoughtfully distributed.

A significant part of leadership is learning when the most valuable thing you can do is get out of the way so that good people can employ their skills and knowledge to do good work. This is not a laissez-faire approach to leadership; instead, it is based on learning—learning to judge how people are contributing and when to let them know you recognize this. After all, leaders must learn to reward people for their contributions in ways that are meaningful to them. There is no point praising or recognizing good work if the persons receiving that recognition devalue the way it is given. Leaders must learn how to help people in one part of the group learn what people in other parts of the group are doing in order to increase learning and promote cohesion. They must learn what sort of compelling vision can emerge from the group as a whole, and how to inspire its pursuit.

PERSONAL CODAS: OUR OWN LEARNING LEADERSHIP

We would like to end on a highly personal note by describing how the two of us have tried to exercise learning leadership in very concrete ways in our own lives. First, Stephen B describes his intentional attempt to fight the stigma associated with depression and anxiety through his own small efforts to use his opportunity as a keynote speaker, writer, and workshop leader to exercise some form of leadership on this matter. Then he explores how he has tried to use his position of relative prominence in his field to encourage White colleagues to engage directly with questions of race and racism. Finally, Steve P describes a recent leadership effort in a pedagogic context in the face of apparent student disinterest.

Challenging the Stigma of Depression

Stephen B has over the last ten years fought depression that at times brought him to suicidal thoughts and took over his life completely. For many years, his energy was devoted chiefly to keeping this condition private at all costs, for fear of what people would think of him if they learned his shameful "secret." After hitting rock bottom and then finally getting onto a long-term combination of successful antidepressant medications, Stephen has vowed to exercise whatever leadership he can in making depression as accepted as asthma or diabetes. Stephen has tried to exercise leadership in this regard by going public at every opportunity with his struggle with depression. He is in an unusual position to do this in that he is often invited to deliver keynote addresses to national and international conferences. Whenever possible, he weaves references to his own struggle with depression into his remarks.

The first time he did this, at an international conference on reflective practice in Cambridge, England, a woman came up after his speech to thank him for putting into words her own experience. A month before writing these words, he gave the keynote address to the annual convention of the American Association for Adult and Continuing Education (AAACE), and the same reaction occurred. From unsolicited e-mails (some from people who had not attended the conference but had heard about the speech secondhand), Stephen learned that a significant number of people wished to show their appreciation to him for talking publicly about a problem that plagued them. Twice he has tried (unsuccessfully) to present a paper at the national Adult Education Research Conference (AERC) on his autoethnography of learning about depression.

It is important to note that Stephen's speaking publicly about his depression is not done in a narcissistic act of self-indulgence. When he refers to it, he does so to illustrate more general themes he is examining in his speech. For example, his Cambridge reflective practice conference speech explored how we come to assess the accuracy of our assumptions, and Stephen's assumptions about depression were used as an example of this. The AAACE convention speech was titled "What It Means to Be Critical," and Stephen argued that one dimension of that task focused on dispelling myths about mental illness. When he teaches workshops on critical theory, he uses his depression as an example of how successfully the dominant ideology of patriarchy (which holds that a man is always in control of himself, rational, and strong enough not to need help) is inscribed within him—a useful illustration of the concept of dominant ideology.

In a workshop called Discussion as a Way of Teaching that Stephen and Steve P delivered at Teachers College, Columbia University (New York), a portion of the workshop focused on modeling differing questioning techniques; Stephen B suggested that Steve P interview him about his depression in front of the participants. The point was for Steve P to model the questioning approaches one can use in discussion to draw people out; for Stephen B, it offered an ideal opportunity for him to do his weekly bit in normalizing depression. As usual, after the workshop several people came up to Stephen to tell him how much they appreciated his talking about something that also afflicted them.

Learning about how to exercise leadership on depression involves many of the tasks we have discussed. Stephen has had to force himself to be open about his condition and invite into conversation others who struggle with this malady. He has had to practice critical reflection as he analyzes how strongly inscribed within him is the dominant ideology of patriarchy. He has tried to model his own public struggle with depression, and his attempts to seek both psychological and pharmaceutical help, as a means to support the growth of others who also struggle with this. In normalizing depression, he has stressed the importance of forming alliances not just with certified professionals but with family members and colleagues, in an effort to develop collective responsibility for confronting this issue. He has certainly tried to analyze his experience of depression in front of his family, friends, colleagues, and wider audiences of educators. Asking questions of himself about his depression is something he has pursued in his speaking and writing, and also by encouraging colleagues such as Steve P to pose questions about this to him.

Finally, Stephen has sought to sustain hope in the face of struggle by speaking and writing about his own successful (for now, at least) experimental quest to find a cocktail of tricyclic and tetracyclic antidepressants that work for him. His intent in going public about his own depression is partly to offer an example of hope to those who struggle with it. After all, throughout this struggle he has continued to publish frequently, teach his classes, run faculty development workshops at his own and other universities, and deliver keynote addresses to major conferences. He has also managed to pursue his passion for music by leading, and writing for, a punk surf band, The 99ers.

Engaging with Race and Racism

For most of Stephen B's career, he has been race-blind. Read pretty much anything of his that was written before 2000 and there is an almost complete lack of attention to how questions of racial identity, or the presence of racist practices, inform adult and higher education. But although he spent his fifty some years on the planet without attending to race, he has been lucky to work in the last decade with some extraordinary individuals who have prompted him to face this issue. Chief among them is Professor Scipio A. J. Colin Jr. III of the department of adult and continuing education at National-Louis University in Chicago (Closson, 2006).

"Dr. C," as she is known to students, has, through her scholarship on and commitment to developing an Africentric paradigm of adult education, inspired in Stephen a whole new area of study and practice. Stephen helped design the doctoral program in adult education at National-Louis University and has been an adjunct faculty member at the institution since the program's inception. He has thus had the opportunity to co-teach multiple courses with Prof. Colin, and also to co-teach with Prof. Elizabeth Peterson, another NLU faculty member and editor of the groundbreaking book *Freedom Road: Adult Education of African Americans* (2001). The fortunate accident of co-teaching with these two colleagues has caused Stephen to vow to make dealing with race a central part of his work from this point on.

There are several ways Stephen has tried to exercise leadership on this issue. The first is through his writing. Colin introduced Stephen to the work of Lucius T. Outlaw (1996) and to his concept of racialization: the way an area of practice or body of thought is viewed primarily through the lens of one distinctive racial group's experience. In the United States, for example, adult education is racialized through the lens of Whiteness, with Whiteness regarded as the positively valued, unspoken norm—though this is rarely commented on. In the *Adult Education Quarterly* (Brookfield, 2003a) and the *Harvard Educational Review* (Brookfield, 2003b), Stephen applied this concept to how the discourse of criticality in adult education might be racialized, and how adult education as a field of theory and practice might be racialized, drawing on the work particularly of African American scholars such as Outlaw himself, Maulana Karenga, and Cornel West.

Stephen then sought to use various *Adult Education Research Conference Proceedings* (Brookfield, 2005a, 2005b, 2006, 2007; Guy and Brookfield, 2007; Peterson and Brookfield, 2007) to try to challenge the way the field of adult education is racialized in favor of White Euro-Americans, and to model a White scholar's attempt to engage with race-based scholarship outside of the dominant Euro-American framework. Some of this work is solo authored, some written with African American colleagues. In this writing Stephen has sought to identify the ideology of White supremacy and use himself as an example of how racism as a learned ideology moves in him as a White person. For example, the presentation "Race and Racism: A Critical Dialogue," which he gave with Peterson at the 2007 Adult Education Research Conference (Peterson and Brookfield, 2007), contained examples of how racist instincts and inclinations were evident in some of his small-scale actions and judgments.

Although this was not a pleasant thing to address in public, he felt it important that in conversations about race Whites show direct and specific evidence of how the ideology of White supremacy is deeply embedded in their daily microdecisions.

He spoke about this at the paper session and then decided to put the paper containing these comments on the Web so anyone interested could see them (http://stephenbrookfield.com/pdf_files/Peterson_Bfield_AERC_2.pdf).

Stephen has also proposed, and now conducts at least twice a semester, a regular faculty development workshop, "Teaching About Racism: Common Mistakes of White Professors," at the University of St. Thomas, his home institution. In this workshop, he deliberately uses his own practice as an example of the subject of the workshop. As someone with the elevated title of Distinguished University Professor he believes it is important to model public engagement with the realities of one's own learned racism, and that before he can ask colleagues to engage with their own racism he must first do it himself, and very publicly. To underscore this conviction, he published an article on the topic of the workshop—using himself as an example—in *Synergia*, the monthly faculty development newsletter sent to all professors at the university.

To Stephen's way of thinking, he is using the power that his White privilege has granted him as a public figure in his field to force those who have not engaged with this work to at least be aware of it. But he is very aware that not all colleagues of color, nor indeed all White colleagues, will see it this way. Stephen hardly needs another publication to add to his resume, so why has he written so much about race and racism, and about educators of color? For him it is because he feels some responsibility to pry open the doors of mainstream practice and theorizing a little wider so that those who enter the arena of adult education theorizing truly represent those engaged in its practice.

He also does this work because he feels it is important that White educators engage with questions of race and racism and that this should not be seen as solely the province of authors of color. If only authors of color produce articles, books, and papers dealing with race and racism, then the White majority can easily marginalize these issues as the province only of non-White adult educators, as something "they" (the generalized non-White "other" whose only distinguishing characteristic is defined as their lack of Whiteness) should take responsibility for exploring. This effectively keeps racial analysis conveniently (for the White majority) on the periphery. But if White adult educators acknowledge and critique their own complicity in a field racialized in favor of Euro-Americans, and if they engage seriously with racialized analyses drawn from a range of racial perspectives, many of which will focus on racism as the salient experience of people of color in a racist country, questions of race and racism cannot so easily be pushed aside by White colleagues.

Despite his efforts to model leadership in White critical engagement with the ideology of White supremacy, race, and racism, it should be emphasized that Stephen's efforts amount chiefly to a public description of his continuing struggle with this and his failure to put racism behind him. It should also be stressed that in no way does he consider himself an exemplar in dealing successfully with racism. His only contribution is perhaps to talk more publicly about it than some other Whites are willing to, and to draw attention to his own unintended acts of racial microaggression (Solorzano, 1998). As an example of his continuing failure, the week before this paragraph was written he was teaching in a class in which he deliberately asked each student to propose a topic for further study but missed a student of color as he went round the group. In the CIQ responses to this incident, some students wrote that they were "disappointed," "shocked," and "horrified" at his action, and at his doing so little to remedy it.

THE LEADERSHIP OF FOLLOWERSHIP

Now we turn to Steve P, who wishes first to talk about the way leadership is modeled in terms of what he calls "followership." To speak of the leadership of followership is an oxymoron unless you accept, as we do, that leadership must be conceived as a collective process. Followership sees leadership as constantly moving around a group, organization, or community, with people sometimes being directive, at other times being supportive, sometimes taking responsibility to develop vision, at other times working to listen attentively so as to support and extend the envisioning of others.

Steve P has served in a positional leadership role as department chair or division director four times in his academic career. Unfortunately, none of these tenures was particularly noteworthy or distinguished. Still, he did learn a lot about leadership. He came to understand that it is important both to get out of colleagues' way to let them be creative and also show them ongoing support for their contributions. He learned it is essential to maintain positive relationships and keep the conversation going despite periodic blow-ups. He discovered that people must connect their work to some sort of mutually agreed vision or overriding purpose. Despite his lack of accomplishment as a positional leader, Steve is quite proud that he has learned how to become a highly effective follower and that in this role he has been most successful in exercising leadership.

An article in the *Harvard Business Review*, called "What Every Leader Needs to Know About Followers," by leadership scholar Barbara Kellerman (2007) prompted Steve to reflect on his experience as a follower. Kellerman begins the article by noting that few observers have anything at all to say about followers. "Good followership," she laments, "is the stuff of nearly nothing" (p. 88). Her purpose is to introduce a new typology of followership, sorting followers into five types according to their level of engagement. She labels them *isolates*, *bystanders*, *participants*, *activists*, and *diehards*. Because as a follower Steve has always seen himself as a highly engaged and active group member, his interest is in describing how he has served his positional superiors as an activist. Although some of what he has to say connects to Kellerman's article, much of it doesn't. Her piece, however, offers a timely backdrop for these reflections and is an authoritative source for the view that following remains a viable form of leading.

The Follower as Receptive Learner

One of the most important ways in which Steve has learned to lead as a follower is as a person open to absorbing new ideas and eager to profit from the perspectives offered by students and colleagues. When he first entered higher education, he thought his primary job was to keep his head down, teach his students in a relatively authoritative way, and do the writing and publication that was expected of him. There wasn't much more to learn; hadn't he learned it already in graduate school? He soon realized that this not only wasn't true; it was, in any case, a pretty boring way to live. He started to go out of his way to talk about the books he was reading, the interesting articles he was encountering in the daily newspaper and scholarly journals, and just as important, the valuable lessons he was gaining from his students and the exciting innovations his colleagues were trying in their classrooms. He modeled the fact that in many ways his students knew and understood things he could never comprehend so well, and that part of his purpose was to share with others what these things were and how he profited from learning them. Similarly, he gained a reputation as someone who was not just willing but eager to visit the classrooms of colleagues and who usually got much more out of what he saw than he could ever hope to give back in advice or suggestions for improvement. As a follower who was also an open and receptive learner, he gained a perspective on the places where he taught that few others enjoyed, especially positional leaders, and this allowed him to play a role in helping everyone get better by building on their strengths.

The Follower as Curious Questioner

For a long time, Steve was primarily a person who questioned others to express skepticism. He had learned the method of critique rather well and was ready and eager to subject what his colleagues said to withering critical assessment. The questions he asked were expressed in a tone of doubt or were overtly leading so as to catch them in a trap of logical contradiction. In time, though, he found this not only wasn't much fun but meant that for others his questions were something to be feared and avoided, rather than an entry point for achieving new understanding, experiencing simple wonder, or promoting meaningful human connection.

As he began to see the power of asking open-ended questions for which he had no answer, he completely changed his questioning habits. Now he got in the groove of asking questions to learn, grow, and show curiosity. When others would speak in a meeting, he would make sure to ask a follow-up question to show that he wanted to know more or that he was intrigued by what had just been said. He would also ask questions to help people see connections to a larger purpose, or to underscore the lack of connection to such a purpose. The questioning he did was perhaps most of all related to a disposition he wanted to communicate: toward learning and constantly deepening one's understanding of the world. He found that this kind of curious questioning can be very contagious and that when you do it persistently, almost stubbornly, others will follow your lead and begin to make the habit of positive questioning a part of their own practice.

THE FOLLOWER AS CRITICALLY REFLECTIVE PARTICIPANT

There is no question that one of the most important contributions followers can make to an organizational or community culture is to keep the power of positional leaders in check. Followers do this by insisting that leaders keep their eye on the prize of the most important aspects of the institution's mission. Not endowments. Not enrollments. Not awards. But maintaining an unrelenting commitment to doing something for the public good—and in the case of colleges of education, often to serving the least advantaged members of the community. They do this by keeping the focus on alleviating poverty, or on decreasing racism, or on improving urban schools, or giving needy kids greater access to college, and so on. As a member of many such organizations, Steve has learned to tolerate references to higher enrollment or more alumni contributions or recognition from *U.S. News and World Report*. But he has also learned to keep the conversation going about larger purposes.

We need to learn to insist that positional leaders explain how they wish to assist all members of the organization in working in some critically important area, or what their plans are to help colleagues address a social crisis that bears a close relationship to their work. Steve thinks he has learned as a follower how to help positional leaders stay mission-driven, how to judge progress made by the college in terms of the commitments to society the institution has promised. This means that followers must ensure that accreditation reports and annual messages emphasize these critically important aspects of the work. The positional leader may ultimately be responsible for the final version of such pronouncements, but Steve has learned that followers have the responsibility and the opportunity, if seized, to keep the pressure on them to promote some greater common good.

THE FOLLOWER AS ADVOCATE FOR DEMOCRACY

What Steve has learned most in this area is that followers can do a great deal to ensure that graduate students in particular have a voice in the education they receive. The greatest conflicts he has experienced with colleagues are over the degree to which these students will be given a say in shaping requirements, in rethinking curriculum, or even in diversifying the pedagogies that are employed by faculty. As a follower, but also as a strong voice for democracy, Steve has tried to make the case that the more authority we give students the more engaged they will be and the more able they will be to fully benefit from their schooling. He has learned that he must model this in the classroom by using the Critical Incident Questionnaire (CIQ) in order to have the moral authority to persuade faculty that they should adopt something similar to open a critical dialogue with their students. As a follower, he has learned that he must have a clear idea of what he means by democracy in practice, and that it has relatively little to do with recording votes and much more to do with taking the voices and opinions of students seriously. It also means understanding how to facilitate discussion so that many student perspectives can be heard and dissenters be fairly represented.

The same, of course, holds true for faculty. If you believe in democracy, you must model democratic process with your colleagues and find ways to honor all voices, however harsh or discordant. Steve's record is hardly perfect in carrying out these responsibilities, but he does believe he became known as someone who believed strongly in democracy and wanted to find ways to live it in the classroom and the institution as a whole. Far more than any positional leader, he was regarded as a leading advocate for making educational practices as democratic as possible.

THE FOLLOWER AS APPRECIATIVE COMMUNITY BUILDER

Finally, despite being a follower for most of his career, Steve has invariably led as an unabashed appreciator of the learning communities of which he has been a part. He has found that by expressing appreciation for his colleagues and co-workers openly and frequently, the result is positive and energizing. Additionally, by recognizing others in specific and concrete ways, he has found that trust increases and the willingness of people to speak honestly and respectfully also goes up. What develops is the enhanced sense that people are working together for some common purpose that matters to them. No one person can create an appreciative, communal environment for others. But Steve has found that when he models simple appreciation it spreads quickly.

When followers are leaders, they do things that others find worthy of emulation. Steve has learned again and again that even when he is not a positional leader he can influence the learning environments he is in for the better. What he has learned over time as a follower corresponds closely to the learning tasks we have identified for leaders. It is probably fair to conclude, therefore, that learning is not only a way of leading but also a way of following. What Kellerman says at the end of her *Harvard Business Review* article is entirely consistent with Steve's experience: we need a broader, more reciprocal view of leadership, "one that sees leaders and followers as inseparable, indivisible, and impossible to conceive the one without the other" (Kellerman, 2007, p. 91).

LEADERSHIP PEDAGOGY IN THE FACE OF STUDENT DISINTEREST

Steve's second example of his leadership focuses on a specific classroom in a specific college. In 2007 he accepted a position as a professor of leadership studies at a small women's college in North Carolina. Aware that the responsibilities associated with this position would pose special challenges, he underestimated just how much of an adjustment this new situation would require. In the prior decade, Steve had become pleasantly accustomed to working with a roughly equal mix of female and male graduate students at the University of New Mexico. For the most part, these were highly engaged adult learners, brimming over with life experiences they were excited to share with one another. It often seemed that all Steve had to do was open class with a provocative question or put forward some controversial pronouncement, and the students would be off and running, eager to explore all the possible connections to their own lives.

At the small women's college where Steve was now an instructor, things seemed to be starkly different. Students entered class with yawns and droopy eyes, frequently dressed in pajamas and slippers, appearing lethargic and bored. They often sat at their awkward desk chairs with their heads nestled in their arms, unexpectant and mute. There were others who arrived chronically late, bursting into the room with a surge of energy, artificially stimulated by hastily grabbed café lattes, mochas, and cappuccinos.

Steve responded to all of this, at least at first, hardly at all. He continued to ask his provocative questions and throw out his outlandish declarations, while particularly making a special effort to invite comments, queries, and critiques from his young pupils. But in most cases the students were unmoved. They seemed to say behind their icy stares, "Go ahead: teach me. I dare you." As a result there were all too many periods in class punctuated by prolonged, gloomy silences.

Once it dawned on him that something needed to be done, the first thing he did was to get feedback from the students about their experience in the class by using the anonymous Critical Incident Questionnaire. As he accumulated data about the students' most engaging, distancing, affirming, confusing, and surprising moments in the class, and as he shared a summary of this data and then got further feedback from them, a few underlying problems emerged. Steve realized that the content struck the students as incoherent, that the text came across as irrelevant, and that few of the students could relate their own experiences to what appeared to be the focus of the class. After a number of sessions in which Steve and the class conferred, a number of changes were proposed:

- Focus leadership dilemmas and cases on contemporary issues, on issues in the news right now.
- Set aside more time for the instructor and the students to tell their stories.
- Incorporate brief lectures into the opening of class to give a focus for the content.

- Introduce small group work to increase participation, and work through content from short lectures and reading before reengaging with the large group.
- Target assignments toward the most important part of the reading.
- Don't rush through topics; linger over important issues like teaming, change processes, and ethics.
- Stick to clear consequences for latecomers.

What seemed to unite the concerns the students registered were two seemingly contradictory feelings: that they wanted to help construct their own learning experiences, and that they needed guidance in approaching and structuring the content to extract maximum value from it. In a very real sense, this brings us back to the multiple responsibilities of the leader: to guide and include, to facilitate and involve. What Steve had lost sight of was that the students, by virtue of their lack of experience, were not necessarily ready to participate actively in linking their own past to the content assigned. At the same time, however, he remained convinced they did have stories to share and ideas to put forward that needed to be aired in a low-risk, nonthreatening space. He had assumed they were as ready and eager to dialogue as he was, but he had not done the developmental work to get them prepared. In a very real sense, he had imposed his own templates for processing ideas on the students and had not been particularly empathic; that is, he had not worked hard to see and feel things from their standpoint.

Even more to the point, Steve had not been sufficiently *open* to the students' perspectives, had not allowed time for the them to *reflect* on their own experiences, had forgotten to think in terms of what he could do to help the students *grow* and do their best work, had lost sight of how the *questions* asked must be shaped by the context we find ourselves in, and had not made provision to hear and respond to the students' authentic *voices*. As a teacher who is also a leader, he had neglected many of those very qualities that he knew were most likely to foster learning in both himself and his co-learners, the students.

Of course, being aware of these qualities and putting these changes in place did not result in a miraculous turnaround in the classroom. Steve still had to deal with latecomers and lack of engagement and limited comprehension of the content. But there was a different feel to the class. Instructor and students were now experiencing a renewed sense that they were all in this together and that their continued success would depend on making this a shared, collaborative effort in which each had a chance to teach, learn, lead, and be led. Reawakened to these goals and possibilities, it was hard to imagine any other way to teach ... or to lead.

REFERENCES

Adams, F. *Unearthing Seeds of Fire: The Idea of Highlander*. Winston-Salem, NC: John K. Blair, 1975.

Addams, J. *Jane Addams: A Centennial Reader*. New York: Macmillan, 1960.

Addams, J. *Twenty Years at Hull House*. New York: Signet Classic, 1961.

Albert, M. *Parecon: Life After Capitalism*. London: Verso, 2004.

Albert, M. *Realizing Hope: Life Beyond Capitalism*. New York: ZED, 2006.

Asante, M. K. *The Afrocentric Idea*. Philadelphia: Temple University Press, 1998a.

Asante, M. K. *Afrocentricity: A Theory of Social Change* (rev. ed.). Trenton, NJ: Africa World Press, 1998b.

Avila, E. B., et. al. "Learning Democracy/Democratizing Learning: Participatory Graduate Education." In P. Campbell and B. Burnaby (eds.), *Participatory Practices in Adult Education*. Toronto: Erlbaum, 2000.

Baker, E. "Developing Community Leadership." In G. Lerner (ed.), *Black Women in White America: A Documentary History*. New York: Vintage, 1972, 345–352.

Baldwin, J. *Notes of a Native Son*. Boston: Beacon Press, 1955.

Baptiste, I. "Beyond Reason and Personal Integrity: Toward a Pedagogy of Coercive Restraint." *Canadian Journal for the Study of Adult Education*, 2000, *14*(1), 27–50.

Baptiste, I., and Brookfield, S. D. "Your So-Called Democracy Is Hypocritical Because You Can Always Fail Us: Learning and Living Democratic Contradictions in Graduate Adult Education." In P. Armstrong (ed.), *Crossing Borders, Breaking Boundaries: Research in the Education of Adults*. London: University of London, 1997.

Barber, B. *A Passion for Democracy*. Princeton, NJ: Princeton University Press, 2000.

Barth, R. *Learning by Heart*. San Francisco: Jossey-Bass, 2001.

Belenky, M., Bond, L., and Weinstock, J. *A Tradition That Has No Name: Nurturing the Development of People, Families and Communities*. New York: Basic Books, 1997.

Bennis, W. "Thoughts on the Essentials of Leadership." In P. Graham (ed.), *Mary Parker Follett: Prophet of Management*. Boston: Harvard Business School Press, 1996, 177–181.

Bordas, J. *Salsa, Soul and Spirit: Leadership for a Multicultural Age*. San Francisco: Berrett-Koehler, 2007.

Boyte, H., and Kari, N. *Building America: The Democratic Promise of Public Work*. Philadelphia: Temple University Press, 1996.

Branch, T. *Parting the Waters: America in the King Years, 1954–1963*. New York: Simon and Schuster, 1988.

Branch, T. *Pillar of Fire: America in the King Years: 1963–1965*. New York: Simon and Schuster, 1998.

Branch, T. *At Canaan's Edge: America in the King Years: 1965–1968*. New York: Simon and Schuster, 2006.

Brookfield, S. D. "Racializing Criticality in Adult Education." *Adult Education Quarterly*, 2003a, *53*(3), 154–169.

Brookfield, S. D. "Racializing the Discourse of Adult Education." *Harvard Educational Review*, 2003b, *73*(4), 497–523.

Brookfield, S. D. "On Malefic Generosity, Repressive Tolerance and Post-Colonialist Condescension: Considerations on White Adult Educators Racializing Adult Education Discourse." In *Proceedings of the 44th Adult Education Research Conference*. Athens: University of Georgia, 2005a.

Brookfield, S. D. "Problematizing White Engagement in Racial Talk." In *Proceedings of the 44th Adult Education Research Conference*. Athens: University of Georgia, 2005b.

Brookfield, S. D. "'Here I Stand': Paul Robeson on Adult Education as Cultural Work, Pan-Africanism and Socialist Persuasion." In *Proceedings of the 45th Adult Education Research Conference*. Minneapolis: University of Minnesota, 2006.

Brookfield S. D. "Radical Questioning on the Long Walk to Freedom: Nelson Mandela and the Practice of Critical Reflection." In *Proceedings of the 46th Adult Education Research Conference*. Halifax, NS: Mount Saint Vincent University, 2007.

Brookfield, S. D., and Preskill, S. *Discussion as a Way of Teaching: Tools and Techniques for Democratic Classrooms* (2nd ed.). San Francisco: Jossey-Bass, 2005.

Brown, C. S. *Ready from Within: Septima Clark and the Civil Rights Movement*. Trenton, NJ: Africa World Press, 1990.

Buber, M. *I And Thou* (trans. W. Kauffman). New York: Free Press, 1971.

Burns, J. M. *Leadership*. New York: Harper and Row, 1978.

Cantarow, E. (with O'Malley, S., and Strom, S.) *Moving the Mountain: Women Working for Social Change*. Old Westbury, NY: Feminist Press, 1983.

Cantarow, E., and O'Malley, S. "Ella Baker: Organizing for Civil Rights." In E. Cantarow (Ed.), *Moving the Mountain: Women Working for Social Change*. Old Westbury, NY: Feminist Press, 1980, 52–93.

Clandinin, D. J., and Connelly, F. M. *Narrative Inquiry: Experience and Story in Qualitative Research*. San Francisco: Jossey-Bass, 2004.

Clark, S., with Blythe, L. *Echo in My Soul*. New York: Dutton, 1962.

Closson, R. B. "Righteous Commitment: A Portrait of Dr. Scipio A. J. Colin III." *New Horizons in Adult Education and Human Resource Development*, 2006, *20*(2), 50–56.

Colin, S.A.J., III. "The Universal Negro Improvement Association and the Education of African American Adults." Doctoral dissertation, Department of Adult Education, Northern Illinois University, 1988.

Colin, S.A.J., III. "Marcus Garvey: Africentric Adult Education for Selfethnic Reliance." In E. A. Peterson (ed.), *Freedom Road: Adult Education of African Americans* (rev. ed.). Malabar, FL: Krieger, 2002.

Colin, S.A.J., III, and Guy, T. A. "An Africentric Interpretive Model of Curriculum Orientations for Course Development in Graduate Programs in Adult Education." *PAACE Journal of Lifelong Learning*, 1998, *7*, 43–55.

Colin, S.A.J., III, and Heaney, T. W. "Negotiating the Democratic Classroom." In C. A. Hansman and P. A. Sissel (eds.), *Understanding and Negotiating the Political Landscape of Adult Education*. New Horizons for Adult and Continuing Education, no. 91. San Francisco: Jossey-Bass, 2001.

Collins, J. *Good to Great and the Social Sciences: A Monograph to Accompany Good to Great*. New York: Harper Collins, 2005.

Dallard, S. *Ella Baker: A Leader Behind the Scenes*. New York: Silver Burdett Press, 1990.

Daloz, L. P., Parks, S. D., Keen, C., and Keen, J. P. *Common Fire: Lives of Commitment in a Complex World*. Boston: Beacon Press, 1997.

Dalton, F. *The Moral Vision of Cesar Chavez*. Maryknoll, NY: Orbis Books, 2003.

Damon, W., and Colby, A. *Some Do Care: Contemporary Lives of Moral Commitment*. New York: Free Press, 1994.

Davis, A. F. *American Heroine: The Life and Legend of Jane Addams*. New York: Oxford University Press, 1973/2000.

Delgado, R., and Stefancic, J. *Critical Race Theory: An Introduction*. New York: NYU Press, 2001.

Denning, S. *The Secret Language of Leadership: How Leaders Inspire Action Through Narrative*. San Francisco: Jossey-Bass, 2007.

De Pree, M. *Leadership Is an Art*. New York: Dell, 1989.

De Pree, M. *Leading Without Power: Finding Hope in Serving Community*. San Francisco: Jossey-Bass, 1997.

Dewey, J. *Democracy and Education*. New York: Macmillan, 1916.

Dewey, J. *Experience and Education*. New York: Macmillan, 1938.

Diliberto, G. *A Useful Woman: The Early Life of Jane Addams*. New York: Scribner, 1999.

Duberman, M. B. *Paul Robeson*. New York: Knopf, 1988.

Du Bois, W.E.B. *Dusk of Dawn, An Essay Toward an Autobiography of a Race Concept*. New York: Schocken Books, 1971.

Du Bois, W.E.B. *The Souls of Black Folk*. Harmondsworth, UK: Penguin Classics, 1996.

Elbow, P. *Embracing Contraries*. New York: Oxford University Press. 1986.

Fisher, R., Patton, B., and Ury, W. *Getting to Yes: Negotiating Agreement Without Giving In* (2nd ed.). Boston: Houghton Mifflin, 1992.

Flader, S. *Thinking Like a Mountain: Aldo Leopold and the Evolution of an Ecological Attitude Toward Deer, Wolves and Forests*. Madison: University of Wisconsin Press, 1974/1994.

Follett, M. P. *The New State: Group Organization as the Solution of Popular Government*. University Park: Pennsylvania State University Press, 1919/1998.

Follett, M. P. *Creative Experience*. New York: Longmans Green, 1924.

Forman, J. *The Making of Black Revolutionaries*. New York: Macmillan, 1972.

Foucault, M. *Power/Knowledge: Selected Interviews and Other Writings, 1972–1977*. New York: Pantheon Books, 1980.

Fox, E., and Urwick, L. *Dynamic Administration: The Collected Papers of Mary Parker Follett* (2nd ed.). London: Pitman, 1973.

Freire, P. *Pedagogy of the Oppressed*. New York: Seabury Press, 1973.

Freire, P. *Pedagogy of Hope*. New York: Continuum, 1994.

Fromm, E. *Escape from Freedom*. New York: Holt, Rinehart, and Winston, 1941.

Fromm, E. *The Sane Society*. London: Routledge, Kegan, and Paul, 1956.

Gardner, H. *Leading Minds*. New York: Basic Books, 1995.

Glen, J. *Highlander: No Ordinary School, 1932–1962*. Lexington: University Press of Kentucky, 1988.

Graham, P. (Ed.). *Mary Parker Follett: Prophet of Management*. Boston: Harvard Business School Press, 1996.

Gramsci, A. *The Modern Prince and Other Writings*. New York: International, 1957.

Gramsci, A. *Selections from the Prison Notebooks* (Q. Hoare and G. N. Smith, eds.). London: Lawrence and Wishart, 1971.

Grant, J. *Ella Baker: Freedom Bound*. New York: Wiley, 1998.

Greenleaf, R. *Servant Leadership*. Mahwah, NJ: Paulist Press, 1977.

Greenwood, D. J., and Levin, M. *Introduction to Action Research: Social Research for Social Change* (2nd ed.). Thousand Oaks: Sage, 2006.

Griswold del Castillo, R., and Garcia, R. *Cesar Chavez: A Triumph of Spirit.* Norman: University of Oklahoma Press, 1995.

Groopman, J. *The Anatomy of Hope: How People Prevail in the Face of Illness.* New York: Random House, 2005.

Guevara, C. *Che Guevara Reader.* New York: Ocean Press, 2003. (Originally published in 1958.)

Guy, T. C., and Brookfield, S. D. "W.E.B. Du Bois and the Basic American Negro Creed: The AAAE, Censorship, and Repressive Tolerance." In *Proceedings of the 45th Adult Education Research Conference*, Halifax, NS: Mount Saint Vincent University, 2007.

Habermas, J. *Theory and Practice.* Boston: Beacon Press, 1973.

Habermas, J. *The Theory of Communicative Action, Volume One: Reason and the Rationalization of Society.* Boston: Beacon Press, 1984.

Hagstrom, D. *From Outrageous to Inspired: How to Build a Community of Leaders in Our Schools.* San Francisco: Jossey-Bass, 2004.

Holst, J. D. *Social Movements, Civil Society, and Radical Adult Education.* Westport, CT: Bergin and Garvey, 2002.

Horton, A. *The Highlander Folk School: A History of Its Major Programs, 1932–1961.* New York: Carlson, 1989.

Horton, M. *The Long Haul: An Autobiography.* New York: Teachers College Press, 1998.

Horton, M., and Freire, P. *We Make the Road by Walking: Conversations on Education and Social Change.* Philadelphia: Temple University Press, 1990.

Jacobs, D. (Ed.), *The Myles Horton Reader: Education for Social Change.* Knoxville: University of Tennessee Press, 2003.

Kellerman, B. "What Every Leader Needs to Know About Followers." *Harvard Business Review,* Dec. 2007, 84–91.

King Jr., M. L. *A Testament of Hope: Essential Writings and Speeches of Martin Luther King, Jr.* (J. M. Washington, ed.). New York: HarperCollins, 1986.

King, M. L. *Freedom Song.* New York: Morrow, 1987.

King, M. L. *The Autobiography of Martin Luther King, Jr.* (C. Carson, ed.). New York: Warner Books, 1998.

Knight, L. W. "Biography's Window on Social Change: Benevolence and Social Justice in Jane Addams's 'A Modern Lear.'" *Journal of Women's History,* Spring 1997, *9*(1), 111–138.

Knight, L. W. *Citizen: Jane Addams and the Struggle for Democracy.* Chicago: University of Chicago Press, 2005.

Kohl, H. *The Discipline of Hope*. New York: Simon and Schuster, 1998.

Lagemann, E. S. *Jane Addams on Education*. New York: Teachers College Press, 1985.

Ledwith, M. *Community Development: A Critical Approach*. Bristol, UK: Policy Press, 2006.

Leopold, A. *A Sand County Almanac: With Essays on Conservation from Round River*. New York: Ballantine, 1949/1969.

Levy, J. *Cesar Chavez: Autobiography of La Causa*. New York: Norton, 1975.

Lewis, J. *Walking with the Wind: A Memoir of the Movement*. New York: Simon and Schuster, 1998.

Lindeman, E. C., and Smith, T. V. *The Democratic Way of Life*. New York: New American Library, 1951.

Lorbiecki, M. *Aldo Leopold: A Fierce Green Fire*. New York: Oxford University Press, 1996.

Mandela, N. *Long Walk to Freedom: The Autobiography of Nelson Mandela*. Boston: Little Brown, 1994.

Marcuse, H. *One Dimensional Man*. Boston: Beacon Press, 1964.

Marcuse, H. "Repressive Tolerance." In R. P. Wolff, B. Moore, and H. Marcuse (eds.), *A Critique of Pure Tolerance*. Boston: Beacon Press, 1965.

Marton, F. "Phenomenography: A Research Approach to Investigating Different Understandings of Reality." In R. R. Sherman and R. B. Webb (eds.), *Qualitative Research in Education: Focus and Methods*. Philadelphia: Falmer Press, 1988.

Matusak, L. *Finding Your Voice: Learning to Lead ... Anywhere You Want to Make a Difference*. San Francisco: Jossey-Bass, 1997.

McDermott, C. "Teaching to Be Radical: The Women Activist Educators of Highlander." In *Proceedings of the 48th Annual Adult Education Research Conference*, Halifax, NS: Department of Adult Education, Mount Saint Vincent University, 2007, 403–408.

Meine, C. *Aldo Leopold: His Life and Work*. Madison: University of Wisconsin Press, 1988.

Metcalf, H., and Urwick, L. (eds.). *Dynamic Administration: The Collected Papers of Mary Parker Follett*. Bath: Management Publications Trust, 1941.

Mills, C. W. *The Sociological Imagination*. New York: Oxford University Press, 1959.

Moses, R., and Cobb, C. *Radical Equations: Math Literacy and Civil Rights*. Boston: Beacon Press, 2001.

Newman, M. *Defining the Enemy: Adult Education in Social Action*. Sydney: Stewart Victor, 1994.

Newman, M. *Teaching Defiance: Stories and Strategies of Social Activists.* San Francisco: Jossey-Bass, 2006.

Newton, J. L. *Aldo Leopold's Odyssey: Rediscovering the Author of a Sand County Almanac.* Washington, D.C.: Island Press, 2006.

Obama, B. *Dreams from My Father: A Story of Race and Inheritance.* New York: Three Rivers Press, 2004.

Opdycke, S. "Julia Lathrop". In J. Garraty and M. Carnes (eds.), *American National Biography,* vol. 13. New York: Oxford University Press, 1999.

O'Toole, J. *Leading Change: The Argument for Values-Based Leadership.* New York: Ballantine, 1996.

Outlaw Jr., L. T. *On Race and Philosophy.* New York: Routledge, 1996.

Palmer, P. *A Hidden Wholeness: The Journey Toward an Undivided Life.* San Francisco: Jossey-Bass, 2004.

Park, P., Brydon-Miller, M., Hall, B., and Jackson, T. (eds.). *Voices of Change: Participatory Research in the United States and Canada.* Westport, CT: Bergin and Garvey, 1993.

Payne, C. *I've Got the Light of Freedom: The Organizing Tradition and the Mississippi Freedom Struggle.* Berkeley: University of California Press, 1995.

Peterson, E. A. *Freedom Road: Adult Education of African Americans* (rev. ed.). Malabar, FL: Krieger, 2001.

Peterson, E. A., and Brookfield, S. D. "Race and Racism: A Critical Dialogue." In *Proceedings of the 45th Adult Education Research Conference,* Halifax, NS: Mount Saint Vincent University, 2007.

Raelin, J. *Creating Leaderful Organizations: How to Bring out Leadership in Everyone.* San Francisco: Berrett-Koehler, 2003.

Ransby, B. *Ella Baker and the Black Freedom Movement: A Radical Democratic Vision.* Chapel Hill: University of North Carolina Press, 2003.

Reyes, E. De Los, and Gozemba, P. A. *Pockets of Hope: How Students and Teachers Change the World.* Westport, CT: Bergin and Garvey, 2002.

Riesman, D. *The Lonely Crowd.* New Haven, CT: Yale University Press, 1965.

Robeson, P. *Here I Stand.* Boston: Beacon, 1958.

Robeson, P. *Paul Robeson Speaks: Writings, Speeches, Interviews 1918–1974* (P. S. Foner, ed.). New York: Bruner/Mazel, 1978.

Robnett, B. *How Long? How Long?: African American Women in the Struggle for Civil Rights.* New York: Oxford University Press, 1997.

Rodriguez, C. *Cesar Chavez.* Philadelphia: Chelsea House, 1991.

Ross, F. *Conquering Goliath: Cesar Chavez at the Beginning.* Keene, CA: El Taller Grafico Press, 1989.

Ryan, J. *Inclusive Leadership.* San Francisco: Jossey-Bass, 2005.

Seifter, H., and Economy, P. *Leadership Ensemble: Lessons in Collaborative Management from the World's Only Conductorless Orchestra*. New York: Times Books, 2001.

Shapiro, I. *Democratic Justice*. New Haven, CT: Yale University Press, 2001.

Shor, I. *Critical Teaching and Everyday Life*. Chicago: University of Chicago Press, 1987.

Sklar, K. K. *Florence Kelley and the Nation's Work*. New Haven, CT: Yale University Press, 1995.

Smock, K. *Democracy in Action: Community Organizing and Urban Change*. New York: Columbia University Press, 2003.

Solnit, R. *Hope in the Dark: Untold Histories, Wild Possibilities*. New York: Nation Books, 2004.

Solorzano, D. "Critical Race Theory, Racial and Gender Microaggressions, and the Experiences of Chicana and Chicano Scholars." *International Journal of Qualitative Studies in Education*, 1998, *11*, 121–136.

Sunstein, C. *The Second Bill of Rights: FDR's Unfinished Revolution and Why We Need It More Than Ever*. New York: Perseus Books, 2006.

Terkel, S. *Hope Dies Last: Keeping the Faith in Troubled Times*. New York: New Press, 2003.

Tjerandsen, C. *Education for Citizenship: A Foundation's Experience*. Santa Cruz, CA: Emil Schwartzhaupt Foundations, 1980.

Tonn, J. *Mary P. Follett: Creating Democracy, Transforming Management*. New Haven, CT: Yale University Press, 2003.

Urwick, L. (ed.). *Freedom and Co-Ordination: Lectures in Business Organization by Mary Parker Follett*. London: Management Publications, 1949.

West, C. *Democracy Matters: Winning the Fight Against Imperialism*. New York: Penguin, 2004.

West, C., and Sealey, K. S. *Restoring Hope: Conversations on the Future of Black America*. Boston: Beacon, 1997.

Wheatley, M. *Turning to One Another: Simple Conversations to Restore Hope to the Future*. San Francisco: Berrett-Koehler, 2002.

Wigginton, E. (ed.). *Refuse to Stand Silently by: An Oral History of Grass Roots Social Activism in America, 1921–1964*. New York: Doubleday, 1991.

Williams, R. *The Long Revolution*. New York: Columbia University Press, 1961.

Williams, R. *Marxism and Literature*. New York: Oxford University Press, 1977.

Zinn, H. *Declarations of Independence: Cross-Examining American Ideology*. New York: HarperCollins, 1990.

Zournazi, M. (ed.). *Hope: New Philosophies for Change*. New York: Routledge, 2003.

INDEX